An Archaeology of the Early Anglo-Saxon Kingdoms

An Archaeology of the Early Anglo-Saxon Kingdoms has for nearly a decade been used by students seeking an introduction to the field. In this new, fully revised edition of Arnold's essential text all of the key recent finds and developments in the field of Anglo-Saxon studies have been incorporated. With an expanded text and an increased number of informative illustrations, C.J. Arnold confronts the key questions facing students who seek to understand how the foundations of medieval England were laid:

- How did kingdoms form out of the chaos of the Dark Ages?
- How was it that a deeply superstitious people came to embrace Christianity?
- What was the fate of Britain's native populations at the hand of invading peoples?

Firmly basing its arguments upon archaeological evidence, the book introduces students to the fascinating dichotomies of Anglo-Saxon society. It acts both as a reliable guide to historical fact and as an invaluable introduction to the key debates currently spurring research in the field.

C.J. Arnold is a Senior Lecturer at the University of Wales, Aberystwyth and is a widely regarded authority on Anglo-Saxon and medieval Welsh history. His numerous previous publications in these fields include *Roman Britain to Saxon England* (1984).

An Archaeology of the Early Anglo-Saxon Kingdoms

New edition

C.J. Arnold

London and New York

First published 1988
Second edition 1997
by Routledge
11 New Fetter Lane, London EC4P 4EE

Simultaneously published in the USA and Canada
by Routledge
29 West 35th Street, New York, NY 10001

© 1988, 1997 C.J. Arnold

Typeset in Garamond by Florencetype Ltd, Stoodleigh, Devon
Printed and bound in Great Britain by Biddles Ltd,
Guildford and King's Lynn

British Library Cataloguing in Publication Data
A catalogue record for this book is available from the British Library

Library of Congress Cataloging in Publication Data
    Arnold, C. J.
        An Archaeology of the Early Anglo-Saxon Kingdoms / C.J. Arnold.
            p. cm.
        Includes bibliographical references (p.) and index.
        1. Great Britain–History–Anglo-Saxon period. 449–1066.
    2. England–Social conditions–To 1066. 3. Excavations
    (Archaeology)–England. 4. Anglo-Saxons–Kings and rulers.
    5. Archaeology, Medieval. I. Title.
    DA152.A76 1997
    942.01'5–dc20   96-28369
                                                           CIP

ISBN 0–415–15635–1 (hbk)
ISBN 0–415–15636–X (pbk)

For M. and D.
and
M.I.B.

Contents

Figures

Tables

Preface to the first edition

It has taken a long time for the contents of this book to be translated from diagrams on a blackboard, which gave students considerable amusement, into words. It has been encouraged by the nervous laughter of my seniors, hindered by the lack of dialogue between them. I hope that those who gave me the confidence to write this book will not now regret having done so, and wish that those who follow gain as much pleasure and excitement in unlocking the many doors that have remained barred for too long.

A number of colleagues, family and friends have always been willing to discuss the problems posed by early Anglo-Saxon archaeology, and to share their ideas, especially Richard Morris, Paul Reilly, Janet Arnold (née Bell), Jeremy Huggett, Julian Richards and the ducks, to whom I am most grateful.

Preface to the revised second edition

Eight years have passed since the completion of the text that formed the first edition of this book. As the publisher's stocks dwindled I was given the chance to bring the work up to date. My immediate reaction was to encourage someone else to write *their* book on early Anglo-Saxon archaeology but their diffidence seemed stronger than my own doubts about the task. The revision of the text was completed in 1996. The volume of data has increased in some areas, research has greatly advanced some topics and in a few areas there has been substantial rethinking; the changes to the text reflect this. The first edition was quite strictly dictated by one theme, the development of the kingdoms. While retaining that concept, restructuring and re-ordering certain key sections has reduced its impact and I have attempted to broaden the usefulness of the work especially in its illustrative material. The intention has been to provide a broader based introduction to the evidence.

Over the last few years I have been greatly encouraged by the directions of research and have continued to enjoy a dialogue with other specialists. I am also grateful to those who read the various drafts and offered me alternative narratives where required. The ducks, however, have long since passed on and so too has their usefulness.

Introduction

By AD 700 there were seven principal English kingdoms: the West Saxons, the South Saxons, Kent, the East Saxons, East Anglia, Mercia and Northumbria. Although their precise boundaries are unclear the respective areas of their kingdoms correspond roughly with central southern England, Sussex, Kent, Essex, Norfolk and Suffolk, the Midlands and the area to the north of the River Humber. They were created from a larger number of smaller and less well documented groups. This was achieved by a process of amalgamation during the two centuries after the migrations of Germanic people to England in the fifth century. Northumbria, for instance, was an amalgamation of two earlier kingdoms: Bernicia, which was roughly equivalent to modern Northumberland, and Deira, modern Yorkshire. At one stage during this formative period there were at least ten separate royal families ruling simultaneously over much that is now England. The success of individual kingdoms was largely dependent on their achievements in the political and economic arenas. It was the more successful of the kingdoms that were most frequently attacked and that were annexed into larger configurations by the more obscure kingdoms. This process of peaceful and aggressive fusion was to continue in succeeding centuries down to the present day.

The written records greatly enhance our knowledge of England's political structure at the end of the seventh century. Little of the surviving written tradition was set down before the second half of the seventh century. Its reliability is determined by the limit of living memory and the vagaries of oral tradition. Many of the written sources stem from the seventh-century conversion of the English to Christianity. This was the successful conclusion of missionary efforts from Rome in AD 597 and Iona in AD 635.

The greatest scholar of the period was Bede (c. AD 672–735) who was born in Northumbria and trained at the abbeys of Wearmouth and Jarrow. He completed his most famous book, the *Ecclesiastical History of the English People* (Colgrave and Mynors 1969), in 731. It was primarily intended as a contribution to Christian teaching, and its main theme was the conversion of the English, but there is considerable information about the development of the kingdoms. Bede's knowledge and the sources available to him affect the value of his *Ecclesiastical History*. He provided many details about Northumbria and Kent, but for other areas he was dependent on informants, where they existed, and the sparse earlier records. He was writing about the period before his life and says less about his own time. Nevertheless, he provides us with details of kings' lives, royal courts, statesmanship, the names of people and places and their conversion to Christianity.

We may also trace the political history of early England through the annual entries of the *Anglo-Saxon Chronicle*. The *Chronicle*, in its various versions, was compiled in Wessex, so it is particularly informative about the development of that kingdom, but less so about others, and there is confusion in many of the entries down to the middle of the sixth century. The inconsistencies between the various sources, however interesting in themselves, must urge caution in our dependence on the information provided.

A symbol of the extent of kingship during the seventh century is the various law-codes issued as a method of regulating society, but which throw light on contemporary attitudes towards justice and perceptions of the structure of society. King Aethelberht of Kent issued the first vernacular laws at the beginning of the seventh century, whereas Ine produced the earliest West Saxon laws between AD 688 and 694.

The greatest influence on modern historians and archaeologists has been the content of the available written sources. The sources' apparent bias and inaccuracy have restrained them. Some of the early kingdoms, for instance, remain very obscure. Despite the relative silence of the written records about them, the archaeological data may demonstrate that similar developments were taking place there as in the well documented examples. However, the archaeological data are prone to similar problems of distortion. One can never be sure that an adequate cross-section of archaeological data, if there is such a thing, has been recovered in any one area. It is the archaeologist who decides what emphasis to place on a particular piece of evidence. The inevitable desire to dove-tail the two forms of evidence together exacerbates the problems of interpreting the archaeological data. If such problems can be overcome it should be possible to push back our knowledge of the development of the kingdoms, even beyond the date at which the written sources are reliable; it will also amplify our understanding of the structure and content of these societies throughout the period.

The early Anglo-Saxon cemeteries provide just such a challenge to interpretation and yet must contain the greatest potential resource for an understanding of the evolving social structure. Encoded within the inhumation and cremation cemeteries are many contemporary attitudes to life, death, the individual, gender, status and social identity as interpreted by those responsible for the funeral; it is the archaeologist's difficult task to disentangle the various strands of information, to isolate the different messages.

The written sources document the conversion of the English to Christianity, through which we learn so much about the kingdoms. The change in religion may account for some of the changes in the archaeological record, but we have limited knowledge of beliefs and the extent and nature of religious practices, both before and after the conversion. The nature and precise function of the earliest churches are obscure, and to extrapolate the wide range of individuals' beliefs from their graves is difficult. If problems of interpretation exist regarding any aspects of early Anglo-Saxon archaeology, it is only bold experimentation and optimism that will produce the tools required to overcome those problems.

We may appraise the development of the Anglo-Saxon kingdoms on the basis of their permanency and their success in the military, economic and political arenas. We may gain glimpses of the struggles for power and supremacy that were taking place from the written sources, but we may only obtain a detailed appreciation of the nature of the societies that permitted such developments to occur from the archaeological evidence. The basis of the continued growth of the kingdoms was the subsistence farmers whose settlements and cemeteries, daily and less regular activities, make up the bulk of the archaeological record. The collections of timber buildings on their farms may be difficult to understand and there remains uncertainty about the details of agriculture, animal husbandry, the extent of surplus and storage facilities, fields, and the density of settlement. Even the nature of the land-scape in which such activities took place is obscure. It is only by approaching that data from as many angles as possible that any worthwhile information will come out of it, and thus we can prepare ourselves to ask the right questions when the opportunity arises to excavate further examples. The practitioners of early medieval archaeology have rapidly passed from a period of having virtually no theory, through a phase of testing general theories developed elsewhere, to the present where much powerful theory is being generated about the development of societies.

The few artefacts recovered from such settlements and the larger quantities deposited as grave-goods in the nearby cemeteries, amply demonstrate the richness of technology and design during the period. They also form the basis of our knowledge of economic life, from so humble an aspect as the source of clay used to make pottery to the origins of gold to adorn extravagant pieces of metalwork. It is such small pieces of information that combine to help us understand the dynamics of the whole society.

The cemeteries present us with two principal burial rites, inhumation and cremation. Most of the graves are difficult to date adequately but in their variations of burial rite, grave structure, container or grave-goods, they hold conscious and unconscious reflections of the societies responsible for them. They contain varying quantities of dress items, containers and weapons, some lavishly decorated, but there are many perplexing problems. The deposition of so many possessions, and the raw materials used in their manufacture, might reflect a successful society that could afford such extravagance. On the other hand this might indicate a society that was being strangled by, or forced to change because of, its own beliefs and practices. There is no doubt that it is difficult to put some of the burial practices into perspective; how are we to make sense of a society that was prepared to consign large quantities of precious metal to the ground but which rarely buried everyday tools?

An appreciation of the sources and uses of raw materials allows us to examine the movement of internally produced goods and of those from overseas. From this we may begin to reconstruct the natures of the economies of the kingdoms. The production of first gold and then silver coinage before AD 700 emphasises their increasing complexity. The evolving social organisation visible in the cemeteries and the development of a greater variety of settlement types also reflects their growing complexity. The largely undifferentiated farms in the earlier part of the period later take their place in the landscape alongside ports, royal centres and religious institutions. Again, the frequent isolation of the archaeological and written evidence comes sharply into focus. Bede mentions royal settlements such as *Gefrin*, identified with Yeavering in Northumberland, and Rendlesham in Suffolk. There are other, unnamed, settlements which archaeologists have identified as 'palaces' and the written sources are almost silent about the earliest ports.

These structures and institutions are an indication of the growing power and complexity of the early Anglo-Saxon kingdoms. Developing as they did after the collapse of Roman Britain and the Germanic migrations of the fifth century, the establishment of the kingdoms is a reflection of human society's ability to recover from such turbulence and to create new order. It forms an exciting period of rapid change. It terminates with a period of relative stability in the kingdoms reflected in the establishment of towns. The blurred picture that we have of these 200 years will only be brought into focus by assessing the state of knowledge at regular intervals. In this way we provide the foundation for future scholars to build on.

The text generally only makes reference to cemeteries and settlements that have been published in more recent years. The reader will find the sources for older excavations in Meaney (1964) and Rahtz (1976, Appendix A). To avoid confusion the pre-reorganisation (1974) county names have been used when appropriate. Some confusion is inevitable as there have been many boundary changes and major local government reorganisation in 1974 and 1996. Such changes are not always reflected in the titles of published books and papers.

Chapter 1

A history of early Anglo-Saxon archaeology

'Wrapped round with darkness'

Judith, translated by R. Hamer

The purpose of this book is to explore the development of English society during the 200 years AD 500–700 following the migrations of Germanic settlers to the British Isles. The aim is to bridge the gap between the work of specialists whose significance to a general understanding may seem obscure, and generalised accounts that may seem remote from the data. To achieve this we shall be drawing upon the products of archaeologists' research mostly carried out during the present century. The desire to understand the development of early Anglo-Saxon society as a specific contribution to the more general study of past human behaviour has only emerged in recent years.

Each chapter examines a particular aspect of early Anglo-Saxon society. Such a division is purely a literary convenience and the reader must see each of the topics as intertwined and forming a complex whole. The kingdoms provide the ideal framework for the study of early Anglo-Saxon society as they were developing during the period under consideration. Within that evolving framework there is both complexity and variety, for change involves redundancy as well as novelty, and each region was subject to different pressures stemming from its past and its neighbours.

The archaeological evidence comes from two main contexts: settlements and cemeteries, although earlier archaeologists concentrated on the latter, and especially the artefacts derived from them. The emphasis here is not on a description of the evidence but on its interpretation. To achieve this the data require varying degrees of manipulation if we are to understand the society whose everyday activities constitute the origins of the archaeological record. We will see how the development of Anglo-Saxon archaeology, in which the number of practitioners has always been relatively small, has engendered a conservative approach to the period not suited to answering the fundamental questions relating to human social evolution. In more recent years there have been signs of a change in emphasis. This is reflected in those chapters of this book that deal with the agriculture of the farms and the homes in which our subjects lived, the craft skills in use, trade in commodities and finished products, and their ideas and beliefs, not least the religious beliefs of the population which Christian missionaries so persuasively altered and adapted.

The combination of all such social activities gave a particular character to early Anglo-Saxon society and the manner in which it developed. A major consideration, therefore, has to be a definition of the structure of society, in as far as that is possible, and of the beliefs and bonds that held it together. Naturally the inherent constraints of the archaeological evidence, our caution and increasing enlightenment about the relationship between the archaeological record and the activities that formed it, and the extent of the research that has been carried out determines the cohesion and balance of a work of this type. However, a definition of the current state of understanding and uncertainty should also serve as a diagnosis to guide future research.

The early Anglo-Saxon period is unspectacular and has not been brought to popular attention, except for those rare and fabulous discoveries such as the ship burials at Sutton Hoo (Suffolk). Indeed, there are many people for whom the knowledge that the earliest Anglo-Saxons came immediately after the 'Romans' and before the 'Vikings' would be a revelation, a shortcoming that the new National Curriculum may manage to overcome. The period is also something of a 'Cinderella' within teaching and research in British universities and colleges, there being less than ten specialists teaching undergraduates.

Post-Roman archaeology is one of the younger branches of British archaeology; older established areas of study, such as prehistory, have inevitably tended to form the vanguard of archaeological research, and are more firmly printed on the popular imagination. This may, in part, explain why until recently approaches to early Anglo-Saxon archaeology seemed so distant from those applied to other periods of the past. There has been a degree of innocence in much research, with time-honoured methods being applied despite their failure to deepen understanding of the past; techniques applied to other periods tended to be excluded as though they were not relevant to a historic period. While there are indications of increasing experimentation, the reasons for the subject being pervaded by such conservatism and isolationism lie in the history of its development. Its comparative youthfulness and exclusiveness cannot be the sole explanations. A great deal of research in the field during the twentieth century has been carried out by scholars trained, in the first instance, as historians. Eminent scholars working in museums have made an equally significant contribution. They tended to introduce a strong art-historical bias whose techniques are still utilised, in the rarity of stratigraphic evidence, as a first approach to data in preference to other parameters. These may be the principal factors that have tended to control and limit the nature and scope of research.

Anglo-Saxon remains were first identified correctly in 1793, when an appreciation of the true age of mankind was only just beginning. Possibly the first mention of Anglo-Saxon graves is that by the thirteenth-century chronicler Roger of Wendover in his *Flores Historiarum*. He describes the excavation of ten human skeletons at Redbourne, Hertfordshire, by monks from St Albans in 1178. They believed some of them were the bones of St Amphibalus (Hewlett 1886: 115). Early Anglo-Saxon objects were first illustrated, but not identified as such, by Sir Thomas Browne in *Hydriotaphia, or Urne buriall* (1658), in which he described the 'Sad sepulchral pitchers . . . fetched from the passed world'. To Browne the cemetery at Walsingham, Norfolk, was a reminder of the power of the culture of Rome. One of the forty or fifty burial urns survived in the 'closet of rarities' at Lambeth known as Tradescant's Ark, which in 1682 formed the basis of Elias Ashmole's bequest to the University of Oxford (Daniel 1981: 42). The urns were reported to contain burnt bones accompanied by decorated combs

> handsomely wrought like the necks of Bridges of Musical Instruments [and] long brass plates overwrought like the handles of neat implements; brazen nippers to pull away hair . . . and one kind of *Opale*, yet maintaining a blewish colour.

Not until the second half of the eighteenth century did any systematic excavation of any early Anglo-Saxon archaeology, a cemetery, take place. The Revd Bryan Faussett carried out a considerable number of excavations in east Kent between the years 1757 and 1777, amassing a total of over 700 graves. It was he who managed the now-famous and hurried disinterment of twenty-eight graves in one day, and nine barrows before breakfast to avoid the disturbance of spectators. Such haste inevitably resulted in cursory recording being a characteristic of research at the time. This is particularly regrettable in Faussett's case because of the scale of his activities in Kent. Faussett failed to appreciate the true significance of his discoveries. In his journal, kept for the years 1757 to 1773 and published as *Inventorium Sepulchrale* under the editorship of Charles Roach Smith in 1856, he attributed the remains to the period of Roman occupation; Smith preferred a purely British origin.

The credit for first recognising that the 'small barrows' were not Roman or Danish, but burial places of the Saxon period, belongs to the Revd James Douglas. He also excavated in Kent, from 1779–93, and published the results in 1793 in his *Nenia Britannica* (Figure 1.1). Douglas's work marks a turning point in early Anglo-Saxon archaeology; in the words of Horsfield in his *History, Antiquities and Topography of Sussex* (1835: 11): 'Up to this time no genuine attempt had been made to acquire knowledge of our early inhabitants, no extensive plan for a generalisation of known excavations.' Douglas made notable advances in archaeological method, fully appreciating the value of dating by association within and between grave groups. As his biographer has pointed out, in a detailed survey of this period of British archaeology, it was to be a long time 'before he had an equal in the study of archaeology on a scientific basis or as an illustrator of archaeological relics' (Jessup 1975: 109).

NENIA BRITANNICA:

OR,

A SEPULCHRAL HISTORY

OF

GREAT BRITAIN;

FROM THE EARLIEST PERIOD TO ITS GENERAL CONVERSION TO CHRISTIANITY.

INCLUDING

A COMPLETE SERIES OF THE BRITISH, ROMAN, AND SAXON SEPULCHRAL RITES AND
CEREMONIES, WITH THE CONTENTS OF SEVERAL HUNDRED BURIAL PLACES,

Opened under a careful Infpection of the AUTHOR.

THE BARROWS CONTAINING

URNS, SWORDS, SPEAR-HEADS, DAGGERS, KNIVES, BATTLE-AXES, SHIELDS, and
ARMILLÆ:—Decorations of Women; confifting of GEMS, PENSILE ORNA-
MENTS, BRACELETS, BEADS, GOLD and SILVER BUCKLES, BROACHES ornamented with Precious Stones; feveral MAGICAL INSTRUMENTS; fome very
fcarce and unpublifhed Coins; and a Variety of other curious Relics depo-
fited with the Dead.

TENDING TO ILLUSTRATE THE EARLY PART OF

And to fix on a more unqueftionable CRITERION for the STUDY of ANTIQUITY:

TO WHICH ARE ADDED,

OBSERVATIONS on the *CELTIC, BRITISH, ROMAN,* and
DANISH BARROWS, difcovered in *BRITAIN.*

BY THE REV. JAMES DOUGLAS, F.A.S.

CHAPLAIN IN ORDINARY TO HIS ROYAL HIGHNESS THE PRINCE OF WALES.

Quis autem eft, quem non moveat clariffimis monumentis tefata confignataque Antiquitas?
Cic. de Div. lib. i.

LONDON:
PRINTED BY JOHN NICHOLS;
FOR BENJAMIN AND JOHN WHITE.
M.DCC.XCIII.

Figure 1.1 The title page of *Nenia Britannica* published in 1793 by the Revd
James Douglas

Figure 1.2 Grave-goods excavated by Thomas Bateman at Benty Grange, Derbyshire, in 1848, including the remains of a helmet (source: Bateman 1861: 31)

During the second half of the nineteenth century archaeologists advanced the subject in three ways. The first way in which progress was made was by the publication of the results of the excavation of individual cemeteries or of campaigns of excavations. Typical examples include: Wylie's *Fairford Graves* (1852), the researches of Lord Londesborough in Yorkshire (1852), and Thomas Bateman's *Ten Years' Diggings in Celtic and Saxon Grave Hills in the Counties of Derby, Stafford and York, from 1848 to 1858* (1861) (Figure 1.2). Progress was also made by incorporating such reports into early regional studies, such as Knox's *Descriptions Geographical, Topographical and Antiquarian in Eastern Yorkshire, between the rivers Humber and Tees* (1855) or George Hillier's *The History and Antiquities of the Isle of Wight* in 1856 (Arnold 1978; Hockey 1977), and in more general works such as C. Roach Smith's *Collectanea Antiqua* (1848–80). Third, there were early attempts to survey the material as a whole, for instance Akerman's *Remains of Pagan Saxondum* (1855). The first attempt to study the subject on a broader basis was by Kemble in his *Horae Ferales* (1863). For comparative purposes he arranged together types of artefacts from a number of north-west European countries. From these he drew conclusions about the connectedness of artefact types. Although he excavated extensively

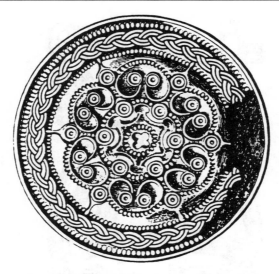

Figure 1.3 An applied saucer brooch from Fairford, Gloucestershire, illustrated by E.T. Leeds in his typological study (source: Leeds 1912: 164)

in Germany, Kemble's greatest contribution in England was as a historian of the period (1863, 1876). The dominance of the study of grave-goods from cemeteries until the end of the nineteenth century was unavoidable. This source of distortion on our understanding of the period has remained almost to the present day; archaeologists accepted them as a reflection of daily life because they were the only source of data.

A characteristic of the early twentieth century was the collection of data and their presentation *en masse*, seen at its best in G. Baldwin Brown's exceptional study of much of the material of Anglo-Saxon archaeology, *The Arts in Early England* (1903–37). Apart from the accumulation of material in this manner the study of early Anglo-Saxon archaeology progressed little. R.A. Smith's county-by-county surveys appeared in early volumes of the Victoria County History from 1900 to 1926. Such surveys formed the basis for research for many years and still remain the principal source for some categories of data. The format, however, was not conducive to typological study which was beginning to have an impact on archaeology in Britain. In *Origin of the English Nation* (1907) H.M. Chadwick was the first to attempt a general work on the origins of the Anglo-Saxons by combining historical and archaeological evidence, a theme that has tended to dominate the subject for much of the twentieth century.

The foundations of a mature Anglo-Saxon archaeology were the work of nineteenth-century archaeologists, amongst them Akerman, Roach Smith, Kemble and Wylie. It was the new technique of analysis, typology, which

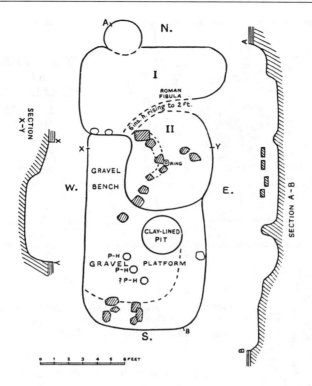

Figure 1.4 Plan of a building at Sutton Courtenay, Berkshire, excavated by
E.T. Leeds (source: Leeds 1936, Figure 9)

caused the greatest shifts of emphasis in the early years of the twentieth
century. Following the publications in England of Oscar Montelius and R.A.
Smith (1908; 1905), Edward Thurlow Leeds (Assistant-Keeper and Keeper
at the Ashmolean Museum, Oxford from 1908 to 1945) produced the first
typology of a form of early Anglo-Saxon metalwork, a brooch type (1912)
(Figure 1.3). Both he and R.A. Smith, in his British Museum guide to Anglo-
Saxon Antiquities (1923), accepted the importance of the work of the scholar
Bernhard Salin, *Die altgermanische Thierornamentik* (1904). Salin's analysis
of the animal motifs used in migration period art provided a chronology for
the English material. Using Smith's county surveys Leeds was able to extract
various classes of object and formulate typologies and chronologies by
comparison with the dated developments in Continental art styles.

E.T. Leeds was also responsible for the first major excavation of an early
Anglo-Saxon settlement at Sutton Courtenay, Berkshire (Leeds 1923, 1927,
1947) (Figure 1.4). He also reported on a number of cemeteries (1916, 1924;
Leeds and Harden 1936; Leeds and Riley 1942; Leeds and Shortt 1953).

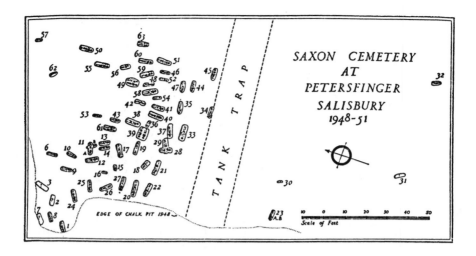

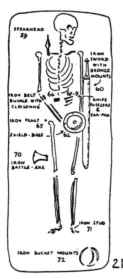

Figure 1.5 Plans of the excavated cemetery and grave 21 at Petersfinger, Wiltshire (source: Leeds and Shortt 1953, Figures 2 and (part of) 4)

The style of reporting of such excavations changed little, with a plan accompanied by descriptions of graves and their contents. Drawings of cremation urns were provided on a small scale, but with no details of the 'grave' or the disposition of the contents. He treated inhumations in a similar fashion, with only some details of the grave, and only late in his career did Leeds provide plans of individual graves (Figure 1.5). Generally, he published photographs of the grave-goods confining line-drawings to more ornate pieces.

Leeds was a pioneer in the typological study of artefacts, producing detailed analyses of various brooch types (1912, 1949, 1971 posthumously with M. Pocock). He also grasped the opportunity to synthesise and in 1913 published *The Archaeology of the Anglo-Saxon Settlements*. This was the first attempt to summarise all of the known archaeology of the period in England and is of interest because it describes the aims and methods of Anglo-Saxon archaeology as Leeds perceived them; there was apparently still a market for the book in 1970 when the publishers reprinted it. He compared the distribution of types of artefact dated by typological methods with historical information, particularly recorded battles between the Anglo-Saxons and the native population. These he saw as marking stages by which the migrants conquered the country. We should note that Leeds was making the distinction between the two races on the basis of the artefacts. For him, an individual using and being buried with an artefact of, ultimately, Continental type was a person of Germanic origin.

This misconception has led many researchers in more recent years to discuss the apparent absence of evidence for members of the native population. We see Leeds, the culture historian, at his peak in his *Early Anglo-Saxon Art and Archaeology* (1936) and his paper entitled 'The distribution of the Angles and Saxons archaeologically considered' (1945). He believed that if he could attribute the distribution of an artefact type to a particular race or tribe it could indicate the course of the invasion and settlement of England and the origins on the Continent of the settlers. This type of preoccupation was prevalent for much of the twentieth century. During this period Åberg (1926) and Kendrick (1938) produced other valuable studies that also concentrated on art-styles and artefact types.

The method of study developed by Leeds can be traced back in his career as early as 1912; however, it was the prehistorian Gordon Childe who formulated the theoretical framework that stated that prehistoric archaeology should be 'devoted to isolating such cultural groups of peoples, tracing the differentiations, wanderings and interactions' (1933: 417). Leeds was undoubtedly encouraged to adopt this approach by the historical information provided about the distribution of the Germanic peoples in England by the *Anglo-Saxon Chronicle* and Bede's *Ecclesiastical History of the English People*.

Fox took a similar approach in his *The Archaeology of the Cambridge Region* (1923). In this detailed regional study Fox was concerned with the Anglo-Saxon invasion and settlement; he also attempted to reconcile distribution maps of artefact types with supposed ethnic groups to the extent of drawing political boundaries. The work of Leeds on Anglo-Saxon metalwork did not encourage other scholars to follow him immediately, perhaps as a result of the more spectacular possibilities opened by the birth of prehistoric studies at Edinburgh and Cambridge in the late 1920s and 1930s. It was not until the 1950s that J.N.L. Myres and D.B. Harden generated new interest with their work on pottery and glass (Harden 1956a). This division of labour by artefact type epitomises attitudes towards archaeology generally at that time, and such divisions have to a large extent persisted to this day, emphasising how artefact-based early Anglo-Saxon studies have remained; new categories of data or ways of thinking have merely encouraged new configurations of this proprietorial attitude.

The *Festschrift* presented to E.T. Leeds (Harden 1956a) provides an important assessment of the state of the subject at the time. The contributors developed many of the traditional themes. C.F.C. Hawkes' study of the Jutes of Kent, stimulated by the latest typologies and chronologies of grave-goods on the Continent (Werner 1935; Kuhn 1940), was one of the last studies employing the traditional methodology, although one may still find its influence in more recent work.

Despite the increase in the number of scholars studying the period, the same preoccupation with art-history and the origins of peoples persisted through and beyond the 1960s in studies of pottery (Myres 1969, 1970, 1977) and metalwork (Hawkes 1961; Hawkes and Dunning 1961). Myres believed that 'it should be possible to extract . . . some valuable information on the origin and distribution of settlers, their relationship to the pre-existing population, their social and economic development, and their notions of religion and decorative art' (1969: 11). He only achieved the first and last of these aims to any degree via the pottery (Figure 1.6). Published works of the 1950s, 1960s and 1970s tended to follow this approach, and while there were occasional signs of shifts in direction, these were mere rustlings in the undergrowth compared with the revolution taking place elsewhere in British archaeology.

The production of the numerous studies of artefact types was important as they form the basis for the chronology of the period, but beyond that their relevance to an understanding of Anglo-Saxon people has not been demonstrated (Evison 1955, 1958, 1963, 1967, 1968; Swanton 1974; Avent 1975; Avent and Evison 1982; Hills 1981; Leigh 1984b). Redefinitions of chronology are claimed to be part of the process of improvement of understanding, but may as easily be viewed as an infinite series of alternatives none of which is demonstrably correct unless it is somehow related to the reality of the society in question.

The Archaeology of Anglo-Saxon England (Wilson 1976a) was the first major attempt at synthesis since Leeds in 1913, but the work ignored most of the early evidence, and there was very little discussion of method. Most significantly it did not cover cemeteries 'because of the lack of competent studies' (ibid.: 3). It replaced traditional topics with studies of the form and pattern of settlement, made possible by the great increase in their rate of discovery and excavation from the 1970s onwards. The traditional dependence on a literal version of written sources is absent, although elsewhere such a dependence may still be found, particularly in discussion of the origin of the Anglo-Saxon kingdoms (Biddle 1976; Hope-Taylor 1977: 276–324).

In the 1950s and early 1960s the then Ministry of Public Buildings and Works (now English Heritage) sponsored the rescue excavation of a considerable number of cemeteries, but the enthusiasm of that support has not been matched by the rate of publication, to the extent that it is very difficult to comment on excavation methods during that period (Hills 1993). Reports on some of these excavations are now appearing (e.g. Evison 1988, 1994) although they do not always provide information about the methods used and in reporting the excavations sometimes give primacy to the grave-goods over other considerations. More recent years have seen the continuation of such rescue work with a much better publication standard, and there have

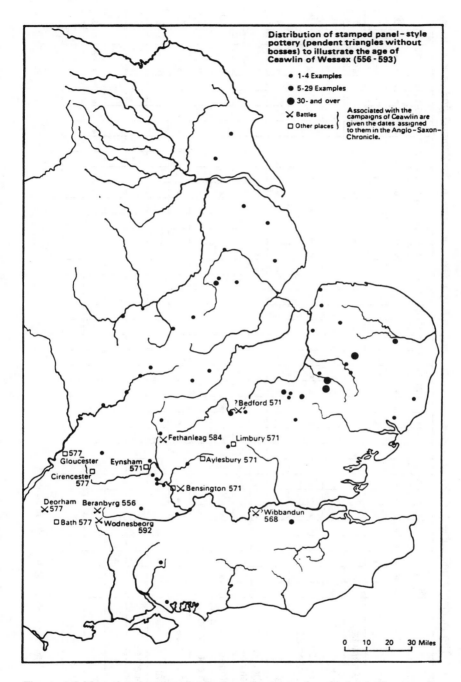

Distribution of stamped panel – style
pottery (pendent triangles without
bosses) to illustrate the age of
Ceawlin of Wessex (556 - 593)

● 1-4 Examples
● 5-29 Examples
● 30- and over
✕ Battles
□ Other places

Associated with the
campaigns of Ceawlin are
given the dates assigned
to them in the Anglo – Saxon-
Chronicle.

?Bedford 571
✕Fethanleag 584   Limbury 571
□577   □Aylesbury 571
Gloucester   Eynsham
Cirencester   571□
577   ✕Bensington 571
Deorham Beranbyrg 556
✕577   ✕
□Bath 577 ✕Wodnesbeorg   ✕?Wibbandun
                 592   568

0   10   20   30 Miles

Figure 1.6 Map showing the distribution of a type of early Anglo-Saxon
pottery and its supposed coincidence with battles recorded in the *Anglo-
Saxon Chronicle* (source: Myres 1969, Map 9)

Table 1.1 The incidence and subject matter of articles on or pertaining to Anglo-Saxon archaeology in *Medieval Archaeology* 1–38

	'57	'58	'59	'60	'61	'63	'64	'65	'66	'67	'68	'69	'70	'71	'72	'73	'74	'75	'76	'77	'78	'79	'80	'81	'82	'83	'84	'85	'86	'87	'88	'89	'90	'91	'92	'93	'94	
Metal	•	•	•	•	•	•	•	•	•					•		•	•			•				•		•		•	•	•	•	•	•	•	•	•	•	26
Pottery			•									•																•	•	•	•					•		6
Other Artefacts	•									•		•									•						•			•	•				•			9
Art Style	•															•	•				•					•		•		•		•	•			•		10
Rural settlements/ buildings/industry	•			•	•	•	•							•	•	•						•	•	•		•	•	•		•				•				15
Towns										•			•	•				•	•								•		•	•					•			9
Churches & monasteries								•			•	•										•	•						•	•								7
Cemeteries	•					•				•	•		•						•								•	•		•					•			10
Settlement Patterns																								•			•								•			3
Written sources	•						•					•															•				•	•		•	•			7
General			•	•							•																											3
Place-names									•	•																												2
Coins				•							•																											2
Economy																															•		•		•			3
Theory																																				•		1

Source: Dickinson (1983), Figure 4 with additions

been three major projects at Mucking, Essex, Spong Hill, Norfolk and Sutton Hoo, Suffolk. Published reports reveal the greater desire for detail and the development of new techniques to cope with the particular problems of excavating early Anglo-Saxon cemeteries. A major improvement in recent years has been the inclusion in such reports of at least some analysis and interpretation of the data (see, for instance, Cook and Dacre 1985; Sherlock and Welch 1992). Earlier reports tended to be content with inventories of graves and their contents although there may be special reasons for this in some circumstances (for instance, Green and Rogerson 1978). This state of affairs is due in part to publication policies.

Dickinson (1983) and Hills (1979) surveyed the more recent years of early Anglo-Saxon studies. Both rightly stressed the shift away from cemetery excavation to the examination of settlements but overlooked the important point that while there was an apparent shift away from the limiting aim of integrating the archaeological and historical data, this was not accompanied by any reassessment of the appropriate aims and methods of studying the archaeology. Dickinson considered the nature of relevant articles published in the journal *Medieval Archaeology* (ibid.: 36–7, Figure 4); we can usefully extend the chronology of this (Table 1.1). She identified a number of limiting factors in the exercise that still apply, such as whether that journal is actually an accurate barometer of current thinking amongst archaeologists of the post-Roman period. It is also worthwhile querying whether the nature of what has been published is governed by the nature of the archaeological evidence or by other considerations. Studies of metalwork, especially decorated metalwork, have consistently dominated other materials. Papers relating to types of settlement have been sporadic but consistent, with perhaps rural settlements and buildings increasing in frequency since the late 1970s. Of other categories the written sources have been most commonly pursued. New categories have had to be added since Dickinson began this exercise, all concerned with analysis: settlement patterns and economics made their appearance from the 1980s but theory has remained largely absent. Dickinson's view that early Anglo-Saxon archaeology lacked a good theoretical framework was an extraordinarily isolationist one, when archaeology had been undergoing a revolution in thinking since the beginning of the 1960s and was dominated by theoretical considerations appropriate to all archaeological periods. While it was true that the literature of the 1970s and 1980s hardly reflected those changes, experimentation was taking place and traditional methodologies were being challenged. It is only in the 1990s that it has been possible to see the more widespread adoption of contemporary archaeological thinking on early Anglo-Saxon archaeology.

The principal reasons for that state of affairs lay in the explanations given at the beginning of this chapter; scholars with museum backgrounds laid the foundations for an artefact-based subject in the first half of the twentieth century, heavily influenced and directed by the written sources. To many scholars of the early Anglo-Saxon period the study of artefacts with a view to placing them into dated sequences *was* archaeology rather than forming the basis for research into the period. Such work was accompanied by little or no questioning of the methodology. Many of the changes that occurred in archaeology generally from the 1960s onwards came about through the development of independent dating techniques that removed the need for the grouping of artefacts to represent 'cultures' using typologies, in part, to provide the time-scale. The release from such constraints allowed for different ways of looking at the data in pursuit of an understanding of society.

The 'New Archaeology' of the 1960s onwards had as its main aim the explanation of societal change rather than the description of the data. It viewed societies as systems whose workings could be understood by examining the inter-relationship between its components. In keeping with the contemporary philosophy of science, theories should be explicit and conclusions should be testable. The result was a very functional, scientific approach to society that viewed it in a mechanistic manner. This is hardly the place for an analysis of the New Archaeology – more important here are its effects on early Anglo-Saxon archaeology. Much of the criticism in this section of the first edition (Arnold 1988a: 9–12) was aimed at the apparent unwillingness of others to embrace archaeological theory and see its benefits; it is now part of the history of the period. The first edition of this book was the result of varied research in the 1970s and 1980s very much in the hypothetico-deductive mould that was designed to explain early Anglo-Saxon society rather than merely describe it within a framework driven by the historical sources. Much of that work centred on the quantitative analysis of cemeteries (Arnold 1980) aimed at an understanding of social structure based around the idea of status. This book itself was strongly influenced by theories of state formation that formed a higher level of generalisation.

There was resistance to the application of such new theories within early Anglo-Saxon archaeology although there was little explicit criticism of the theories from within the specialisation (Evison 1987). For many, the New Archaeology passed by like a skirmishing army on a distant ridge. Students of the history of archaeology would probably agree that it had a significant effect on archaeology and this is also now reflected within early Anglo-Saxon archaeology. As the teaching of archaeological theory became more widespread in British universities students expected new ideas to be applied across the board and when this did not occur some decided to respond themselves. What characterises much of the exciting published research of the last decade or so is the desire to look at horizontal relationships, to move away from the earlier emphasis on vertical relationships. In the 1980s attempts were made to examine the social context of some of the evidence through synchronic analysis, much of it computer-based (Arnold 1983; Richards 1987). Structuralist approaches to cemeteries are demonstrating the ways in which social and ideological relationships can be examined and emphasise that there is not a direct relationship between mortuary rituals and life (Härke 1990; Huggett 1995); analysis of metalwork decoration is seeking to understand the language of the motifs (Leigh 1984a); there is a growing desire to engender work on the period (Brush 1988) and to reach the social identity of individuals (Pader 1982; Fisher 1988). The influence of Critical Theory is also visible in studies of attitudes to early Anglo-Saxon archaeology (Hamerow 1994). There is now a great vibrancy within the discipline with researchers looking forward to a secure innocence, and the discipline has 'the critical awareness of available approaches and techniques that is essential if we are to begin interrogating the social and economic aspects of the archaeological record rigorously' (Scull 1993: 66). At the same time the work of providing basic order to the material and of re-assessing earlier work has continued (Dickinson 1993a; Hines 1984, 1992a; Leigh 1984b). There has also been a greater willingness to summarise the archaeology of the period particularly with a view to seeing the contribution of the early Anglo-Saxon period to later times (Hinton 1990; Welch 1992; Higham 1992)

It has taken the best part of a century to reach the stage where such studies are possible, during which time the evidence has been described and ordered. If the development of theoretical archaeology became possible within prehistoric studies in the 1960s because of the development of scientific dating techniques, the difficulties of using those techniques within the early Anglo-Saxon period might, in part, explain the desire to retain traditional methodologies. The degrees of confidence that can be applied to scientific dates are inadequate for a period that can be viewed in terms of generations (Campbell, Baxter and Alcock 1979) and timbers that might be used to provide dendrochronological dates are extremely rare. Thus scientific methods of dating are probably less accurate than the traditional methods based on the study of artefacts, although their accuracy is very difficult to establish. It is important to stress, therefore, that there is no absolute, only a relative, chronology for the period.

The unreliability of the written sources and the more obvious difficulty of actually relating the majority of historical events to archaeological data, make their use for dating early Anglo-Saxon archaeology very limited. It is important to understand how chronologies for the period have been constructed as even synchronic studies have at their root the knowledge that data belongs to the period and dating becomes even more critical when seeking to understand change in society. E.T. Leeds worked hard to use the sources to provide a chronology of the development of brooch types (1933) and the extremely dubious assumptions he made have coloured a great deal of thinking to this day as most typologies assume evenly paced evolution of form and decoration. There was rarely any regard for the context that actually determined the series of choices that were made to achieve a particular end product and the transformations undergone in the creation of the archaeological record. Even if they are accurate, the written accounts are principally concerned with conscious expressions of political life, while archaeology is concerned with a mixture of conscious and unconscious actions. The little history of the period that has survived is an invaluable asset, but there are great dangers in using archaeological data to elucidate chronologically-based historical problems when the span of as little as a generation is so crucial. In addition the surviving texts are not contemporary with the period and say as much about the aspirations of the writers in their own time as about the past they were presenting.

One of the earliest detailed discussions of how the artefacts of the period might be dated was provided by Åberg (1926: 149–58), although typically there was no consideration of what such chronology could be used for beyond using it to relate the archaeological data to a historical narrative:

> the chronological position of the Anglo-Saxon antiquities has been esti-mated partly from the typological characteristics of the material and from the occurrence of the various objects in closed finds in association with other objects, partly from datable coins.
>
> (ibid.: 149)

From these cases, similar artefacts could be dated by comparison. In using this method it is rarely clear whether the date applies to the manufacture or deposition of the artefact. Some of the earliest material (i.e. object-types which are found both on the Continent and in England) was dated by refer-ence to the historical sources: 'the oldest brooches belong to the time of the invasion' (ibid.: 156). Artefacts found on both sides of the North Sea provide an important reference point, although it would be easy to question the basis of the chronology of such objects on the Continent. The use of English material to support Continental chronologies creates additional problems.

Åberg (1926) discussed the value to chronology of the Crondall (Hampshire) coin hoard (Sutherland 1948) and graves at Sarre (Kent) and Compton Vernay (Warwickshire) which contained coins (Rigold 1975: 71–2; Avent 1975: 47). A number of other graves containing coins have been added to the list since Åberg was writing in 1926 (Rigold 1975: 69–70; Avent 1975: 6; Rigold and Bayley 1977; Grierson and Blackburn 1986) as well as the one case of coins from a building at Mucking (Hamerow 1993: 64). The *termini post quos* of these finds could be tabulated with the diagnostic contents of each context, but the value of such an exercise must be tempered by the fundamental problems of the chronological association of the coins and the other artefacts and their respective use-life.

A great stride forward was made after 1931 by J.N.L. Myres who began the systematic investigation of early Anglo-Saxon pottery (Myres 1969.: 1–5; 1977), yet there was no clear statement about the methods used to establish the chronology of the vessels under review, despite quite specific dates being ascribed. Myres fitted the material to a five-phase evolution of Anglo-Saxon society to which dates were attributed, but the basis for it was not discussed.

The supposedly most securely dated vessels are those which can be related to Continental chronologies; vessels that occur on the Continent but not in England date to before the migration (or after if contact was lost), those on both sides of the North Sea to the migration period itself (or after if contact was maintained), and those which are only found in England must have developed after the migration period. The method involved making important assumptions about the nature of the migrations and the rate of change in the style of the English pottery if potentially 'early' vessels were not to be confused with those of the following centuries. In the event very few vessels had date ranges given to them (Arnold 1981a). The flexibility employed in making comparisons with Continental pottery has also been questioned, for instance the problem posed when the shape of two vessels is similar but whose decoration is totally different. The artefacts found within cremation vessels were generally ignored and appear at times to conflict with the given dates (Morris 1974; Kidd 1976; Dickinson 1978; Richards 1987).

Most discussions of the chronology of specific artefacts, or artefact-types, of the period are couched in predictably vague terms. This is in a sense unavoidable, but inevitably the flexibility that must be allowed can lead to varying opinions. Fundamental to all such discussions are assumptions about the rate of evolution of decorative styles and the definition of the circumstances in which such evolution took place. It could be argued that until those important issues have been resolved the role of subjective opinion in dating many artefacts is unavoidable.

When dates for particular artefact-types are given it is rarely made clear whether the date is one of manufacture of the artefact, its period of use, or the context in which it was found. The dating of an artefact to the span of a single generation would be to a degree of accuracy that would provide a powerful tool for the study of Anglo-Saxon society. Because the length of the period is so short and can be measured in generations, considerable caution has been shown in the accuracy of dates given (Avent 1975: 56). Some writers quote dates to an accuracy of twenty-five years, others favour thirty years, but rarely is it made clear why or how such dates are obtained. There is unlikely to be any advance in the accuracy of dating early Anglo-Saxon archaeology in the near future whereas the assumptions upon which such dates are based are likely to come under close scrutiny. Most writers have a framework for the development of the society in question to which their chronology is related, whether stated or not. It may therefore be more productive to work within the limitations imposed by the data than to continue to explore art-styles as a route to chronological precision when this does not seem possible because of the unknown number of unknown variables. What is most apparent is that when chronologies are put forward the resulting data either cannot be, or are not, used to study early Anglo-Saxon society in any more detail, and, even when a pattern appears, it is noted as an aside to the central issue.

The aim of this book is to demonstrate how recent archaeological excavation and research have markedly changed our understanding of early Anglo-Saxon archaeology during the period AD *c.* 400–700. This was a society that had complex structures and ideologies and which was undergoing rapid change following the migrations. Rural communities were expanding their social and political networks as the Anglo-Saxon kingdoms gradually formed and coalesced. These changes are paralleled by a growing economic complexity as production and exchange that was embedded in the social structure increasingly took on an institutionalised, commercial appearance. Christianity became a powerful religious force towards the end of the period, superseding a traditional set of beliefs of great antiquity. Archaeology is the principal source of data for informing us about the complexity of this society and the manner in which it was evolving, how change affected the individual as well as the larger groups.

Chapter 2

Migration theory

These new-comers were from the three most formidable races of Germany, the Saxons, Angles, and Jutes.

It was not long before such hordes of these alien peoples vied together to crowd into the island that the natives who had invited them began to live in terror

Bede, *A History of the English Church and People*

Given the material and linguistic dominance of the Germanic migrants on the indigenous population it is interesting that there are so few migration myths and legends (Figure 2.1) but heroic stories are normally the antidote to failure, real or perceived. The principal story is that related by Bede and acceptance of that story has determined much modern opinion regarding the migration period (for a recent discussion, see Hines 1994: 50–2). Thus the archaeological evidence was expected to match the story and little comment

"Take care of yourselves, you hear? Watch out for Angles, Jutes, Saxons, Scots, Picts, Danes and Normans."

Figure 2.1 Cartoon published by *Punch*

was aroused even when it did not (see Figure 1.6). The fact that Bede knew so little of what had occurred may be a reflection of the actual nature of the Germanic settlement of England; that there was no single shared story. The only expansion on the story that has been attempted concerns the numbers of migrants and the true fate of the native population: the various possible models regarding these issues, the very nature of the migrations and our ability to recognise ethnic identities in the archaeological record, have largely determined modern opinion. Surprisingly the applicability of the concept of the 'frontier' to fifth-century England has hardly been debated (Arnold 1984a: 13–16) and at least the principal conceptual dichotomy of frontier as a place of domination and opportunity as opposed to hardship and suffering should form part of the equation; whether or not it is relevant it is implicit in some of the principal models that have been put forward, for instance those models that assumed mass genocide of the native population. A fuller understanding of historical migrations may assist us – a comparison has been made between the archaeological evidence for a fifth-century Saxon settlement at Mucking and the experiences of the Mayflower Pilgrims in New England in 1620 (Dixon 1993) – but it would be dangerous to place too much reliance on comparative studies given the number of potential variables. Due to periodisation of the past, the actual migrations, sandwiched between the collapse of Roman Britain (Arnold 1984a; Esmonde Cleary 1989, 1993) and the establishment of Anglo-Saxon society, have tended to be overlooked in favour of debates about the date of the *adventus Saxonum*.

Few would dispute that during the fifth century Germanic peoples migrated from the Continent to England and settled amongst the native population. While some immigrants may have served as mercenaries in the early stages there is no evidence for a military invasion. It might therefore be assumed that the 'migration' was in reality a large number of different events and that the immigrant and the native populations co-operated in the continuance or development of an agrarian and economic system that was to their mutual benefit. As a result any distinctions gradually blurred despite the very real dominance of one material culture and language. While the seemingly wholesale adoption of Germanic traits might seem powerful evidence for large-scale Germanic migrations, no such explanation is apparently required to explain the wholesale change in religion that occurred in the seventh century. With a desire to maintain, or even create, separate identities, segments of the population at some stage began to bond together under the leadership of dominant lineages, not necessarily of Germanic origin, from which, after a period of competition and emulation, identifiable kingdoms emerged in the later sixth century.

The principal competing theories have been, on the one hand, large-scale migration and population displacement and on the other a British population dominated by a small Germanic warrior élite (for example see the discussions by Scull (1993: 70–2) and Hamerow (1994: 164–6)). Such models, as extreme positions, have been presented as though they represent a choice. The reality may have included both, and the whole spectrum in between, in a particular time or place. This may be supported by the hints that the ethnic identities described by Bede may have been arrived at by different routes (Hines 1994: 52–4). Others see them as a simplification of a contemporary and/or earlier complex pattern of regional and local identities. The reason why such theories are able to float is that the speed and nature of the migrations cannot be demonstrated archaeologically.

Hines views ethnic identity as an ideologically based attribution that is 'qualified for, on the basis of variables such as birth, language, culture and location', that is 'theoretically exchangeable' (1994: 49–50). It would obviously be of great assistance if there was some objective test of past ethnicity, for instance if there was a simple method of determining ethnicity from skeletal remains. While methods of measuring biological distance are being assessed and the search for epigenetic traits is being carried out, we should not overlook the implications of imposing a contemporary pre-occupation with ethnicity onto the past, especially one that is wholly biological. However, the value of physical anthropology to the debate has not been fully tested although observations have been made regarding the coincidence of cultural and genetic traits leading to conclusions regarding the presence of particular peoples (Härke 1990, 1992a; Putnam 1984: 16). Some studies of particular genetic traits have indicated that it is possible to distinguish between native and migrant populations which are found in the same cemeteries although with different types of grave-good (Jackson 1995). Others studies have pointed to continuity in population between Romano-British and Anglo-Saxon samples which, in those samples, would support cultural replacement rather than migration (Lloyd-Jones 1995). It would also be helpful if we could define the sex and age profiles and social cohesion of migrant groups.

The development of theories about the nature of the migrations has tended to reflect the writers' time and place. In the nineteenth century it was polit-ically expedient for historians and the few archaeologists of the period to trace the 'origins' of English society back to their Teutonic roots (Higham 1992: 1–16). This implied a denial that the native population of England or of the other parts of the British Isles had made any major contribution to post-Roman society. This was possible at a time when a simple opposition was being constructed between the mythical Celt who was 'spiritual, imprac-tical, rural, natural, and poetic' and the 'materialism, "Saxon" philistinism, utilitarianism, excessive rationalism, artificiality' of the Germans and the contemporary modern Europe (Sims-Williams 1986: 72). Writers went to considerable lengths to emphasise difference even at the level of physical type (Beddoe 1885). Whatever the extent to which that tension remains in Britain today, political events of the early twentieth century encouraged the gradual, if at times temporary, moderation of such views.

The settlement by Anglo-Saxons was most commonly described as 'invasion' until the end of the Second World War, thereafter 'migration' was the acceptable term. 'The departure of the Romans and the coming of the Teutonic invaders' was virtually all E.T. Leeds had to say on the question in 1913 (Leeds 1913: 9). Writing after the First World War, in 1926, Åberg described the arrival of the Anglo-Saxons as an 'invasion . . . undertaken with large and organised forces' with no mention of the native population. Between the world wars a variety of views are evidenced: Jolliffe (1933) saw 'Kentish civilization' as purely Teutonic while Myres in 1936 could see evidence of 'a slow penetration of humble Saxon cultivators' in East Anglia and of 'military conquest' in southern England (Collingwood and Myres 1936). Twenty years later, after the Second World War, writers went to greater pains to define the stages by which the Germanic peoples may have taken control and to emphasise the resistance, both culturally and militarily, of the British (Harden 1956a; Myres 1969).

The Europe of today is very different from that which was coming to terms with the end of the Second World War, and since the formation of the European Community new concerns have developed regarding the distribution of economic and political power. These have taken a new twist since the implosion of the Communist bloc in 1989. Writers have suggested that migrations should be reinstated as an historical reality and that any attempt to emphasise continuity by playing down the Germanic impact would be a distortion (Härke, quoted by Hamerow 1994: 166). While there is a growing desire to be more precise about the Anglo-Saxon migration there remains a polarity of opinion. One vision is of the remarkable achievement of 'tens of thousands' of migrants imposing 'their language, their law, their political system and their material culture' on a native population 'numbering in the millions' (Esmonde Cleary 1989: 204). An alternative view seeks to explore what 'imposing' means albeit with the involvement of smaller numbers from the Continent; Higham suggests that gradual change was brought about by the 'infiltration' of small warrior groups rather than by a mass migration (Higham 1992: 228). Such groups benefited from the removal of the late Roman aristocracy and took over their estates thereby creating warrior lordships; their leaders therefore had no role model for the acquisition of Roman social, cultural and religious norms, except that which could be transferred from a depressed peasant population. As a variant on this idea Scull suggests that it was the Romanised superstructure that had disappeared leaving the subsistence economy still in the hands of magnate families, a society very similar to that which the migrants had left. It was into such a society that the migrants settled and soon took political control (1992: 8–15; 1993: 70). This implies that a degree of organisation and leadership existed in the societies of the Continental homelands. The study of building traditions in the area first settled by the migrants, eastern England, failed to demonstrate any marked differentiation in building types but élite migrant families might be those building in the new tradition on Roman villa sites (Marshall and Marshall 1991, 1993).

The nature of the migrant groups is rarely defined but it is implied that there was a predominantly male contribution to the bloody or peaceful events. This overlooks the fact that one of the principal indicators of the migration is the female dress-fastener and the number of pre-migration weapon types that the migrants might have been expected to bring to England, such as spears, are few in number (Swanton 1974: 5). As presented, the whole debate hinges on a number of key alternatives that apply to both the native British and the migrants, such as: passive or violent; male and/or female; numerically large or small; dominant or subservient; individualistic or corporate. To Bede's assertion that the country was settled by Angles, Saxons and Jutes, with secondary movements such as that of the Jutes to the Isle of Wight, archaeology contributes a more detailed picture of the migrants' places of origin and destinations in England. On the Continent as in England there were no clearly defined cultural regions, rather core areas with overlapping edges. Analysis of the distributions of dated types of artefact reveals much about the process of acculturation following the migrations but does not explain it (Scull 1993: 71).

The origins of the settlers may be identified through pottery, metalwork and the burial rite used in disposing of the dead (Hines 1984, 1992a, 1992b, 1994). Settlers predominantly from the Anglian area of Schleswig-Holstein and the island of Fyn were in mid, eastern and northern England from early in the fifth century along with some Saxons. Shortly afterwards in the late fifth century there appears to have been a migration from western Norway into Norfolk and Humberside. Saxons left their homeland in the areas south and west of the River Elbe in north Germany during the fifth century, and there is evidence for their settlements in the Thames valley and the area to the south as far east as the River Medway indicated by brooch types such as saucer brooches. On that basis some Saxons also settled in eastern England (Scull 1993: 71) although, ultimately, the greatest concentration is in northern Wessex and Sussex. The view that Jutes migrated from Jutland in the mid-fifth century to east Kent is supported by the presence in east Kent of cruciform brooches and pottery. While that 'identity' rapidly disappeared with the adoption of Frankish forms, square-headed relief brooches and gold bracteates indicate that connections with the homeland continued into the early sixth century (Hawkes and Pollard 1981; Gaimster 1992) and their presence served to reinforce Scandinavian origins in the aristocratic ideology (Hedeager 1992; Hatch Wicker 1992). Kent was to be the source of several of the new dress-forms that were transmitted to and adopted in other areas of England. Indeed, the manner and speed with which the symbolisation of ethnic identity changed with time, especially in styles of dress, have been viewed as the result of their adoption by élite groups of society and promoted by exchange (Hines 1994: 54). Scull views the presence of key immigrant lineages as being crucial to political development (1993: 71–2).

It is difficult to determine the nature of these movements of peoples in terms of numbers, gender structure and frequency although it would not appear to have been a uniform process. Examination of the distribution of some of the earliest types of metalwork indicates that there was not a moving frontier through which new migrants advanced northwards and westwards from coastal enclaves (Hines 1992b). Hines has argued that before the end of the fifth century 'there was a relatively intense forging of new identities amongst the groups of folk of mixed origins settled in England' (1992a: 317). However, studies of early Anglo-Saxon metalwork and pottery are bedevilled by the difficulties of establishing the meaning of the distributions. For instance, the distinction between the colonisation of an area by a distinct ethnic group, implicit in the paragraph above, and of the spread of a fashion visible through artefacts, may forever elude us. We should add to this the obvious problems that the wearing of a diagnostic artefact does not necessarily prove the ethnic affiliation of its wearer and that the principal source of information available is the presence of diagnostic artefacts. It is at least possible to determine where the demand for new products existed, even if the cultural, social and economic factors determining the choice, and the origin of the person making the choice, may be more difficult to define. Similarly, the fact that many of the earliest imported metalwork types are female clothing fasteners only demonstrates that women were dressing in a certain manner, not necessarily that such women came from across the North Sea. Studies of burial rites, dress-fasteners and pottery have emphasised how they were used to distinguish groups on a large scale, such as Anglian or Saxon and also the ethnic identity of the individual for instance through female dress (Dickinson 1991). However, the chosen identity of an individual may, on Higham's model, have more to do with the origins of dominant groups or families in a region and the development of political structure than with the origins of the population as a whole and there is considerable evidence for the mixed origins of the immigrant population in any area. Comparative studies of burial rites have emphasised how communities using particular cemeteries interpreted the specific elements of the rites in a local manner (Richards 1987; Härke 1990; Huggett 1995). The forms of artefact types introduced to England in the fifth century can be used to monitor the patterns of migration. Naturally they only contribute to an understanding of those patterns at the time of death of the individuals with whom they were buried. These burials may come after a period of invisibility of both the native and earliest migrant populations (Scull 1993: 70). In all such studies it is assumed that the earliest objects are contemporary with the migrations whereas they may have been antique when they arrived.

For example, sleeve clasps (wrist or sleeve-fasteners or clasps) introduced to eastern England in the last quarter of the fifth century (Figure 2.2) tend to occur near rivers that emptied into the Wash. They appear in clusters in Cambridgeshire, Norfolk and Suffolk that is in contrast to their wider

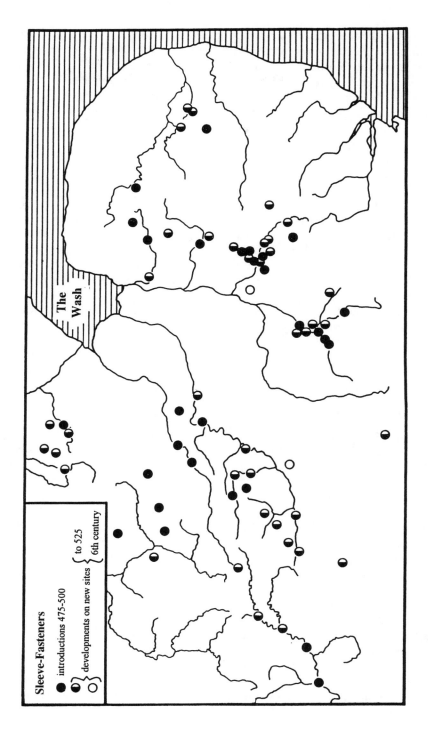

Figure 2.2 Map showing the phased distribution of sleeve-fasteners in eastern England (data: Hines 1994)

Within the map:

Sleeve-Fasteners

● introductions 475–500
◐ developments on new sites } to 525
○ 6th century

The Wash

dispersal in Leicestershire, Northamptonshire and Warwickshire. The distribution is not coastal, suggesting that there was either little effective resistance to the migration and that the settlers enjoyed considerable freedom of choice regarding where they settled to farm, or that such resistance as there was had evaporated by the time of the death of the individual. The actual number of individuals being buried in a given cemetery with such clasps is, as with other signifiers, always very small. The subsequent developments of these metalwork forms tended, until AD 525, to occur in areas around the original clusters and in regions where the early forms were more dispersed. The final developments of the clasps down to about AD 550 are rarely found on new sites. This suggests that migration, colonisation and/or the adoption of the new dress-style had by then ceased and that the settlement pattern had stabilised. In other words localities colonised in the first two phases are still in use later indicating either a stability in the population and settlement pattern or social controls over the spread of a fashion. The fact that there are few new cemeteries after the early sixth century may support the view that the adoption of this new dress-style occurred within a stable settlement pattern.

The square-headed brooches that appear to have supplanted earlier brooch types, such as the cruciform brooch, in eastern England reveal a similar pattern (Figure 2.3). Those of the earliest phase AD 500–20 are thinly and widely dispersed in areas away from the coast. Those of the second, and overlapping, phase AD 510–50 tend to cluster around the earlier sites and in new areas such as Berkshire. In the third and final phase AD 530–70 there are again few new locations brought into use. In Norfolk and areas along the coast to the north the brooch only appears at this time, not because there was late settlement there, but because it was slower to replace other forms. In complete contrast the earliest Jutish evidence in Kent, for instance the cruciform brooches (Figure 2.4) dating from AD 450 onwards, is concentrated mostly in east Kent, again not on the coast, with a few further west along the northern edge of Kent.

Taken literally, the patterns might suggest that groups of Germanic brooch-using or brooch-making migrants quickly settled inland and that the limited additional expansion could simply be the result of population expansion or exchange with previously non-brooch-using groups. They tell us nothing about the nature of the migrant groups, of the non-brooch-using individuals or of migrant and native relationships.

Attitudes about the fate of the British during and after the period of migration have changed considerably over the last one hundred years. At one time the view was propounded that many were annihilated, as Bede suggested, but more recently there has been a gradual acceptance that they were present but invisible. There is now a growing desire to see them in the archaeological record. Previous work had been blinkered by the belief that everything new in the fifth and sixth centuries must be the result of Germanic domination;

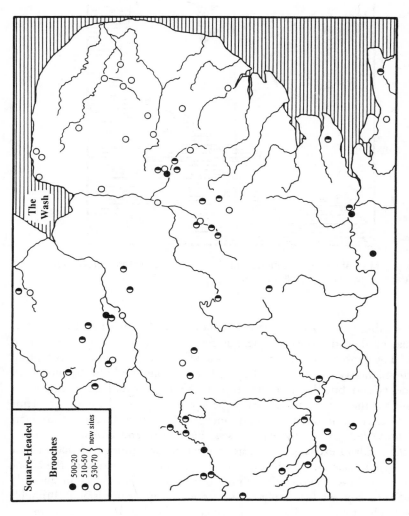

The Wash

Square-Headed
Brooches

● 500-20
◐ 510-50 } new sites
○ 530-70

Figure 2.3 Map showing the phased distribution of square-headed brooches in the Midlands and eastern England (data: Hines 1994)

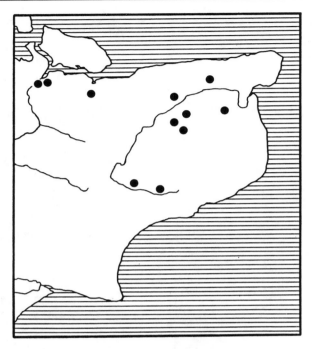

Figure 2.4 Map showing distribution of fifth-century cruciform brooches in east Kent (data: Hawkes and Pollard 1981)

but in seeking the native population it should not be forgotten that there is an equal need to demonstrate the existence of Germanic people in a given region. The problem has been compounded by the all-too-easy assumption that Germanic-style artefacts in England can automatically be equated with settlements and burials of those peoples. While it would be foolhardy to suggest that there were no Germanic people in England there are problems of consistency of argument. For instance, sixth-century Germanic artefacts found in Wales, principally glass vessels, metalwork and beads, are claimed to be the result of exchange, whereas we have already concluded that in East Anglia such a dispersal may be due to an expanding population or the adoption of new dress fashion. The ethnic origin of an individual in an early Anglo-Saxon context has not yet been conclusively demonstrated although studies made of communities on the fringes of the distribution of Germanic artefacts have argued for a strong native cultural contribution (Faull 1977). A characteristic such as crouched burial can no longer be viewed as a good indicator (Whyman 1993). Even if a mixing of traits can be demonstrated it still says nothing about the origin of the individual. The manner in which a group's ethnic identity was indicated may have changed through time and it may not always or only have been represented through the durable component of material culture.

It would be helpful if the known distribution of (dead) people in early Anglo-Saxon England (Figure 8.1) could be compared with the distribution of people in the equivalent area of fourth-century Roman Britain. However, such a catalogue of evidence has not been published. Such a comparison made in East Anglia (Scull 1992: 10–14) revealed a strong coincidence between the distributions suggesting the Romano-British pattern strongly influenced the Anglo-Saxon: it 'suggests that the earliest Germanic settlement took place within a British society in which elements of the settlement hierarchy most closely associated with the cantonal administration and Romano-British economic structures still exercise some pull'. However such a similarity may be as much the result of topography and continuity in land-use as any other factor and does not demonstrate a particular form of ethnic interaction. Early Anglo-Saxon period artefacts, known principally from their use as grave-goods, are found in many parts of England although they are as rare in western areas as they are in Wales and Scotland where they are mostly found on settlements. Within the regions where they are found in any quantity there are particular concentrations and areas devoid of any evidence. The major concentrations are in east Kent, on the north shore of the Thames Estuary in Essex, in Norfolk and Cambridgeshire, Lincolnshire and Humberside. Areas such as the Weald, Derbyshire and Northumberland have produced considerably less evidence. Those areas of England where no Germanic style artefacts are found merit greater attention as they may provide a base-line for comparison.

Hines has examined the question of language as an ethnic identifier in the light of the known history of linguistic change in north-west Europe around the time of the migrations (Hines 1994). However analytically convenient it is to think in terms of a linguistic geography of discrete variants it is more probable that there was a linguistic continuum around the North Sea. It was a continuum that had been established by the Late Roman Period and was quickly re-established 'after the demographic disruptions of the Migration Period' reflecting 'a high degree of linguistic flexibility that is directly correlated with the intense redefinition of group identities that took place in Germanic Europe between circa 200 and 600 AD' (ibid.: 57). It is seen as likely that the various known forms of Old English 'represent the separate identities of distinctive and influential interest groups of Early to Middle Anglo-Saxon England' (ibid.: 56). Such interest groups may be the élite of the developing kingdoms and as the kingdoms emerged as political realities 'both language and ethnic identity began to be "nationalised" in a recognisably modernistic, political way, and the boundaries of language varieties and group identity began to rival the foci of these phenomena as determinative factors' (ibid.: 57). As a hypothesis for the eventual emergence of a language it sits most comfortably with the 'élite dominance' theory of the migrations rather than with the 'mass-migration' alternative. The manner in which language acted as an ethnic identifier, particularly if it was driven by a small segment of society, need not be mirrored exactly by other means of ethnic identification. Analysis of the sources for understanding language variation and change also needs to be carried out as they may only reflect the language of a few.

The interpretation of the buildings and settlements of the period has been coloured by ignorance of late Roman 'native' rural settlements. It is becoming clear (James, Marshall and Millett 1984) that the common rectangular buildings of the period do not have a unique origin, but are a hybrid that perhaps owes most to Romano-British building techniques (Dixon 1993). The only unadulterated 'import' may be the sunken buildings, *Grubenhäuser*, which were used as dwellings and workshops. The presence of rectangular timber buildings amongst the masonry buildings of a Roman villa, such as Orton Hall Farm, Northamptonshire, (Mackreth 1978) might be interpreted as the re-use of an estate and its headquarters by Germanic people. Alternatively this might be viewed as the replacement in timber of Roman buildings that could not be repaired as the materials and technology were no longer available. The ethnic origin of the builders need not be paramount and is in any case not known. Timber buildings were being erected in parts of fifth- and sixth-century England, the plans, method of construction and external appearance of which were, at most, a mixture of Romano-British and Germanic traits and which were built both on the fringes of the area of Anglo-Saxon settlement as well as at its heart (Scull 1991). The majority of the earliest buildings are known from eastern England, where the building tradition evolved most slowly, from where it appears to have spread to other areas with greater fusion with native traits (Marshall and Marshall 1993). This is the type of hybridisation that might be predicted if the two elements of the population were co-operating, although such a merging of ideas is less apparent in language and artefacts. The type of buildings and settlement layout of post-Roman Britain outside the areas of Germanic settlement are perhaps exemplifed by Poundbury, Dorset, although the differences should not be allowed to distract us from the similarities (Green 1987). What is most challenging is the apparent speed with which hybrid buildings appeared over a wide area and this might support the view that they are as much a hybrid as a native form of architecture. The analysis of animal bone from settlements as an indicator of husbandry practices and diet emphasises that there was little change between early Anglo-Saxon settlements and earlier ones whereas there are marked differences with patterns on the other side of the North Sea (Crabtree 1989a, 1989b).

The contribution of the native population has been detected in various types of ornamental metalwork, such as quoit brooches and certain forms of penannular brooch. Both developed in, and out of, a late Roman milieu and occur in early Anglo-Saxon period graves, albeit in small numbers (White 1988; Ager 1990) as though some of the native people hung on to their identity for longer than others. The difficulty of identifying the native population's contribution to material culture is of paramount importance in any analysis of the relationship between them and the incoming population.

There may be considerable scope for comparisons between burial customs of Migration Period northern Europe and late Roman Britain with those in early Anglo-Saxon England. By these means it would be possible to determine the nature and extent of change following the period of migration. What is clearer now is that a number of the burial forms that are claimed to be purely British can be found on the Continent. A change from cremation to inhumation was occurring on the Continent during the migration period. The preponderance of cremation in eastern England (Figure 3.9) has been used to support an early date for settlement there and while this might also be used to explain the, real or apparent, preference for inhumation in certain regions in the Anglo-Saxon period it must be tempered by the fact that such a burial rite was preferred in late Roman Britain. If the latter tradition was influential in determining funerary custom, especially in southern England, it is necessary to ask why it was of less relevance in the areas where cremation was preferred. The timing of the colonisation of particular areas has normally been seen as critical to the resulting pattern but it may also serve to emphasise that the migrations and subsequent developments were not uniform processes.

The availability of detailed analyses of late Roman burial customs makes it possible to begin to identify a much greater contribution to post-Roman funerary practices than might once have been thought (Black 1986; Philpott 1991). Certain burial forms, such as decapitation, north–south alignment and prone burials, have been claimed as exclusively native; such burials always form a minority of the graves in an Anglo-Saxon period cemetery. This should be seen positively as the continuation or re-introduction of some burial customs rather than an indication of the proportions of native and immigrant in the population. The number of inhumation graves in a cemetery that can be claimed to demonstrate an exclusively Germanic burial rite is also relatively few. The information gleaned from burials about dress fashions also points to native traditions, for instance the burial of unworn bracelets and of single brooches on the shoulder (Owen-Crocker 1986; White 1988). More attention might also be given to those 'Anglo-Saxon' cemeteries that contain overtly 'late Roman' forms of burial to determine the actual number of traits that are carried through. Many writers have suggested that such an opportunity, albeit a rare one, exists at Wasperton, Warwickshire, where a late Roman cemetery is stratigraphically earlier than one in which cremations and inhumations were accompanied by early Anglo-Saxon grave-goods (Crawford 1983). This need not be seen as a result of a change in the population so much as a change in material culture and custom. The populations may have been assimilated with the adoption of certain aspects of different cultures.

In the absence of an objective test of an individual's origin, as opposed to a given identity expressed in part through material culture, the question of the nature of the migrations will continue to flow with the tide of contemporary thought. The precise points on which disagreement turns are now much clearer but the debate is continually scuttling sideways to new unresolved areas without any greater resolution. The question of identity has focused minds and encouraged a new way of thinking about material culture as something active that has wide-ranging possibilities and not only with regard to this issue.

Chapter 3

Farm and field

An Anglo-Saxon farmstead could draw on a variety of environments to maintain the supply of essential resources. The evidence recovered from excavations emphasises that the landscape was being fully utilised by the inhabitants of farms, or groups of farms, dispersed across the landscape. The extent of utilisation is exemplified by the settlement and cemetery excavated on a hilltop overlooking the English Channel at Bishopstone, Sussex, (Bell 1977). In the fifth century buildings were erected over an earlier farm and fields. In the pastures stood sheep, cattle and a few horses and roaming more freely were geese, fowl and cats (Figure 3.1). Growing in the arable fields during the summer months would have been a crop of barley amongst which various weeds were growing, including fat-hen, common orache and black bindweed. The food produced in this way was supplemented by marine resources: mussels, limpets and periwinkles gathered on the foreshore, conger eel from the lower shore and whiting taken from the sea; nets were made on the farm. The animals not only provided dairy products, meat, leather and wool for clothing; bone was used to make such things as combs, weaving tools and netting needles. In nearby woodland pigs were reared, and red and roe deer were hunted. Also taken from the woodland were oak, hawthorn and hornbeam used for building, for fuel and for the wooden implements found in the adjacent cemetery. Clay and ironstone were brought from the Weald to manufacture pottery, spindle-whorls, loomweights and a variety of iron implements including nails, knives, spears and shield fittings. Copper-alloy and silver items were manufactured or acquired and eventually buried, along with considerable quantities of other material, as grave-goods in the community's cemetery (Figure 3.8).

This picture of subsistence agriculture varies little between settlements and any minor variations may be seen as the result of local environmental, social or cultural differences, survival or the recovery technique used in excavation (Table 3.1). Some of the differences are most marked; for instance at Cowdery's Down, Hampshire, the large proportion of cattle bones is the result of the discovery of a complete cow on a site where generally few animal bones were found. There is generally little variation in the quantities of bones

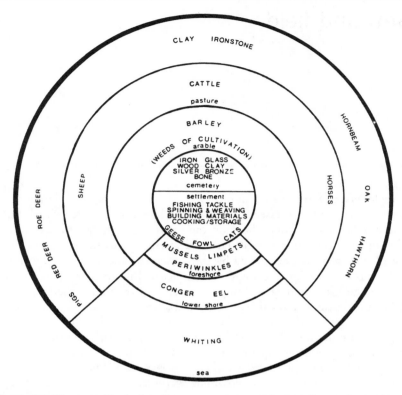

Figure 3.1 Diagram illustrating the resources exploited at the early Anglo-Saxon settlement at Bishopstone, Sussex. The evidence from the buildings and the cemetery is shown in the centre, surrounded by the resources derived from the sea-shore, arable fields, pasture and the Weald (data: Bell 1977)

of each species found on settlements; at West Stow, Suffolk, the proportions of animal species and the particular bones were the same in all types of context.

The settlement of West Stow was located on the banks of the River Lark in the relatively dry Breckland region of East Anglia. This is reflected in the animal bone recovered (West 1985; Crabtree 1985, 1989a, 1989b). The environment was quite different from that at Bishopstone: the valley provided good pasture, while the river itself was home to fish and water fowl; the river terraces supplied good farmland; and away from the river terraces the higher slopes provided rough grazing. Analysis suggested that hunting of deer and other wild mammals and of birds was rare and that at all stages in the settlement's history cattle, sheep and goat, pig, horse, geese and chickens provided the majority of the meat diet; cats and dogs were present but apparently

Table 3.1 Quantities of animal bones from early Anglo-Saxon settlements by percentage of fragments (x = present). Data is generated and presented by different methods: for significance of figures see original reports.

Site	cattle	sheep/goat	pig	horse	deer	bird
Walton	38	31.8	21	3	0.7	4.2
Bishopstone	25	39.5	17.2	2.2	1.4	7.8
Cowdery's Down	71.3	4.3	3			
Old Down Farm	37.5	42	7.5	2.4		4.2
West Stow Phase 1	34.27	44.04	21.69	x	x	x
West Stow Phase 2	36.3	49.98	13.71	x	x	x
West Stow Phase 3	34.66	45.69	19.65	x	x	x
Mucking	46	16	25	12	x	x

were not eaten. Typically the commonest domesticated animal was the sheep or goat, which was increasing in importance throughout the period in preference to cattle, unlike Continental settlements where sheep are less common. The sheep at West Stow were being used mainly for a combination of meat production and dairying, with a small amount of wool being used for domestic purposes (West 1985: 93). Cattle at this time were generally good-sized, perhaps the result of the provision of reasonable grazing and implying successful husbandry. Horseflesh was more commonly eaten in earlier periods and on contemporary settlements on the Continent than at West Stow. The third most common animal found at West Stow was the pig which was being consumed in large numbers during the early fifth century. This is surprising when the Brecklands are more suitable for sheep-rearing. Pigs were comparatively rare on the Continent at this time. Crabtree suggests (1989a: 210) that this may be because of the time it would have taken settlers to establish their herds of sheep and cattle; pigs on the other hand 'mature quickly and multiply rapidly' and would be very suitable for such circumstances. This assumes, however, that the shape of the system of animal husbandry was driven by the needs of migrants. However, the differences between meat consumption and kill-patterns in England and on the Continent suggest different cultural influences. In contrast there was no change in butchery techniques and kill-patterns between early Anglo-Saxon West Stow and in local Romano-British samples and there is no evidence for the introduction of new breeds in the fifth century. The evidence indicates that native traditions of animal husbandry were a greater influence than any Continental traditions that might have been introduced with the migrations.

At West Stow wild animals were not commonly hunted, their remains making up less than 1 per cent of the total. As a representation of the make-up of the diet this would seem to be typical although the quantity of wild animal bones does not necessarily convey their social importance. At West Stow these comprised red deer, roe deer, badger, hare, fox, beaver and the

European brown bear as well as large water birds including teal, white-fronted goose, swan and crane. At Walton (Buckinghamshire) beavers, cranes, plover and redwing were identified (Farley 1976) but were equally rare. The infrequency with which wild animals were taken may be reflected in the similar rarity of the bow and arrow (Manley 1985). One bow was described by the excavator as 'about five feet in length' (Hillier 1856: 30). In a Warwickshire cemetery, Bidford-on-Avon, were 'several arrowheads of different patterns with closed sockets' (Humphreys *et al.* 1923: 96–7). The bow and arrow may be used as a weapon as well as for hunting game but it may be significant that not only are they rare in early Anglo-Saxon contexts but so also are other tools. The burial of weapons in graves appears to have been controlled by a particular set of rules (p. 188) and it may be significant that the bow and arrow is not included in that context. The rarity of the bow may also indicate that some hunting was restricted to particular social groups.

Animal husbandry in the early Anglo-Saxon period appears to have been designed to satisfy immediate local needs, but evidence that the situation was changing towards the end of the period can be found by comparing such food resources with those at the earliest post-Roman urban and commercial centres in England; Hamwic, the middle-Saxon port of Southampton, and Ipswich (Suffolk) have both seen large-scale excavation and have produced useful assemblages of animal bone. Middle-Saxon rural settlements, like those earlier, were supplied with domestic animals as well as some wild ones, whereas the latter are rare at Hamwic (Bourdillon 1979; Crabtree 1989b). Although they were eventually eaten, the Hamwic sheep were not reared primarily for that purpose, and there are lower proportions of fowl and poultry than at early and middle-Saxon farms. The numbers of cattle on both rural and urban middle-Saxon settlements are very similar but their size is larger than their earlier counterparts suggesting some improvement, whereas there was no significant development in the size of pigs. The conclusion would seem to be that the early Anglo-Saxon countryside was managed differently, or not as efficiently, as in the following centuries. In the eighth and ninth centuries the killing age of domestic animals was earlier in rural contexts, whereas at Hamwic the bones do not reveal such early mortality, implying that the town, divorced from the wild, was not affected by the immediate hazards of the land or that it was supplied with animals of selected older age groups (Crabtree 1989b: 207). The early killing age at the early Anglo-Saxon settlement at Walton need not reflect success in animal husbandry.

Other similarities and differences between the early Saxon rural settlements and the later urban ones can be found in the butchery techniques used. At West Stow butchery was carried out using a heavy chopping technique with a cleaver or by fine knife cuts especially 'to disarticulate the hock joint' (Crabtree 1989b: 208) and this method is found on earlier and other contemporary settlements. The sawing of bone at West Stow and Hamwic was confined to bone working for secondary uses. The longitudinal splitting of long bones at West Stow was rare in comparison with the later middle-Saxon urban settlements.

If meat from domestic animals made up a significant proportion of the diet the remainder was supplied by crops. Barley was not always the only crop grown as the data recovered at Bishopstone might suggest but it is always the most commonly represented, followed by wheat and then rye and oats. The impressions of two peas on pottery at Mucking may be the first recorded from the period (van der Veen 1993: 81). At Mucking and Stonea, Cambridgeshire, there were impressions of the two principal forms of wheat: the hulled wheat, *Triticum spelta* and naked bread wheat *Triticum aestivum* (van der Veen 1993). At West Stow there were indications that a change from the hulled varieties to the naked bread wheats occurred at some time between the mid-fifth century and the middle-Saxon period. Samples of Roman and of mid-fifth century date contained hulled spelt wheat, suggesting a degree of continuity in production, while in a late seventh-century deposit it was absent (Murphy 1985: 103). Of the crops found in urban environments after AD 700, bread wheat is the most common, whereas the hulled spelt wheat occurred rarely, possibly merely as a contaminant to the crop. Naked wheats are free-threshing and, unlike the hulled varieties grown earlier, grow best on heavy soils. Further samples from settlements in a wide variety of locations will be required before a detailed picture of early Anglo-Saxon agriculture can be produced; generalising from a few samples may well blur regional differences.

There is nothing to suggest that there was any significant change in diet as a result of the migrations and the only changes that occur in the late seventh century could be interpreted as a drive for greater efficiency to feed a growing non-food-producing urban population. It should be remembered however that only a small part of the total diet is visible archaeologically. Similarly the study of past dental health can provide only general indications about the food eaten. During the early Anglo-Saxon period a diet having a coarse physical consistency resulted in a lower incidence of dental caries compared with modern populations. The consumption of naturally occurring sugars in milk, honey and fruit resulted in cavities occurring at different positions to those in modern teeth (Moore and Corbett 1971).

Despite extensive sampling during the excavation of the sixth- and seventh-century settlement at Cowdery's Down the results prompted the excavator to offer a warning about interpreting the results; it was concluded that 'it is impossible to make any assertions about the economy or waste disposal systems associated with the site' (Green 1983: 261). The rarity of evidence for domestic and agricultural activities provoked a number of suggestions. It may simply be the result of little domestic refuse being left around the settlement; cereals may not have been processed there, or, if they were, not in a place likely to have resulted in their being burnt and therefore preserved. It seems unlikely that cereals played a minor role in the diet. Such domestic refuse may have been spread on fields and the removal of floors by later agriculture may have robbed the archaeologist of vital information. This may only be an important curiosity of Cowdery's Down, for, on other contemporary settlements, pits and other deep features contained numerous seeds and animal bones. At West Stow, for instance, there were not only extensive deposits but it was also possible to suggest how they had formed. One feature contained carbonised rye grains, a 'fully processed crop ready for consumption or sowing' that may have been accidentally burnt, while another pit contained rye that had become contaminated and had been burnt as refuse (Murphy 1985: 102). At the same site coprolites, probably human, and found in sunken buildings and pits, revealed a relatively low level of parasite eggs. This implies that the incidence of such infections was low (Walker 1985). It may be significant that deep features, such as sunken buildings and pits, which were common at West Stow were much less common at Cowdery's Down (see p. 51).

The survival of such evidence may be due to a wide range of factors that need have little to do with contemporary activities. Nevertheless, even at Cowdery's Down a pattern is apparent. In the earliest phases of the settlement, when all of the buildings were closely associated with fenced enclosures, the majority of the bone and cereal recovered came from buildings straddling the fence. In the third and final phase the majority of the food remains came from the buildings inside the enclosure, especially from smaller buildings. This change may reflect the growth in size or importance of the settlement and the greater separation of domestic and farming activities.

Very little is known about the layout of fields or of the ploughs that may have been employed on them. It has been suggested that a totally new system of open fields for arable agriculture was laid out in at least one area of England in the seventh century (Hall 1979, 1981). The absence of evidence of a distinctive layout of fields before that time has led to the suggestion that Romano-British fields continued to be used in the early Anglo-Saxon period. Open fields may have been a feature that developed gradually through the Anglo-Saxon period as a whole (Taylor and Fowler 1978). None of the parts of ploughs from the period have survived except for a soil stain from a wooden object in an unusual grave at Sutton Hoo, Suffolk. This has been interpreted as representing a complete ard-type plough (Carver 1992a: 353). Although horses were kept it is not at all clear whether they or cattle were used for traction. Horseflesh was certainly eaten but whether they were used for transport has to be judged against the relatively small numbers of animals represented (Table 3.1) and the rarity of pieces of horse-gear from settlements and cemeteries. The central link of a three-link horse-bit was excavated at Walton; if actually Anglo-Saxon it is a very rare example (Farley 1976: 198). Late prehistoric terrets have been found in Anglo-Saxon cemeteries on the Isle of Wight and in Kent (Arnold 1982a: 68). Snaffle-bits made of two linked iron bars with a small ring at each end are known from a scatter of cemeteries across the country from Lincolnshire to Kent (Welch 1983: 112). That horses at Mucking were kept until *c.* 20 years of age suggests they were kept for work (Done 1993: 79).

The range of tools found on these farms is often limited and unrepresentative of the range of activities known to have taken place. They are found in the deeper deposits of sunken buildings; tools associated with textile production are most commonly recognised. In addition there are rotary querns for milling flour, hand sickles, stone rubbers, awls, knives connected with leather-working, punches and a hammer for metalworking and hones for sharpening edge-tools and weapons. The rarity of tools is particularly emphasised by the number of known woodworking tools: whilst carpentry skills are demonstrated in the construction of houses, furniture, in ship-building and in the production of fine items like cups of stave construction, woodworking tools are extremely rare. The cemeteries of Horton Kirby and Lyminge, Kent, produced axe-hammers and a T-shaped axe, a plane and wedges. A boring-bit and saw have been identified at cemeteries in East Anglia (Wilson 1968; Dunning 1959). At the settlements at Mucking a chisel, awls, gimlet and a round shave were found (Morris 1993). It is not clear why there should be such a high proportion of woodworking tools from Kent, especially the cemetery at Sarre beside the Wantsum Channel, but it may reflect shipbuilding and repairing as much as more general carpentry. It seems probable that most tools were handed on from one generation to the next; their frequency in Kent may reflect a desire and ability to dispose of such items as grave-goods. The only exception to this pattern is the iron knife, an everyday tool that is frequently found in graves, and which may have been more personalised than the more specialised tools and therefore buried with the owner (Härke 1989).

On the farms of the period two main types of building are encountered. Those built at ground level are often called 'halls' in a rather indiscriminate manner, although it provides a useful shorthand to distinguish them from the other type, the sunken buildings. 'Sunken featured building' (SFB) was the rather cumbersome term adopted by Rahtz (1976: 70 ff.) for this latter type which in Germany are known as *Grubenhauser*, while others favour 'hut'.

Sunken buildings are actually small structures erected over a sub-rectangular pit dug in the ground, ranging in size from 3 × 2 m up to the largest so far excavated at Upton, Northamptonshire, that measured 10 × 6 m (Jackson *et al.* 1969). The superstructure was supported by one, two or three posts at each end, represented by postholes on either the upper or lower edges of the pit. A gable roof is implied by such an arrangement and the number of posts may relate to the presence or absence of vertical side walls as much as to the size and weight of the roof (Figure 3.2). At West Stow, the six-post array could be claimed to be the earlier form while generally those with one post at each end are the most common. Larger examples tend to date to the seventh century. A few representatives have central posts, and stakeholes around the

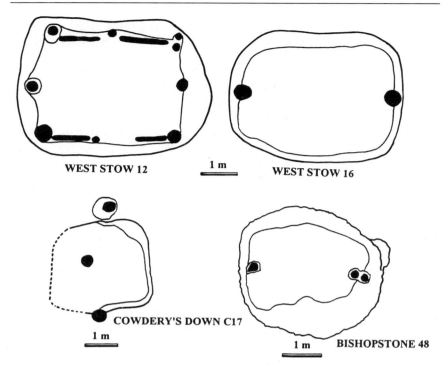

Figure 3.2 Comparative plans of sunken buildings from early Anglo-Saxon settlements, showing the variety in the methods of construction (sources: West 1985, Figures 59 and 75; Millet and James 1983, Figure 56; Bell 1977, Figure 88)

edge of the hollow as revetment. Dixon argues that there was a consistency in the sunken buildings at Mucking and that the arrangement of posts, when present, relates to varying methods of building the walls with cob, wattle and daub and lapped planks; he estimates that such structures would have required a minimum of 140 man-hours to build (1993).

It has been argued that some, at least, of the sunken buildings had plank floors, either at ground level or in the base of the pit. The presence of a hearth in the base of the pit indicates that there was not a plank floor; the absence of material trampled into that surface is ambiguous as it might mean the earth floor was kept clean or that the pit was floored over at either level. The structural evidence is also capable of bearing a number of interpretations (West 1985; Jones 1979b; Dixon 1993, 1995) as indications of timberwork at the lip of the pit may only be connected with the superstructure. Planking in the base may have fallen from the walls or roof-lining. Some may have had plank floors in the pit-base. At Mucking the base of the pit formed the floor in most, if not all, cases (Hamerow 1993: 14–15). If the purpose of the pit was to provide thermal advantages and the maximum headroom using the minimum raw materials in the superstructure, a ground-level plank floor would have been something of a nonsense (Welch 1985: 23, n. 1).

A variety of activities took place in these buildings that served predominantly as dwellings and workshops; the European evidence for the functions of such buildings has been surveyed (Hamerow 1993: 17–19; Dixon 1993). Determining their function is complicated by the fact that once these structures went out of use they became ready depositories for rubbish (Jones 1979b) which can be difficult to distinguish from material reflecting the use of the building. For instance, of the sixty-eight such buildings at West Stow, six had been used for weaving, some producing up to 100 loomweights used to tension the warp-threads of an upright loom (Figure 3.3). At Mucking there was evidence for their use in bone and antler working, metalworking as well as weaving (Hamerow 1993: 10–19).

The term 'hall' includes all of the rectangular timber buildings. Their only remains are the postholes and beam-slots dug into the subsoil. Their function is difficult to determine on internal evidence but their spatial relationship to other buildings and features can at times suggest which were predominantly domestic rather than ancillary. There is considerable variation in size, method of construction and design which may be significant to their function. Some of the smallest examples have been found at West Stow, perhaps because of the weakness of the sandy subsoil on which they were built (Figure 3.4). Three basic types can be discerned on the basis of the position of doors and the presence of internal partitions. First are those with opposed doors and internal partitions. Second are those with opposed doors and no partitions. Third are those with single doorways. At Chalton (Hampshire) the largest structures measured 9 m or more in length, and are characterised by opposed doorways in the centre of the long sides, flanked by pairs of postholes (Addyman, Leigh and Hughes 1972). The doors were hung inside the buildings closing against the back of the door frame. Such doors could have been secured by the use of a drawbar; iron keys for the operation of such devices are known from a small number of women's graves. Internal divisions were positioned at the eastern ends sub-dividing one-third or one-fifth of the area. The provision of separate rooms was not visible at Bishopstone and only present in one building at West Stow. The second group of rectangular buildings, also with opposed doorways, but no internal partitions, vary more in size, clustering at 8.5×5.3 m and 6.5×3.5 m. Third, at the smaller end of the scale are buildings having single doorways in the middle of one side.

Some of the best preserved buildings have been excavated at Cowdery's Down and can be arranged sequentially into a minimum of three phases (Millett and James 1983). The majority of the buildings were of posthole or trench construction and display considerable variation in size and design (Figure 3.5); where buildings overlapped it could be shown that, typically,

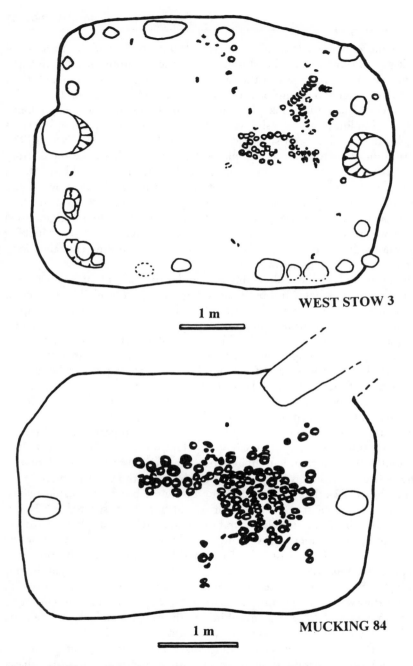

WEST STOW 3

1 m

MUCKING 84

1 m

Figure 3.3 Plans of sunken buildings containing textile manufacturing equipment. Clay loomweights are frequently found lying in the bottom of the pit in rows and irregular heaps (sources: West 1985, Figure 35; Hamerow 1993, Figure 76)

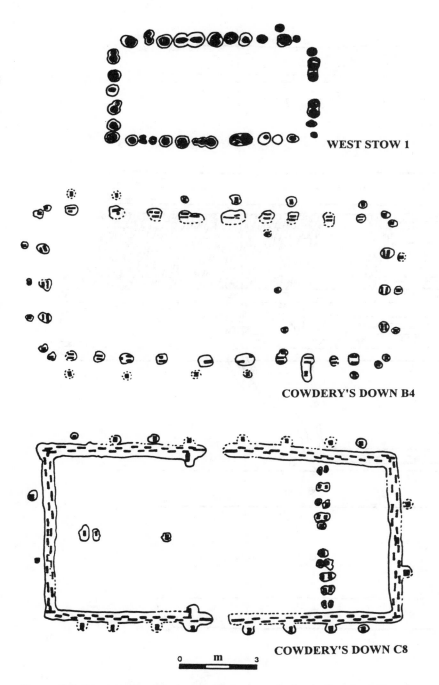

WEST STOW 1

COWDERY'S DOWN B4

COWDERY'S DOWN C8

0   m   3

Figure 3.4 Comparative plans of halls from early Anglo-Saxon settlements showing the variety of methods used in their construction (sources: West 1985, Figure 8; Millett and James 1983, Figures 37 and 39)

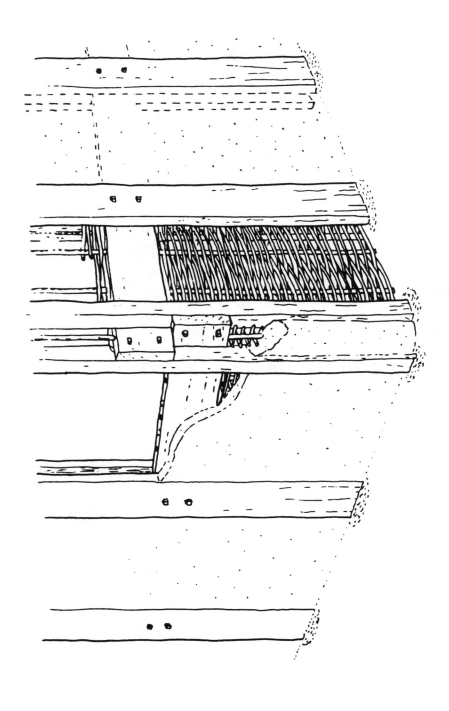

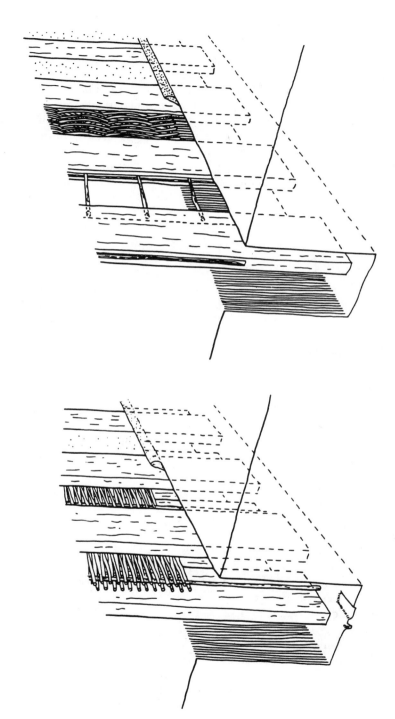

Figure 3.5 Constructional details of buildings from the early Anglo-Saxon settlement at Cowdery's Down, Hampshire, showing the various methods used to build the walls (source: Millett and James 1983)

post-built structures preceded those using continuous trenches. The walls of the buildings most commonly comprised a single row of vertical timber planks or baulks with wattle panels inserted into grooves down their edges. Alternatively, pairs of vertical timbers in holes in the ground clasped horizontal members with wattle and daub infilling, or the uprights were staggered with panels of interwoven wattles between them. The interpretation of the superstructures naturally presents greater problems, but it is argued that most had gabled roofs with rafters resting on wall plates below head height. Some are equipped with raking timbers that, if resting against the wall plate, might have been designed to relieve some of the outward pressures. The floor may have been clear, with crucks across the middle of most of the buildings supporting purlins and a ridge-piece. Some of the more complex structures may have had suspended timber floors. Alternative reconstructions are possible, however, and the use of crucks at this time is contentious (Alcock and Walsh 1993).

It is estimated that the construction of one of the larger buildings at Cowdery's Down, C12, would have required the removal of about eighty tonnes of topsoil, clay and chalk. The total weight of the timber, taken from up to eighteen mature oak trees, daub and thatch would have amounted to some seventy tonnes (Millett and James 1983: M5/02, M5/03). This gives a reasonable impression of the massive quantities of raw materials required and an indication of the effort involved.

The internal arrangements and uses of these buildings are poorly understood. They must have been used domestically, for storage, as byres and workshops; indeed, any building is likely to have had a number of functions. It is not possible to say to what extent the differences in construction relate to their function. Within one hall at Chalton an area of less-worn chalk subsoil at the eastern end near the partition may mark the position of a hearth. Scatters of iron slag in the vicinity of two buildings at Catholme, Staffordshire (Losco-Bradley 1977), strongly suggest that iron smelting and forging took place in them. Two rectangular buildings had a pit sunk in one corner. Of Cowdery's Down the excavator suggested that the positioning of the doors and the size of some of the buildings 'does not seem to indicate an agricultural function' (Millett and James 1983: 247). He preferred to see the stability of the layout as a reflection of social units, whether divided by 'kinship, sex or status' (ibid.). However, the deliberate positioning of the buildings that were physically connected with enclosure fences, outside the fence line, could be seen as a method of separating animals from domestic areas; the small size of some partitioned areas and annexes attached to rectangular buildings might make them most suitable as byres for small animals and which may have required additional minor doors.

The layout of the buildings at Cowdery's Down (Figure 3.6) changed gradually with the number of buildings increasing in each phase, there being three, six and ten in each, always accompanied by two fenced compounds that contained some of the buildings. In the first phase the rectangular compound was divided across the middle with a building in each half. One rectangular building abutted the compound fence with an annexe within the enclosure from which there did not appear to be access to the compound. The annexe need not have been roofed, although there was access to it from the main part of the building. This in turn had doors midway in its long sides, outside the compound. In the second phase of the settlement one of the buildings in the compound was replaced, while the other two remained in use. A new structure was built straddling the fence and with doors outside the enclosure. Another building, similar to the annexe in the first phase, was erected in the compound adjacent to its end wall. In the final phase there was a major change in alignment and structural type of building. Some of the structures around the compound were rebuilt and the enclosure extended westwards, beyond which was a series of six additional buildings erected along the ridge (Figure 8.4).

There were very few artefacts recovered from the settlement, even in areas protected from later ploughing; they included shears, nails, a variety of fragmentary fittings and pottery made up of nine fabric groups. It is thought that this represents a very real social phenomenon, either because of the nature of the settlement or because it was a general policy to dispose of rubbish away from the settlement, perhaps as manure on the fields, and it is clearly not the product of poor preservation as has tended to be assumed (Astill and Lobb 1982: 140). On those settlements where there was a high proportion of sunken buildings (Table 3.2) these tended to be filled with rubbish after ceasing to be used as a building; rubbish pits are also found. On settlements where sunken buildings are rare they again had a secondary function as rubbish pits, but primary rubbish pits are not present in greater numbers to make up any deficit in capacity. There were clearly different rubbish disposal strategies. At Mucking the sunken buildings and pits were largely used for general rubbish disposal. The pits were generally either roughly circular or rectangular and in as far as there was a specific function,

Table 3.2 Ratios of building types in early Anglo-Saxon settlements

Site	Rectangular buildings no.	Rectangular buildings %	Sunken buildings no.	Sunken buildings %	Ratio	Subsoil	Pits no.	Pits: buildings
Mucking	53	19.9	213	80	1:4	gravel	52	1:5
West Stow	14	16.6	70	83.3	1:5	sand	79	1:1
Eynsham	4	19	17	80.9	1:4	gravel	13	1:2
Bishopstone	17	85	3	15	6:1	chalk	5	1:4
Cowdery's Down	16	88.8	2	11.1	8:1	chalk	2	1:9
Chalton	57	93.4	2	6.5	14:1	chalk	2	1:30

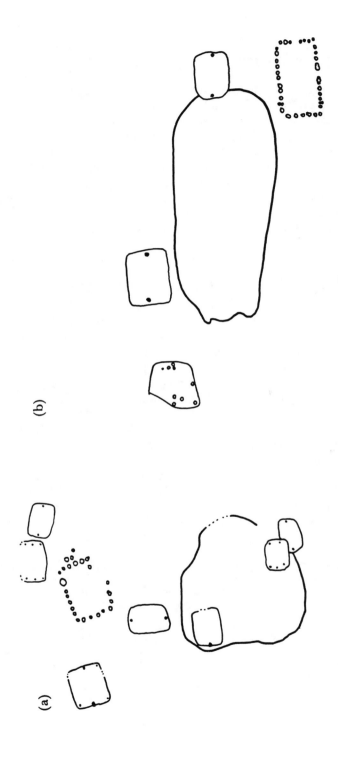

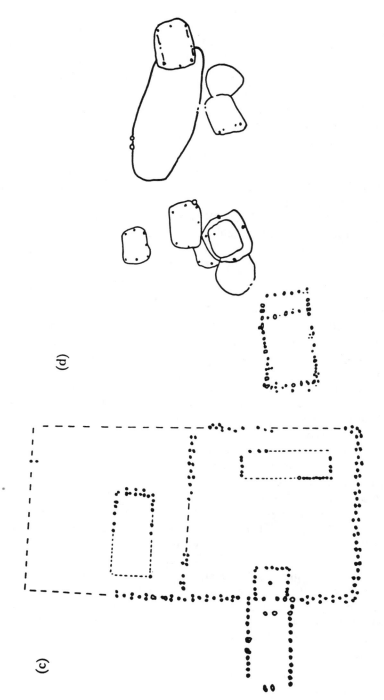

Figure 3.6 Comparative plans of individual farms from early Anglo-Saxon settlements: (a, b and d) West Stow, Suffolk; (c) Cowdery's Down, Hampshire (sources: West 1985, Figure 7; Millett and James 1983, Figure 31)

the pottery from them tended to be undecorated grass-tempered wares of sixth- and seventh-century date. One contained smithing debris and another a layer of charcoal and burnt bone (Hamerow 1993: 19). At Cowdery's Down and Abbots Worthy (Hampshire) pits were associated with animal bones, and sunken buildings were used for more general rubbish. There was a greater variety of pit-forms at Abbots Worthy. They took three forms: oval pits associated with shallow circular ones; rectangular, vertical sided ones; and three very large circular ones measuring 2.7 m diameter × 1.5 m depth.

The farms themselves may be categorised on present evidence into four broad types on the basis of their layout. First there are those consisting of one or a few buildings in isolation or associated with earlier structures. Examples include late prehistoric enclosures or, as at Lower Warbank, Kent, adjacent to a Roman villa (Philp 1973: 156–63). These may only be part of larger settlements. Second, there are individual farmsteads represented by a group of buildings associated with a fenced enclosure or paddock, such as Cowdery's Down (Millett and James 1983). The third category consists of larger settlements with multiples of the previous category, such as Bishopstone, Chalton (Addyman, Leigh and Hughes 1972) and West Stow. Finally, there are large settlements that do not seem to be divided into individual farm units, such as Mucking (Hamerow 1993). The size of such settlements can easily be overestimated as the number of buildings must be viewed as a factor of the length of time the settlement was occupied, the frequency with which buildings were replaced and the functions of buildings; all are difficult to assess. The rarity of artefacts found during excavations of such farms not only effects the archaeologist's ability to date the buildings, but also makes it extremely difficult to understand the details of the activities carried out in them.

The type of farm layout represented at Cowdery's Down is fairly common (Figure 3.6). It accounted for more than half the structures at Chalton. At Bishopstone, where the extent of erosion was even greater and the excavation not complete, there is less evidence for such planning although traces of fence lines attached to buildings were located. At Mucking the conditions of excavation were still more difficult and the absence of fenced areas may not be real. At West Stow the sunken buildings, which were in the majority, cluster around the rectangular buildings in distinct groups. At Catholme a similar pattern of enclosed units was revealed. There was also a large central building surrounded by lesser structures, some interpreted as granaries. One unit was composed of many more buildings than the others and it is suggested that this represents a social difference with specialist activities taking place there.

The common attributes of the building tradition of early Anglo-Saxon England have been summarised as:

> rectangular, precisely laid-out and constructed in substantial earth-fast foundations. Their plans frequently employ simple geometric forms or

length–width ratios; the square is very common and often occurs in pairs. Most buildings have a door exactly in the centre of each long wall, and some have an annexe at one or both ends. Most of the structures stand within, or abut palisaded enclosures, and Grubenhauser are present.

(James, Marshall and Millett 1984: 184)

The writers, as we have seen (Chapter 2), view the evidence in terms of an early medieval building tradition that has not been apparent until recently because of the variable quality of the surviving evidence and the small size of the data-base. They view the building tradition as a merger of traits with Romano-British and Germanic origins, although Dixon (1982; 1993) places greater emphasis on the former. He emphasises how the uniformity of the architecture contrasts with the marked regionalisation seen in artefacts and views this as evidence for the native origin of the tradition (see also Scull 1991). However, metrological studies of some buildings have suggested that a different unit of measure was used in northern England from that in the east of the country (Huggins *et al.* 1982; Huggins 1983; 1991). In addition it has been shown that there was regional variation in the size, shape and the degrees of uniformity within the building tradition with houses tending to become larger with time (Marshall and Marshall 1991, 1993). The elements of the tradition appear to have involved much innovation. It is difficult to measure cultural influence and, despite the importance of the issue, distinguishing between native building traditions and those which spread from the Continent within hybrid forms will remain problematic.

Some regional differences can be discerned in the selection of building types although it is difficult to determine whether these are practical responses to local conditions or whether they have an ethnic or social basis. Those settlements in central southern England on chalk downland, such as Chalton, Cowdery's Down and Bishopstone, are marked by the rarity, but not absence, of sunken buildings (Table 3.2); pits in such locations are also a rarity. Settlements founded on gravel and sands in eastern England tend to have far larger numbers of excavated structures, such as pits and sunken buildings. This may be because of the ease of digging in sand and gravel compared with chalk, or is possibly connected with drainage as clay on chalk surfaces would have resulted in an accumulation of water in holes and pits. This may have made rectangular, surface buildings more practical for ancillary activities. It seems unlikely that the rarity of sunken buildings in southern England relates to the nature of the material excavated from the pit and its suitability for building purposes when the superstructure could be built in a variety of ways. The frequency of sunken buildings may be related to the date of the founding of the settlement as Dixon has argued: they were the principal architecture introduced by migrants and would have been quick to erect. The reasons for such preferences may be related to ethnic, cultural, economic or geological factors. In many cases the proportion of sunken buildings is much higher on subsoils of sand and gravel but there are exceptions: Yeavering was constructed on a sandy soil and has few sunken buildings; Old Down Farm, Hampshire has many on a chalk subsoil. This suggests that there are other factors involved such as ethnicity or particular soil-types being present in those areas settled earliest.While there are differences in the size ranges of buildings on different settlements (p. 218), attributed to social factors, this does not affect the ratios of building types. It might be thought that these differences reflect the availability of suitable timber, but it is difficult to determine the extent and nature of woodland at a sufficient level of detail. With adequate management timber felled to build a house would have regenerated in time to build its replacement and the designs of the houses do not suggest there was any shortage.

Jones suggested that the sunken buildings found on early Anglo-Saxon settlements were dwelling houses, especially in eastern England at the large Thameside settlements of Mucking and at West Stow (1979b) although Hamerow has emphasised that there is no evidence at Mucking for a 'specific function' to be attributed to any of the sunken buildings (1993: 15). The consensus appears to be that they were used as dwellings and workshops (Dixon 1993: 129–30). What is inescapable, assuming that settlements in different parts of England had broadly similar economies, is that those functions carried out in sunken buildings in eastern England were performed in rectangular, ground-level buildings in the south. It is difficult to compare floor areas of settlements in different areas of the country as some types of building may have had a different use-life than others. However, it is interesting that a group of buildings associated with an enclosure at Chalton had a total floor area of c. 99 m². At West Stow, Hall 5 and the associated late sixth-century sunken buildings also measured c. 99 m². In comparison, the buildings of the first phase at Cowdery's Down, which it is suggested is a higher-status settlement, measured 238 m². If buildings are, at least in part, being used for storage, volume becomes an issue. On the settlements where rectangular buildings predominate they tend to be of three sizes, large, medium and small. Within groups of buildings the variation in size appears to be connected with function, for instance the larger building will be that abutting or straddling the fence while those inside the enclosure will be smaller. Social statements about the status of the settlement may also have been made by displaying large buildings. One group of settlements had mostly large buildings, for instance Yeavering (Northumberland), the other had smaller ones, such as Chalton (Figure 3.7) (James, Marshall and Millett 1984). At West Stow, where sunken buildings predominate, the number and size of the rectangular buildings places the settlement firmly in the first group, those with small structures. Those settlements with larger rectangular buildings tend not to have many sunken buildings, suggesting that some craft or agricultural activities were not undertaken there. The variation in size of the sunken buildings is much greater, with no clear clustering when a large sample

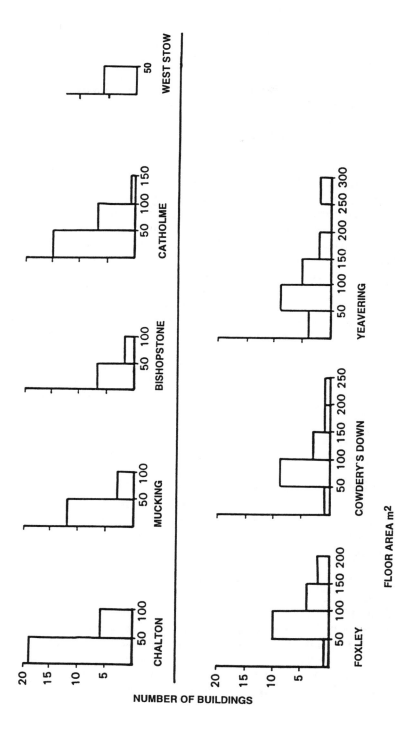

Figure 3.7 Histograms illustrating the different sizes of halls from early Anglo-Saxon settlements by floor area (source: James *et al.* 1984, Figure 5 with additions). Two patterns are revealed on the basis of the proportions of small and large structures

is analysed (Hamerow 1993: 11) although on average they measure *c.* 4×3 m. The apparent variation in construction technique may have more to do with the survival of the evidence (Dixon 1993, 1995).

The study of the buildings found on early Anglo-Saxon farms tells us little about the rural economy. An additional approach to the question is the analysis of the settlement pattern, the search for underlying regularities in the choice of location of the farms. Regional differences may be informative and the manner in which the patterns may change through time. The available archaeological data are the few excavated settlements and the more numerous cemeteries. A full appreciation of the cemeteries, in this context, demands an understanding of the relationship between the settlements and cemeteries during the period. In the absence of information about land tenure the location and inter-relationship of the farms can be assessed by environmental determinants such as soil, geology, height, aspect and proximity to water. The relationship of the settlements to cemeteries can be considered using the results of large-scale excavations as a control, and the actual distances between such features may act as a guide even when a relationship cannot be directly inferred. An understanding of why settlements were deserted and presumably relocated can be revealed from an examination of the chronology of the settlements and by comparison with the locational qualities of later sites. Additional information regarding the settlements of the period might be gleaned from the study of place-names. The chronology of the various early medieval elements has been broadly established, but we remain ignorant of the actual names given to the settlements of the period. It is actually questionable whether the locational analysis of Old English place-name elements has any validity for early Anglo-Saxon settlement patterns. The number of unknown factors is so great and the processes by which place-names have survived so irregular and difficult to assess that their use here is of limited value (Gelling 1978; Arnold and Wardle 1981; Taylor 1983; Welch 1985: 17–18; Copley 1986, 1988).

In the majority of cases where large-scale excavations have taken place, early Anglo-Saxon cemeteries were situated adjacent, within 0.5 km, to the settlement (Figure 3.8). Where a settlement was 'drifting' across the landscape there seems to have been greater conservatism in the location of the cemetery. There has been considerable interest shown in the fact that a proportion of cemeteries is found close to the later parish boundaries as though such boundaries are a later fossilisation of earlier property units and that the boundary was an appropriate place for burial (Bonney 1972, 1976; Goodier 1984). It remains possible that some cemeteries, particularly those on higher ground, may well have been located on, or at junctions of, boundaries as territorial markers. However, the notion that a significant proportion of early Anglo-Saxon cemeteries was deliberately located on the edges of territorial units that later became parish boundaries does not stand up to statistical analysis (Reilly 1988).

Such a close relationship between settlement and cemetery may not have existed throughout the country. Cemeteries in eastern England and the Midlands tend to be very large, infrequent and dispersed, whereas those elsewhere are smaller and more common (Figure 3.9). Cremation was the most common burial rite at such large, centralised cemeteries and if cremation took place near the settlement the remains could more easily be transported to a distant cemetery. It has been noted on occasions that cremated bones are found both in urned and unurned deposits in a small cluster as if placed there in a small bag. There is, however, no evidence for funeral pyres at settlements and the evidence for them at such large cremation cemeteries is extremely rare. A possible example has been excavated at the relatively small, and mixed-rite, cemetery at Snape, Suffolk, (Carnegie and Filmer-Sankey 1993) and an area of scorched clay, charcoal and burnt bone was noted at Sancton, Yorkshire (Myres and Southern 1973: 10; McKinley 1993: 295–6). The barrow burial at Asthall (Oxfordshire) may have been built over a funeral pyre (Dickinson and Speake 1992). It is possible that shallow burials and pyres are under-represented at cemeteries because of later disturbance such as ploughing, although it is surprising that virtually all traces have been removed. A more detailed understanding of cremating can only be achieved through the study of cremated bone and related ethnographic studies (McKinley 1994a: 72–81; 1994b).

The location of rural settlements depends on a balance of both practical and symbolic considerations, for instance the nature of the rural economy, the system of land tenure and attitudes to landscape. The practical aspects could be analysed in terms of a number of factors, such as water, fuel, arable land, pasture, the needs of defence. To this might be added the impact of previous landscape use in the form of fields and roads. Known early Anglo-Saxon settlements are gradually becoming as common as cemeteries (Figure 3.10) even if few have been excavated. Extensive field-walking programmes demonstrate how dense the distribution of settlements actually was, although not all of the farms identified need be contemporary. In the Itchen and Avon valleys in Hampshire the farms were regularly spaced along the valley bottoms (Hughes 1984). Similar research in Northamptonshire also emphasises the widespread distribution of such settlements, some near earlier and later settlements, others having no such connection (Taylor 1983). Within the broad perspective of rural settlement studies it is most apparent that they are not static entities and their mobility results in their frequent desertion. In Suffolk, Sussex and Hampshire, fieldwork has revealed that no village can claim uninterrupted development from earlier than the middle-Saxon period (Newman 1992; Hughes 1984). A similar study of Norfolk villages admirably demonstrated how medieval settlements were frequently relocated, although in that case early Anglo-Saxon settlements were conspicuous for their absence (Bell 1978; Cunliffe 1972; Wade-Martins 1980). The excavated deserted medieval village of Wharram Percy, Yorkshire, may not be unusual in being founded

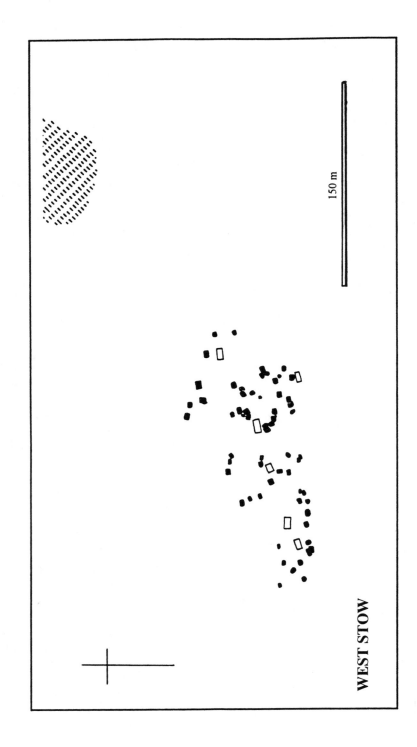

WEST STOW

150 m

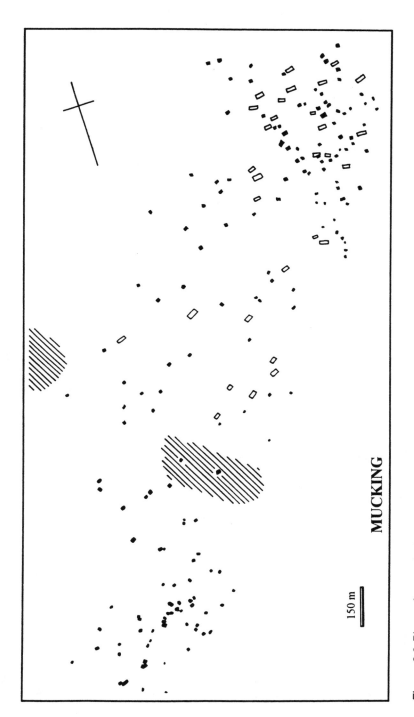

MUCKING

150 m

Figure 3.8 Plans of extensively excavated early Anglo-Saxon settlements and cemeteries showing the close relationship between the two (sources: West 1985, Figure 7; Hamerow 1993, Figure 50; Bell 1977, Figure 86)

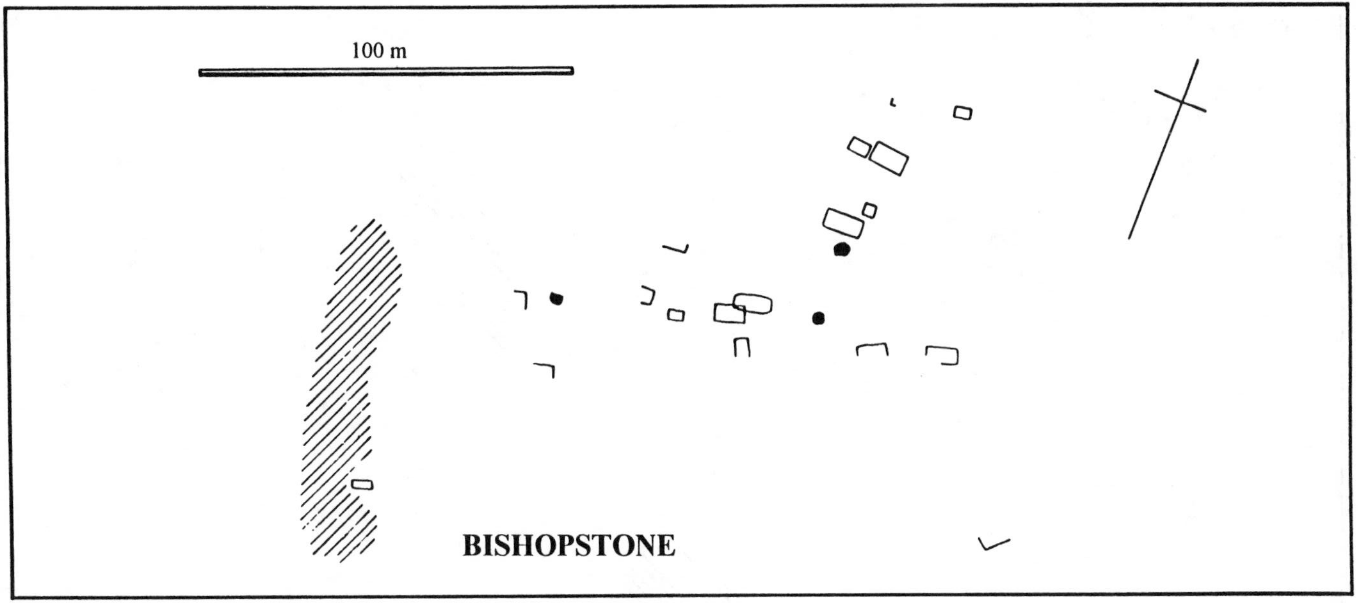

BISHOPSTONE

100 m

Figure 3.8 continued

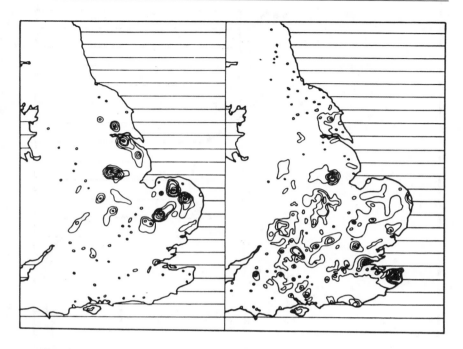

Figure 3.9 The distribution of cremation (left) and inhumation (right) burials by grid generalisation. While cremation was most common in eastern England, inhumation graves have a more general distribution

in the eighth century (Milne and Richards 1992). The excavation of early Anglo-Saxon settlements has produced a number of contrasting patterns of the drift of settlement, but what they have failed to find is an example of settlement drift continuing from the early to the middle-Saxon period. Stability appears to have occurred from the eighth century onwards, although at different times in specific areas (Hamerow 1991).

The mobility of settlements of the period is most graphically demonstrated by the results of the large-scale excavations at Mucking (Hamerow 1993). The first identifiable early Anglo-Saxon occupation of the gravel terrace above the River Thames (Figure 3.8) began early in the fifth century, possibly initially largely of sunken buildings (Dixon 1993). It grew into a dense settlement within which three periods of rebuilding were observed. In the late fifth, or early sixth, century the settlement gradually moved northwards; it was smaller, of briefer duration and more dispersed, and the cemetery belonging to it was defined by Romano-British ditches. In the third phase in this drifting pattern, in the later sixth or early seventh century, the settlement moved to the north-east and was relatively dense with some deliberate

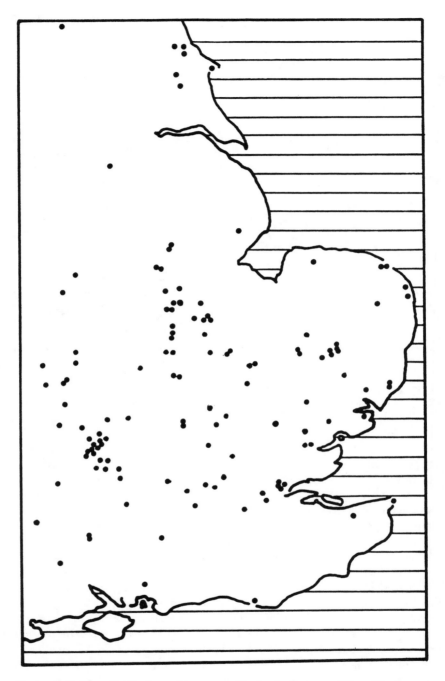

Figure 3.10 The distribution of known early Anglo-Saxon settlements in England. The greatest number are known from the Midlands and eastern England

alignment of buildings and halls being a more prominent building type. In the final phase, in the seventh century, the settlement moved westwards and consisted of more isolated and separate farmsteads. It is apparent from the data that Mucking was not a village but a series of shifting hamlets, a close community changing to one in which there was less interaction. This may be intimately connected with increasingly defined forms of land holding (Hamerow 1993: 86–92).

At Mucking the number of buildings in each phase varied suggesting that there was also considerable demographic change. At West Stow (Figure 3.6) the extent of the drift is more limited as though the ties to the land were even stronger; buildings were replaced by moving in various directions to adjacent sites that had not previously been built on. In the seventh century, in the final decades of the occupation of the site, boundaries were created separating the remaining farms (West 1985: 146–52). The number of building groups remained fairly constant. If there were population increases they must either have been absorbed or were regulated by the movement of people away from the settlement (Scull 1993: 72–5). At Cowdery's Down the number of buildings belonging to each phase increased from three to six to ten. The settlement was founded as a single building group in and around an enclosure. Some of the buildings were replaced on the same site in the two ensuing phases, but in the second phase an additional building was erected 150 m along the ridge. In the third and final phase additional structures were built along the ridge between and beyond the earlier ones suggesting there may have been a marked change in the status of its occupants (Millett and James 1983).

It has been observed that in Berkshire topographical names, particularly those referring to water, are the most common Old English names in areas where early Anglo-Saxon settlement has been attested archaeologically. This is hardly surprising when the most common location for these, and other, settlements is beside a source of water. The great majority are riverbank sites and there is no clear difference between early and middle-Saxon settlements in terms of this variable (Figure 3.11). The high number of settlements very close to water can be equated with the number at low altitudes, sea-level and up to 15 m above sea level. Most are actually riverbank sites that also corre-late with the number of settlements on drifts and clays, and the soil-type developed on drifts, the stagnogleys. Wells are almost unknown on early Anglo-Saxon settlements, emphasising the importance of rivers, but they are more common on urban and rural settlements from the eighth century onwards. The creation of numerous wells at the port of Hamwic, Saxon Southampton, may have been encouraged by the high density of population, but the wells on middle-Saxon farms such as Odell, Bedfordshire, may imply an awareness of the risks from polluted water brought about by a growing population, or the need to extend settlement on to good soils which were not close to water at a time of increased property rights.

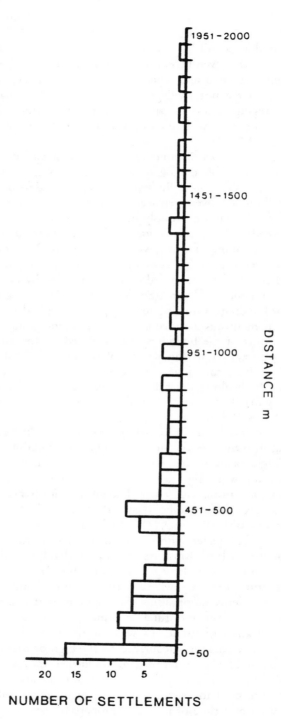

DISTANCE m

NUMBER OF SETTLEMENTS

1951 – 2000

1451 – 1500

951 – 1000

451 – 500

0 – 50

20   15   10   5

Figure 3.11 Histogram showing the distances between early Anglo-Saxon settlements and the nearest (modern) source of water. Over half of the settlements are within 500 m of a water-source (source: K. Hammond)

The greatest proportion of farmsteads are sited on good quality soils, stagnogleys and brown earth (Figure 3.12). Stagnogleys are non-calcareous loamy or clayey soils at moderate depths, light to moderately fertile, moderately well drained and suitable for cultivation; the category includes soils on river terrace gravel. Brown earths are loamy non-calcareous soils, well drained, fertile and excellent for farming. Of the remainder, 10 per cent of the sites are located on rendzinas, shallow calcareous soil over limestone and chalk which is also light and fertile. In the early Anglo-Saxon period poor agricultural soils appear to have been avoided, especially those affected by fluctuations in ground water that would cause waterlogging. In contrast to the proportions of early Anglo-Saxon farms located on rendzinas, no middle-Saxon settlements are known on such soils. This may be the result of siting for ease of farming in the earlier period. Further, it may suggest a drift away from the shallow, light soils favoured in the early period to heavier soils that are more fertile and produce a greater yield per acre. By the late Saxon period, most settlements occur on the heavier soils; indeed by that date settlement is found on a far greater variety of soil types.

The need for wood for fuel, building materials and tools would have required settlers to have access to extensive woodland. It is hard, however, to gauge the effect this demand on woodland had on the landscape at this time. Considerable clearance would have been required to build a large timber building, up to eighteen mature oaks being necessary to build one of the larger examples at Cowdery's Down. Another major demand on woodland that is rarely discussed is the fuel requirement for cremating bodies, especially in eastern England where many thousands of cremations may be represented at a single cemetery. While this might be thought to have a major impact, the effects would have been lessened if the cremating was carried out at dispersed homes. Little research has been carried out on cremating and of the quantities of fuel required. An experiment stemming from the excavation of prehistoric cremations in Orkney indicated that one cubic metre of brushwood and peat was required to reduce a four-stone goat to 0.04 cubic metre of bone and ash in five hours (Hedges 1977: 143); ethnographic evidence suggests that the quantity of wood required is up to 500 kg (McKinley 1994a: 72–81). From a practical point of view Wells's study of Anglo-Saxon cremation (1960) was concerned only with determining the technique of cremating and the temperatures achieved. He found that there were reasons to believe that bodies were placed supine below the pyre and that the average temperature achieved was about 900° C, but the quantity of fuel required was not determined. There are perhaps too many unknown quantities in the complex equation regarding number of bodies, quantity of fuel, rate of woodland regeneration and time, to be able to calculate what impact the presence of a large cremation cemetery would have had on the landscape. There is palaeobotanical evidence for a phase of increased woodland clearance in the sixth and seventh centuries in Britain (Biddick 1984: 108 and Figure 1) but

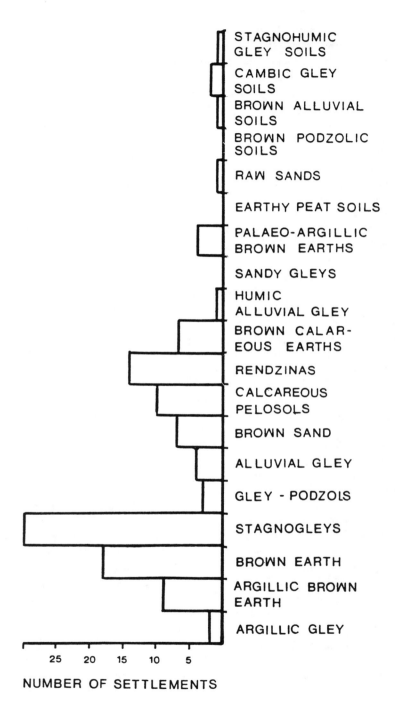

STAGNOHUMIC GLEY SOILS

CAMBIC GLEY SOILS

BROWN ALLUVIAL SOILS

BROWN PODZOLIC SOILS

RAW SANDS

EARTHY PEAT SOILS

PALAEO-ARGILLIC BROWN EARTHS

SANDY GLEYS

HUMIC ALLUVIAL GLEY

BROWN CALAREOUS EARTHS

RENDZINAS

CALCAREOUS PELOSOLS

BROWN SAND

ALLUVIAL GLEY

GLEY - PODZOLS

STAGNOGLEYS

BROWN EARTH

ARGILLIC BROWN EARTH

ARGILLIC GLEY

25   20   15   10   5

NUMBER OF SETTLEMENTS

Figure 3.12 Histogram showing the number of early Anglo-Saxon settlements on specified soil-types. The largest number of settlements is found on light soils such as rendzinas and stagnogleys and fewer are located on heavy soil-types (source: K. Hammond)

the general picture, in as far as it can be reconstructed, is one of continuity of countryside, including woodland, management (Rackham 1986: 75–85).

The extent to which the landscape was being farmed and the efficiency of agricultural practices may be measured by the degree of freedom with which settlements drifted (p. 55). The growth of population and commensurate expansion of settlement is reflected in the increasingly varied soil environments settled through the Anglo-Saxon period. The archaeological evidence suggests that settlements drifted, whether for demographic, agricultural or other reasons, from an initial point and that there was a more severe pattern of relocation that took place between AD 650–750. This occurred at the same time that there was a major dislocation in building traditions (Marshall and Marshall 1993: 400). Successive stages of drift can be identified in many settlements that were then abandoned; resettlement may have occurred in the vicinity but not sufficiently close to be detected in the same way as the earlier drift. It may be that settlement patterns began to be more stable, in part, because of the development of land ownership with established property boundaries (Hamerow 1991). The earliest surviving land charters, documents indicating title to property and defining its boundaries, date from the seventh century indicating that some such change was taking place. The pagan Anglo-Saxon cemeteries are much easier to date because of the larger number of artefacts found in them as grave-goods. However, they are a poor indicator of the extent of shifting settlement because there was an inherent conservatism in the location of cemeteries, a desire to continue to place the dead among the ancestors. So while settlements drifted around an original nucleus the cemetery often remained in use. However, very few cemeteries remained in use throughout the period, and those that did tend to be the large examples in mid- and eastern England that may have had a centralised function and were therefore not subject to the effects of settlement drift. There may of course be special reasons for the development of new cemeteries that are distinct from the factors provoking settlement shift but it must be in part a related issue.

The instability of the rural economy may in part be dependent on the effects of climatic change. A global climatic cataclysm began in AD 536 that was to last for about ten years. A thick cloud of dust that blocked out the sun's heat and light is likely to have been caused by the impact of an asteroid of medium size (Baillie 1994) and resulted in the failure of crops. In the 540s plague swept through Europe. Bede describes how in the 670s the South Saxons were saved 'from a cruel and horrible extinction' as a result of their conversion to Christianity by Wilfrid: 'for no rain had fallen in the province for three years prior to his arrival, and a terrible famine had ensued which reduced many to an awful death' (Colgrave and Mynors 1969: IV 13). Extreme fluctuations in climate are more likely to have a detectable effect on settlement patterns than gradual changes. There is evidence for a minor advance in European glaciers during the period AD 700–900 (Denton and

Karlén 1973). Tooley has demonstrated that there was a period of climatic extremes in addition to a complex marine transgression sequence at this time. Sea-levels rose to a maximum of +1.2 m above sea-level in c. AD 150, falling during the following 500 years to a minimum altitude of +0.4 m above sea-level by c. 650 (Tooley 1978: 182–92). Specific examples of the effects of such transgressions have been noted in studies of settlement patterns in coastal and estuarine regions (Hallam 1961; Hawkes 1968; Thompson 1980). The extent of climatic change and its actual effect on human communities is difficult to define but there remain a number of definite possibilities.

With an assumed growing population in early Anglo-Saxon England there would have been increasing pressure on rural resources, especially by the second half of the seventh century. With the development of urban centres and religious foundations greater demand would have been placed on the hinterland. The predictable result would have been an intensification of agriculture and changes in the nature of landholding and ownership. A reflection of this may be the final relocation of settlements on to more fertile and productive soils and the changes in cereal crops being cultivated. An agricultural surplus would have been required to support the development of urban centres which in turn encouraged craft specialisation. In this way the move to more fertile soils may have been made to improve productivity per person and increase output for similar or less effort.

Chapter 4

Elusive craftspeople

The study of technology is important in its own right, but it also deepens our understanding of a society as a whole because it is intimately connected with both the way in which people are organised and the structure of the economy. We may examine the technologies applied to the basic raw materials used in early Anglo-Saxon society – wood, metal, clay, fibres and minerals – paying particular attention to aspects that are peculiar to the period and leaving the general matters of technology as understood. We must also give some consideration to composite commodities. Of equal importance are the source and nature of the raw materials and the effort and organisation that lie behind the crafts and skills described.

The most prolific source for the study of Anglo-Saxon technology is the vast array of artefacts that have survived as grave-goods in burials. An examination of the results of early Anglo-Saxon industry points to the effort and organisation involved in procuring the raw materials. Detailed studies of particular artefacts direct attention to the varying complexity involved in manufacturing items, many of them designed for specific functions. Much of the variation in the items is indeed directly related to their use, but the variability in the design of objects destined for the same function may point to socio-cultural differences. There have been few detailed studies of the technology of particular types of artefact, or products requiring tools in their manufacture. Rather, individual studies have been made of certain types in the reports on the excavation of cemeteries. Where such detailed studies have been made they tend towards the typological and shy away from the technological aspects. Similarly the sociological aspects are rarely dealt with although there are indications that attitudes are changing (e.g. Dickinson and Härke 1992).

BROOCHES

It is not surprising that the more complex, composite artefacts are rarer than those whose production is relatively straightforward. Despite the level of organisation required to bring together the materials and expertise to produce

Figure 4.1 The face of a keystone garnet disc brooch from Faversham, Kent
(source: de Baye 1893, Figure 17)

complex items, it is surprising how few have survived. Perhaps this may serve
to emphasise the difficulties of actually manufacturing such items during the
period.

An example of this is the disc and composite disc brooches of Kent (Avent
1975; Leigh 1984b). They are found predominately in Kent and are believed
to have been manufactured from *c.* AD 550 to *c.* AD 650. Of such brooches
192 were catalogued suggesting that the average output was at least two per
year. There are three main types of brooch: keystone garnet disc brooches,
plated disc brooches and composite brooches. In Avent's scheme these types
overlap chronologically, each being dated AD 550–630, 600–30 and 610–50
respectively. Such phases may reflect the work of an individual workshop
over three generations with individual jewellers breaking new ground, or the
conservatism of the consumers once a type was fully developed. The greatest
changes in the technology and style of the brooches in Kent occurred in the
last quarter of the sixth century. Gilded silver objects were replaced by solid
gold objects decorated with filigree and *cloisonné* work. It is strange that
although the latter technology was known it was not used by Kentish metalworkers for nearly fifty years. Filigree and *cloisonné* was the preferred style
of the Frankish élite and its introduction to Kent may have had a political
motive. A shortage of gold has also been argued as a reason, emphasising
the importance of the ability to procure the necessary raw materials.

The production of such brooches was a complex procedure, both in the
gathering together of the raw materials as well as the actual production of
the pieces themselves. To manufacture a garnet disc brooch (Figure 4.1) a

two-piece mould would be made in clay from a model, in which would be cast the skeleton of the brooch in silver. This would include the rims, inner and outer, the central setting border, empty cells for the keystones, other settings and the outline, at least, of the animal ornament. The casting would then be cleaned up with a graver to remove residual material and to sharpen the outlines, and then polished. Then niello would be applied to the rim decoration, applied to the recesses as powder, cast, ground and polished. Then the outer band of the rim would be fixed, probably with solder. Gilding, normally done by taking powdered gold mixed with mercury to form an amalgam, was painted on to the surface and then heated so as to drive off the mercury. The settings were usually backed by gold foil stamped with a chequer pattern (Avent and Leigh 1977; Meeks and Holmes 1985). The settings, which were most often of garnet but also glass, stone and shell, were then fixed. Finally the lug to hold the pin would be pierced, that for the catch-plate bent over and the iron wire pin would be attached, pointed at the catch-plate and coiled at the other end to form a spring hinge.

It is known that some of the settings in such brooches are glass, but many, as in other types of brooch, especially in Kent, are of garnet. Garnet is found in such places as Egypt, Britain, Scandinavia and many other parts of Europe. The selected garnet had to be split and then shaped to fit the cells and patterns; alternatively, the cells may have been shaped to fit the pre-cut garnets. Shaping the garnet could have been carried out by one of three methods (Arrhenius 1971). Slices can be cut using an abrasive wheel that results in a smoothly sloping, or faceted, edge. Second, the shaping can be done by flaking or chipping. The third method, for which there is some evidence, is to cut a groove using a diamond, quartz or garnet-tipped point along which the garnet could be snapped into two. Some shapes, however, could not have been produced in this way. Visible garnet edges tend to be smooth, which may suggest wheel-cutting, but if rougher methods were used the slices could be polished afterwards to remove any roughness (Bimson 1985). What is not clear is whether they were cut by the jeweller or imported ready cut. The Kentish examples tend to be simple shapes, discs and rectangles, which are equally common in Europe. Other shapes – square, diamond, triangular, lentoid, drop or half-disc – are much rarer but are found on the Continent in southern Germany, Hungary and south-east Europe in general. The question is difficult to answer especially when complicated by the possibility of re-use.

MUSICAL INSTRUMENTS

The range of craft skills in use during the early Anglo-Saxon period is well, if unevenly, represented in the archaeological record, although not all classes of object have received the same level of study. However, the survival of certain types of object is as much the result of various factors prior to burial

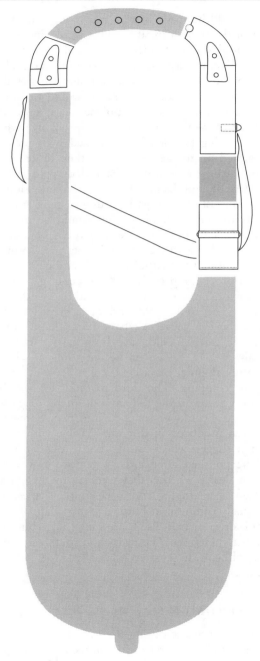

Figure 4.2 Reconstruction of a lyre from grave 22 Bergh Apton, Norfolk (source: Lawson 1978)

as to post-depositional processes. The rare survivals can add an altogether different dimension to our understanding of the period, and serve to sharpen our awareness of the difficulty of establishing precisely how rare certain items were in society at the time. A suitable example is the musical instruments, in particular lyres, which are known from four burials, Bergh Apton (Norfolk) (Figure 4.2), Morning Thorpe (Norfolk) and the well-furnished barrow burials of Sutton Hoo mound I and Taplow, Buckinghamshire (Bruce-Mitford 1970, 1983: 611–731; Lawson 1978; Green *et al.* 1987). The presence of lyres at Bergh Apton and Morning Thorpe in otherwise unremarkable graves and two from 'royal' burials might indicate that there were musicians whose accomplishments were primarily for the ears of the powerful. Such a distinction may be indicated by the position of the instruments in graves. Those at Bergh Apton and Morning Thorpe were found in front and close to the body, unlike those at Taplow and Sutton Hoo which were distant from them. The form of joinery used on such instruments implies 'able craftsmanship and an availability of at least small gouges and chisels' (Lawson 1978: 96). Considerable care was taken in constructing them in hardwoods, and there is a conformity in the known examples which date from the fifth to eighth centuries.

The arch of the Bergh Apton lyre was fixed by mortise and tenon joints, strengthened by metal plates, and carried six pegs holding the strings. The sound board was similarly strengthened by a metal binding strip. To the outside of the frame were attached wrist straps making it possible to support the instrument and use both hands in a performance. The fittings were individually made for each example but there is otherwise a general standardisation.

BOATS

We may compare the intricacy of the production of small objects, such as brooches and musical instruments that were functional as well as objects of beauty, with craftsmanship at the opposite end of the scale that involved more complex carpentry as well as considerable effort, for example boat building and house construction.

The Sutton Hoo lyre was deposited with many other possessions lying around the burial chamber in a ship (Figures 4.3 and 7.10), which remains one of the best examples of contemporary marine engineering. Such a survival is very important, for while we may be largely ignorant of the details of land travel, the role of ships in transporting people and goods across the waters to England is known to have been great. The ship was an open rowing boat driven by thirty-eight oarsmen, and was 24.4 m long, 4.3 m wide at the centre and the depth amidships was 1.4 m, with the prow 3.8 m above the level of the keel plank amidships (Bruce-Mitford 1975). It was clinker-built without permanent decking and no evidence was found for a mast. The hull

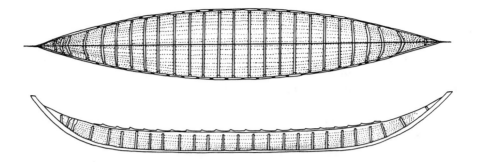

Figure 4.3 Plan and section of the ship from mound I, Sutton Hoo, Suffolk
(source: Carver 1992a, Figure 66)

was stiffened with twenty-six ribs. It was probably steered over the stern by
a large steering oar. The most recent assessment of the coins from the grave
suggests the burial was made after AD 613 (Stahl and Oddy 1992). The ship
in mound I is one of four known boats of the period all of which were associated with inhumation burials, three of them under large mounds. The
others are from Sutton Hoo mound 2 and two from Snape on the River
Alde, 15 km to the north-east. The re-excavation of mound 2 at Sutton Hoo
will add significantly to our understanding of such boats and there is every
indication that it was of similar construction to that in mound I, but smaller,
being about 20 m long (Carver 1992a: 355–7). The larger of the Snape boats
was also clinker-built and riveted, double-ended, at least 14 m long and with
a beam of 3 m. There were nine strakes on each side with the rivets set at
140 mm intervals. It is dated to after AD 550 (Filmer-Sankey 1992: 41).
The last boat, also from Snape, was a 3 m long logboat with a beam of 0.7
m and with 'fins' at each end (Filmer-Sankey 1990; 1992: 48).

The principal limitation of the Sutton Hoo mound I boat, assuming it
was intended to function as such, was that in having a keel plank and not
a keel, it would not have been able to support a sail; a slightly smaller boat
from Kvalsund (Norway) dating to *c.* AD 700 was provided with an incipient
keel and may have been able to bear the greater stresses of a sail. In the
absence of a greater range of evidence it is difficult to be certain about how
representative the known examples are of the actual range of ship types.
There can be no doubt that crossings of the North Sea and the English
Channel were being made; the fifth-century migrations and the international
connections of the sixth and seventh centuries are clear testimonies to such
sea journeys. Experiments and modern calculations suggest that the Sutton
Hoo mound I type of boat could average a speed of three knots for little
more than six hours, so that a crossing of the North Sea from Holland to

East Anglia might have taken a few days, although if sails were available the time would be considerably less (Green 1963).

BUILDINGS

Carpentry was also extensively used to build the houses, barns and byres which were more common and fundamental to everyday life. The skills required were no less than for the intricate metalworking and jewelling skills of the period, but the effort and raw materials required were on an altogether different scale. A variety of building types is represented at some settlements, for instance Cowdery's Down, where building C12, the largest and possibly the most elaborate, may serve to demonstrate the skills required. Any estimates of the quantities of raw materials required must be approximate as they are, in turn, dependent on a preferred reconstruction of the super-structure.

It has been estimated that to construct the rectangular timber building, C12, would have required the movement of *c.* 81 tonnes, or 45 m³, of topsoil, clay and chalk for the footings which would have taken approximately 90 man-hours. The building materials such as timber, daub and thatch would have weighed 70 tonnes (Millett and James 1983, M5/02). Our ignorance of the methods makes it difficult to establish accurate estimates of the effort involved in carrying out the various tasks but we may at least gain some idea of the order of magnitude of the work. The timber work presents more difficulty as we are even more uncertain about the methods used and the tools available. Millett and James take the absence of large saws (1983: 198) literally and assume timbers would have been split radially; as we have already seen tools are generally rare finds during the period and the absence of a surviving saw need not represent the real situation (Wilson 1968; Darrah 1982). If an adze was used, smaller trees might have been more practical so that one finished square might have been formed from a single trunk. We gain an impression of the quantities of oak involved from the estimates for the building; the 55 m³ of oak required would have been obtained from about eighteen mature trees. A conservative estimate suggests that the principal timber work would require trees from two hectares of oak forest to construct the building, excluding any floorboards.

The probable sequence of events in erecting such a structure would begin with the excavation of the flat-bottomed wall-trenches dug into the chalk. Judging from the signs of pecking on the trench sides, the trenches were made with a pointed tool. Gaps were left for the doorways and the resulting rectangular area would have measured 22.1 × 8.5 m, if slightly wider at the middle of the long sides. Staggered vertical timbers (Figure 3.5) were erected in the trench with horizontal members between the verticals to hold the intervening panels of daubed wattles. The most practical means of achieving this would be to partially construct the wall panels on the ground with the

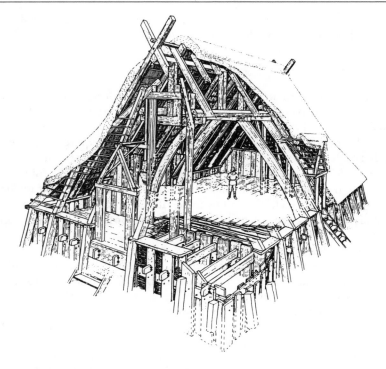

Figure 4.4 Possible reconstruction of building C12 at Cowdery's Down, Hampshire (source: Millett and James 1983, Figure 70)

uprights and horizontals pegged together. The panels could then be raised into position. The wattling would then be inserted and finally the wall-plate. In the absence of internal roof supports, the wall may have been supported by two pairs of curving cruck blades supporting a horizontal beam carrying a king post to support the ridge (Figure 4.4), although other reconstructions are possible (Alcock and Walsh 1993). Rafters would be placed from the wall-plates to the ridge piece, probably supported on purlins. Millett and James (1983) argue for a raised joist and plank floor. As the majority of the roof load, thatch or oak shingles, was placed on the wall-plates, steeply inclined external raking timbers counteracted the thrust of the rafters. The total hours of work required to construct such a building is impossible to estimate. The preparation of the foundations and the timbers alone would have required considerable time and although C12 is the largest building excavated at the settlement, the effort required to build many of the others would not have been much less.

Such timber buildings would have been built using the accumulated experience of the community and would not have seemed such an intricate

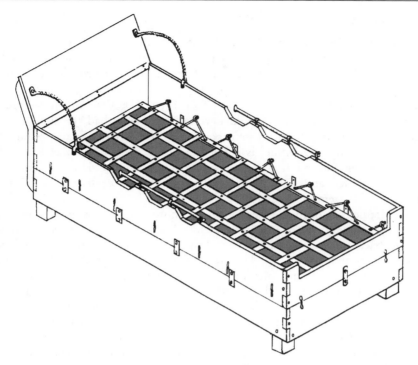

Figure 4.5 Possible reconstruction of bed from Swallowcliffe, Wiltshire
(source: Speake 1989, Figure 81)

task to those who regularly witnessed the activity. Carpentry skills did not
stop there as furniture would have been required within domestic buildings.
What furniture actually stood inside them we can but guess. The rarity of
artefacts from within buildings does not help our knowledge of furniture
fittings. It is only in those rare instances where furniture is incorporated in
funerals, whether specifically made for the funeral or not, that we get a
glimpse of what was possible. There are a number of definite examples of
bed burials especially in Wiltshire, Cambridgeshire and Suffolk. The example
from Swallowcliffe, Wiltshire (Figures 4.5 and 7.11) consisted of ash plank
sides and headboard, iron hand-rails and leather 'webbing' forming the base,
the whole requiring a variety of iron cleats, eyelets and nails (Speake 1989:
82–115). An iron folding stool whose inlaid decoration suggests a sixth-
century date is another known piece of furniture (Wilson 1957). The clay
figure decorating the lid of a cremation urn from Spong Hill is depicted
sitting in a chair (Hills, Penn and Rickett 1987, Figure 82).

HELMETS

The spirit of true craftsmanship is, however, best seen in those items that, as far as is known, were unique in their time and which required a wide range of skills to achieve, irrespective of the inspiration provided by other contemporary pieces. A fine example is the helmet from the Sutton Hoo burial in mound I (Bruce-Mitford 1978: 138–231). One might imagine, perhaps wrongly, that there would have been few who had the skill at any one time to produce such an item because of the variety of skills required. It is possible that the helmet is a Swedish product, or, more likely, as with other traits in mound I, the result of long-term and widespread contacts between Sweden and East Anglia. Whatever the source it exemplifies the strength of contemporary skills.

The framework of the helmet consists of an iron cap, almost hemispherical, which was beaten out of one piece of metal. Over this cap, from the front to the back is a strong iron crest, D-shaped in cross-section and hollow, riveted at its ends to the cap. The crest was of two parts, a flat bottom plate fitting into a U-sectioned piece. It must have been either forged or welded to the cap or fitted hot and allowed to cool into position. Attached to the lower edge of the cap are a face-mask, two cheek-pieces and a neck-guard. The face-mask was rigid and attached by rivets, the neck-guard and cheek-pieces hinged by strips of leather strengthened by bronze bars and riveted. The neck-guard was solid and beaten out of two sheets of metal and held to the cap by two riveted leather hinges with metal reinforcing bars. It is assumed that the interior of the cap was lined with soft leather. The heavy cheek-pieces would have enclosed the face completely. The surface of the helmet was almost totally covered with figural and interlaced ornament. This was applied to the surface of the iron cap in the form of tinned bronze sheeting into which the ornament had been stamped with dies. The bronze sheeting was held to the cap, cheek-pieces, neck-guard and mask by fluted strips of bronze riveted through the edges of the foil to the cap of the helmet. Some jewels were fitted to the surface; there was a line of square-cut flat garnets on the eyebrows, and dragon heads which form terminals to the crest have cabochan garnets for eyes. The iron crest and bronze eyebrows were inlaid with silver wire. Parts of the surface of the helmet were gilded, the boar, dragon heads, the nose and mouth of the face-mask, under surfaces of the eyebrows and the broad fluted strips flanking the crest. Fluted strips holding and framing the decorative panels were of tinned bronze (Bruce-Mitford 1978: 138–231).

There can be no doubt about the time and skill required to produce such an ornate and complex piece of metalwork; the investment required was no doubt matched by the importance of the person for whom it was made. It emphasises the effort that would be expended to symbolise the identity of an individual in a society that, consciously and unconsciously, reflected the hierarchy of identities in almost every activity. The production of an item such as the Sutton Hoo helmet was undoubtedly a great achievement, but there are cases where the complexity and skill involved in the manufacture of even the seemingly most humble item is surprising. This can be demonstrated by examining items made using different raw materials and technologies.

IRON TOOLS AND WEAPONS

Apart from the almost ubiquitous knife, iron was most extensively used in the production of weaponry that is almost all found as grave-goods. Typically for the period the quantity of finished products is far greater than the known examples of production sites (McDonnell 1989). There is however a growing body of evidence for iron-smelting and smithing from settlements. That at Wakerley (Northamptonshire) consisted of a clay-lined furnace set 2½ feet into the limestone bedrock. There was no means of tapping the slag, requiring the furnace to be broken after smelting and then rebuilt (*Medieval Archaeol.* 15 (1971): 132). At Mucking blocks of smelting and smithing slag were recovered, the largest weighing 24 kilograms, and one deposit contained a small quantity of tap slag (McDonnell 1993). That slag was at some times tapped during the period is also shown by the debris at Shakenoak (Oxfordshire), which was accompanied by the clay linings from four furnaces and forging hearths (Cleere 1972). Similarly at Little Totham (Essex) and Romsey (Hampshire) there is evidence for slag block smelting amongst which there was a small quantity of tap slag (McDonnell 1993). At West Stow there was no indication of smelting but smithing slag was present (Macalister 1985) and there was similar evidence at the settlement of Catholme (Losco-Bradley 1977). Leeds noted that '*scoriae*', cinders, were to be found on most of the surfaces within sunken buildings at the settlement at Sutton Courtenay, suggesting to him that 'every man may have been his own smith' (Leeds 1936: 24). The same conclusion was reached with the evidence at Mucking, that smithing and smelting took place at the same location 'on a small scale to satisfy local needs' (McDonnell 1993: 83). There is no evidence for large-scale smelting associated with the major ore deposits of the Weald or the Forest of Dean at this time.

Spears and axes have utilitarian forms whose manufacture would have been within the abilities of anyone with basic smithing experience. Both have sockets for handles or shafts that would have been created by beating the iron around a former. The heads of the spears are usually slightly lozenge-sectioned as a result of beating out the edges, and the socket, normally split on one side, was riveted to the top of the shaft. There are hints of preferred shapes on a regional basis, but there is little distinct typological development discernible. Occasional specimens are decorated with inlaid copper wire (Swanton 1973, 1974) using the same technology as the folding iron stool noted above.

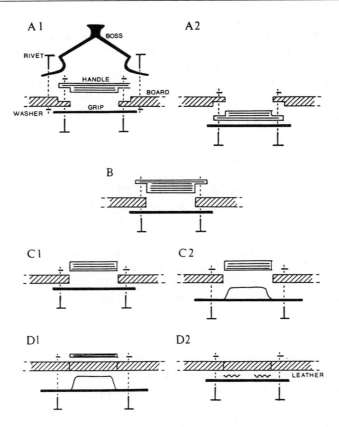

Figure 4.6 Possible reconstructions of early Anglo-Saxon shields (source: Härke 1981, Figure 1). The evidence for the reconstruction comes from the iron fittings and indications of wood found on them

Spear shafts were made of wood, which often survive as corrosion products allowing the species to be identified (Watson and Edwards 1990). From the hafts of spearheads, normally split to allow a firm fit of the shaft, we find the use of hazel and ash, both of which tend to grow straight when pollarded. There is archaeological evidence for such management of woodland at this time from Barton Court Farm (Oxfordshire) (Robinson 1981). The length of such shafts is difficult to determine except where there is an accompanying ferrule binding the foot. With such items we are dealing with a simple use of wood. More complex carpentry was used on this scale in the manufacture of shields (Dickinson and Härke 1992).

Shields were probably circular, of wood with a central hole over which was an iron grip, often mounted off-centre and held in place by rivets burred

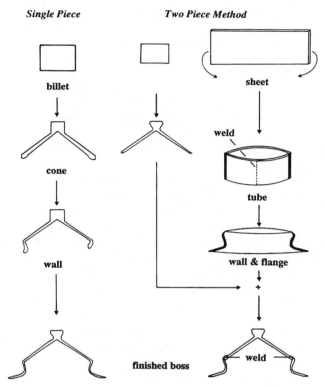

Figure 4.7 Two possible methods of manufacturing a carinated shield boss (source: Härke and Salter 1984, Figure 4)

over on the front (Figure 4.6). A wooden handle may be formed either as an integral part of the boards by cutting two semi-circular openings, or by a separate piece of wood fixed in a variety of ways. The wooden handle may be bound with leather and textile, which may also be applied to the grip where a wooden handle was not used. The opening, and therefore the hand, was protected by an iron boss fixed by rivets passing through a flange and the boards. It is the iron boss and grip that usually survive in graves where they are found. The 'impression' of the wood grain is often preserved on the metal components where they were in contact, sufficient to show whether the boards were of plank or laminated construction. The earliest insular bosses were tall and narrow with a spike apex. These were replaced during the later fifth century by the most common form, having a low and broad shape with an overhanging carination, concave wall and disc-head apex. During the sixth century the preferred form had a convex cone and straight wall that changed gradually until, in the middle of the seventh century, the boss was enlarged into the 'sugar-loaf' form. Two principal methods appear to have been used to make the bosses (Figure 4.7), either being beaten up from a single billet of soft iron or made in two pieces, the cone beaten up from a billet and the wall and flange from sheet metal, welded together. The boss was fixed to the face of the shield by means of four or five rivets whose flat round heads are occasionally tinned. The ends of the rivets were bent over at right angles making it possible to calculate that the wooden boards of the complete circular shields were 0.5 to 1.5 cm thick. Shields appear to have been made in three preferred sizes ranging from 0.34 to 0.92 metres in diameter, the most common being 0.60 metres. Watson has demonstrated that most shields were covered with leather on both sides. The wood chosen was normally alder, ash, birch, lime, maple and willow or poplar, all relatively light woods (Watson 1994). In addition to occasional metal edge-binding, some shields were provided with simple board fittings, such as lozenges, studs and discs and there are a few examples with figural appliqués, such as the fish from Spong Hill (Hills, Penn and Rickett 1984: 80–2) and those from Sutton Hoo mound I; graves with figural fittings tend to have a larger number of grave-goods than those with simple, or no, fittings. There is no regional preference for the choice of wood but some of the boss shapes are more common in particular areas and the highest proportion of shields with board fittings is in Wessex.

The handles of knives were most often of horn, sometimes wood, and were usually made from two pieces riveted through the iron tang. The alder-wood handle of a knife from Christchurch (Hampshire) was of one piece of wood that had been forced over the pointed tang (Jarvis *et al.* 1983).

Swords were the rarest and most prestigious weapons in early Anglo-Saxon England (Davidson 1962). They were two-edged weapons, normally about 90 cm long. The various organic fittings associated with the grip, such as that of horn from Snape (Cameron and Filmer-Sankey 1993), rarely survive. It is the metal mounts and fittings that are most commonly found and it is these that form the basis for a typology (Böhner 1958). The earliest examples have straight pommel bars and guards, the latter slightly broader than the heel of the blade, and capped by a mount in the shape of a cocked hat. The sword hilt offered scope for embellishment; sometimes the pommel and guard are decorated, inlaid or gilded, embellished with runes and given a loose ring (Hawkes and Page 1967; Evison 1967). The blades may also be decorated, by a method known as pattern welding, although this is rarely apparent from the corroded form in which they are found (Wilson 1976b: 265–6; Anstee and Biek 1961; Hodges 1964: 47ff.). Pattern welding was achieved by a complex and skilled process. It is suggested that a channel was left on each face of the blade into which separate strips were laid. The strips were themselves complex; an iron rod was carburised, piled and drawn down and the process repeated until a rod of laminated iron and steel was formed. The bars were then folded or twisted together and beaten out to form the central

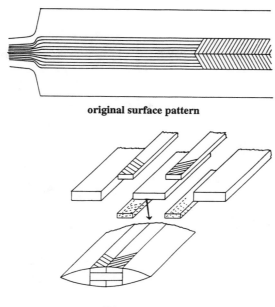

original surface pattern

possible component parts

Figure 4.8 A possible construction method of a pattern-welded sword from Spong Hill, Norfolk (source: Gilmour 1984, Figure 110)

element of each face. The blade was then polished to emphasise the bands of iron and steel. An example from Spong Hill (Hills, Penn and Rickett 1984: 161) had pattern welding but did not incorporate a central channel. The composite rods were partly twisted, partly straight (Figure 4.8) and had probably been formed by welding together four composite rods, or in pairs, to either side of a central strip. The cutting edges were welded on separately.

CASTING

The apparent certainties of knowledge concerning the technology of sword and shield manufacture may all too easily divert attention away from the areas of greater doubt. In discussing the stages in the manufacture of the Kentish disc brooches considerable detail was omitted because of uncertainties regarding the actual methods of jewellery manufacture at the time. Understanding of these methods is critical to our appreciation of the technology employed and, as important, our knowledge of the organisation of metalworking; detailed studies of cast metalwork have shed much light on such matters.

Figure 4.9 A saucer brooch from Fairford, Gloucestershire, and a cruciform brooch from Sleaford, Lincolnshire (source: de Baye 1893, Plates VI and VIII)

The methods of manufacturing and replicating cast-alloy metalwork have been extensively studied, for instance square-headed, saucer and cruciform brooches (Figures 4.9 and 5.20) which occur predominantly in midland, eastern and northern England (Leigh 1990; Dickinson 1993a; Mortimer 1990). The first manufacturing stage was to produce a model, of wax or soft metal, or possibly wood or bone, with most of the decoration put on to the model before casting the brooch. The model was then covered in clay, cut into two sections to produce a two-piece mould and the model removed. If the model was made of wax it could be melted out but, of course, not re-used, requiring a master model to be made if replication was intended. The lugs that would become the catch-plate and pin-holder could have been on the model or might be added to the mould at this stage. The molten metal would be poured in and allowed to cool before the mould was broken open. The brooch would then be cleaned, relief decoration sharpened and any punched decoration added. Mercury gilding could then be applied. Finally the lugs would be prepared and the pin attached.

Each stage in the process of manufacture required a different combination of raw materials and tools that would have had to have been obtained, manufactured and processed. The raw materials would have included – depending on the type of cast metalwork – wood, charcoal, iron, mercury, wax, clay, lead, antimony, tallow, tin, gold, garnets and other stones and abrasive, as well as the raw material for the casting. Various tools would have been required for casting, graving, cutting, bending and polishing. Despite the small scale of production the metalworker would have needed considerable knowledge and skill to accumulate the equipment and materials to produce such brooches.

While the principal stages of casting such brooches may be understood there remains some uncertainty about the precise methods used to produce the two-piece mould. The study of three lead-alloy models of early Anglo-Saxon brooches has focused attention on the problems (Mortimer 1994). While studies of brooches indicate that piece-mould technology may have been used, the actual evidence from England comprises, as we have seen, fragments of a two-piece clay mould from Mucking (Figure 5.17) and another lead model for an English square-headed brooch from Geneva, Switzerland (Bonnet and Martin 1982). Piece-mould technology was in use in Scandinavia and Europe at this time (Holmqvist 1975; Willems 1973) but only later in England. It is possible that the lead 'models' are actually trial castings but because they would be difficult to remove without damaging the mould and given the absence of evidence for their re-use, their function as models seems most likely. The model would be pressed into clay, holes cut for alignment, and then allowed to dry. Clay would then be applied to the other side of the model, the ingate cut and then the two halves parted so that the model could be removed. Additional detail, such as lugs and further decoration, could then be pressed or cut into the mould before it was fired. The method would require great skill but only one casting episode.

If such lead-alloy pieces were not models it would be necessary to consider the possibility that the process was altogether more complicated, involving two models and moulds. The first model would be made from wax, wood or bone around which a mould would be formed of clay and in which a lead-alloy, secondary, model would be cast. Finer detail could be added to the secondary model before another, secondary, mould would be created. This method would have required less skill but two casting episodes. It is not possible as yet, from either the models or the finished products, to be certain which method(s) was used.

While such consideration of the methods used to create moulds might seem over-attentive to detail, an understanding of them has implications beyond early Anglo-Saxon technology. The study of the structure of such industry and the means of dispersal of such artefacts is largely dependent on an understanding of similarity and, therefore, of the means of replication. Hence the methods by which the moulds, be they primary or secondary, were made is crucial. The problems explored here apply to the manufacture of all cast metalwork, brooches and buckles being the most common, although the problems are most easily studied in those types with decorative variation.

CONTAINERS

The technologies considered so far have been those relating to large-scale carpentry and items worn or carried, especially brooches and weaponry. A different range of skills was required for the production of containers, be they 'buckets', glassware, turned wooden vessels or pottery.

Early Anglo-Saxon buckets (Stamper 1978) are of metal-bound stave construction (Figure 4.10). These should not be confused with pails that are cylindrical, handled containers made entirely of metal and mostly imported into England (Richards 1986). Buckets are most usually copper-alloy or iron bound, straight sided and on average 10 cm high and broad; it is their small-ness that perhaps makes the term 'bucket' inappropriate. A few taper to the top, such as the example from the cemetery at Berinsfield (Oxfordshire) (Boyle et al. 1996); some tapering vessels are bound with copper-alloy, for example that from Droxford (Hampshire), others are of mixed construction such as those from Harwell (Oxfordshire). Perhaps the greatest variation is in the decorated mount, or escutcheon, to which the free-moving handle was fixed. These fittings are often very complicated. The principal types are those with bifurcated beaked heads, mounts with zoomorphic or anthropomorphic heads, plate escutcheons with ring suspension loops or inverted triangular openwork mounts. Some have handles without mounts, or none at all. Those with bifurcated head mounts show varying degrees of debasement, one of the earliest being that from Little Wilbraham (Cambridgeshire).

One very notable group with plate escutcheon mounts have arcade and dot decoration in repoussé, which is allied to an extensive Continental group. The English examples, which are concentrated in central southern England, vary slightly from the Continental examples (Arnold 1982a: 58–9). Other escutcheons are kidney shaped or triangular, sometimes having holes drilled to create openwork decoration. Typical examples are those from Portsdown (Hampshire) and Mucking (Jones and Jones 1975: 178) which have ring suspension loops, a feature that is more common on the Continent. A common type of bucket mount on the Continent is that with openwork triangular mounts, although the only definite English example is from Gilton in Kent. Others may be in a British tradition, such as one from Twyford (Leicestershire) with a moulded ox-head on the escutcheon (Hawkes and Smith 1957) and that from Souldern (Oxfordshire) (Kennett 1975) whose stylised anthropomorphic face is reminiscent of the late prehistoric bucket from Aylesford (Kent) (Evans 1890: 363).

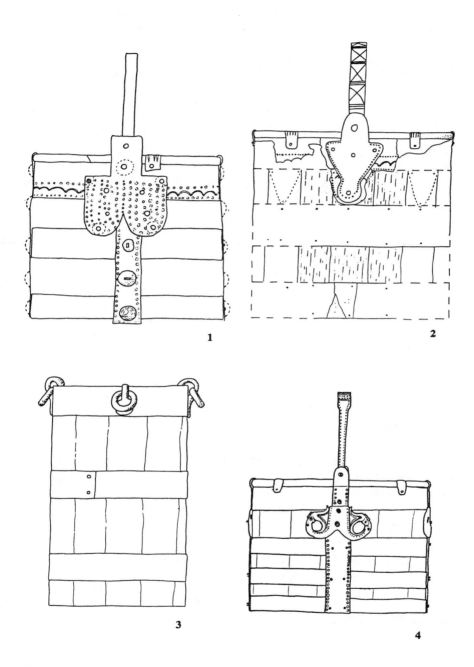

1

2

3

4

Figure 4.10 Examples of early Anglo-Saxon buckets (source: Stamper 1978)

The handles themselves are most commonly formed of a plain bronze strip, pierced at the ends and riveted through the escutcheon or upper binding strip, allowing the handle to swivel. Other handles have terminals that are hooked, passing through a mount or through opposed holes in the vertical bands. They may also be decorated with notches and incised lines and stamped dots, arcs, circles and triangles.

The bindings consist of various combinations; there may be three or four horizontal bands and two or four vertical stays, normally fixed to the staves with rivets. Copper-alloy bound buckets were probably manufactured cold as the metal is unsuitable for shrinking on to wooden staves, unlike iron. Iron bound buckets tend not to have vertical stays, the bindings being both broad iron bands and rod-like hoops. Some of the more ornate buckets have triangular mounts, in copper-alloy sheet, suspended from the top band. Amongst the more ornate are those showing a bearded human face in relief repoussé work that are known in Essex (e.g. Great Chesterford and Mucking) and Kent (e.g. Eastry, Sandgate and Howletts). Others have suspended pendants decorated with circle and dot designs.

The majority of buckets found in early Anglo-Saxon graves are of stave construction, bound with copper-alloy. Such construction required a similar control over materials as a cooper. Experiment has shown that considerable skill is required when making such small vessels with cold-worked copper-alloy bindings; a wooden former with a circular aperture may have been used to hold the staves in place while the bindings are applied and riveted. Generally the staves forming the bucket have constant width and thickness (Table 4.1). Some vary considerably in their width such as that from grave 60 at the cemetery of Petersfinger (Wiltshire) which had staves varying from 2 to 5 cm wide. The edges of the staves have to be cut straight and at a precise angle to ensure that the desired shape is acquired and that the unbound staves can be supported before the bindings are attached.

Unfortunately there are few certain identifications of the species of wood used. Yew is noted from Luton (Bedfordshire) grave 32, Portsdown, Harwell grave 9, Welbeck Hill (Lincolnshire), Roundway Down (Wiltshire) and buckets 2 and 5 from Sutton Hoo. Other species represented are pine or fir at Stowting (Kent) and Ashton Valley (Wiltshire); oak is known at Higham

Table 4.1 Dimensions of staves on early Anglo-Saxon buckets

	Width (cm)	Thickness (cm)
North Luffenham (Rutland)	4	0.5
Louth (Lincolnshire)	4	0.5
Hillersham (Cambridgeshire)	4	0.4
Sleaford (Lincolnshire)	4	0.2

(Kent) and ash at Mucking (grave 600). One surviving base is that from North Luffenham (Rutland) made of a circular piece of wood cut with the grain, 0.2 cm thick, which was clearly fitted before the binding as it was slotted into a groove at the bottom of the staves; such a method of fixing was common.

An alternative form of vessel was that turned from wood. Bowl-turning is thought to have been a Germanic introduction to England. Such vessels are most commonly, but not exclusively, found in male graves, for instance the six turned maple-wood bottles and eight turned walnut burr-wood cups amongst the grave-goods in the ship burial of Sutton Hoo mound I (Bruce-Mitford 1983: 316–408). How common such vessels were is difficult to tell. Most are only recognised because of the metal bindings around the mouth that both strengthened and decorated the vessel. Simple clips and staples are likely to represent repairs. Many others may not have had such embellishment and are more difficult to detect. The majority of turned wooden vessels of the period are in softwood and are likely to have been produced using a pole lathe (Dixon 1994). A tree trunk would be felled and cut into billets that could be split. The half-rounds would then have been trimmed into cones and left to dry. When suitably prepared they would be mounted and turned using the lathe (Morris 1982).

Glass vessels are the product of an entirely different technology, and again most research has been directed towards their typology (Harden 1956b, 1978). There has been considerable debate about the origins of the glassware found in Anglo-Saxon cemeteries and on settlements outside England; some are Roman survivals, and a proportion was imported from glass-houses in the Rhineland and northern Gaul. However, the very large concentrations (Figure 5.10) at Faversham, Kent (Harden 1956b: 146–7) and the fact that some supposed European types are more common in England than on the Continent, for instance the Kempston type cone-beakers (Evison 1972) and bag beakers (Harden 1978: 2), must encourage the view that some at least may have been made in England. Unfortunately the evidence for their production is limited as glass-houses may leave little archaeological evidence when all of the waste can be recycled.

Harden's type-series (1956b: 139–43) divided the total assemblage into a number of distinct categories: beakers with stems or claws, bell-, bag- or cone-shaped, with the related horns, pouch bottles, squat jars, bottles, palm cups and bowls, to which has been added a bucket-shaped vessel from the cemetery of Westgarth Gardens, Bury St Edmunds (Suffolk); slight variations have been made to the original typology (Harden 1978: 2–6) (Figure 4.11).

Attempts to characterise glass with a view to understanding its technology and sources have been made, but glass is a difficult material to work with in this way because of compositional irregularities (Sanderson and Hunter 1980; Hunter 1985). There are, for instance, no apparent compositional differences between Roman and Anglo-Saxon glass vessels (Sanderson and Warren 1984) although there are marked differences in appearance; this may

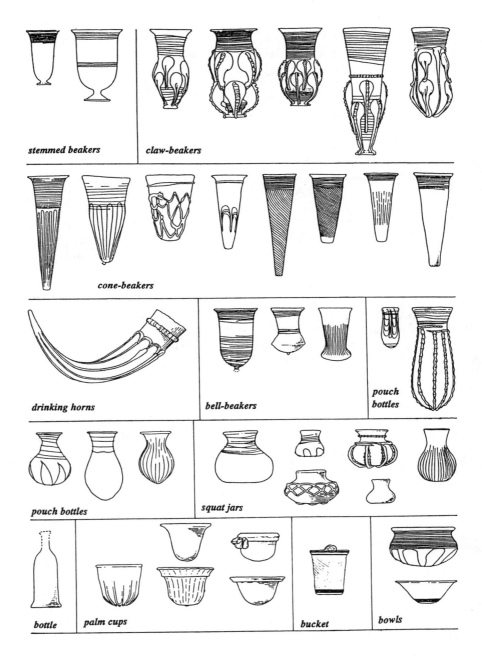

Figure 4.11 Types of glass vessel from early Anglo-Saxon England (source: Harden 1956b, Figure 25 with additions)

be the result of a decrease in technological ability. Anglo-Saxon glass displays a variety of colours, especially brown, ochre, yellow, blue and green, which are probably brought about by a lack of control of the furnace conditions rather than by deliberate colouring. A programme of glass characterisation using a variety of techniques is currently being carried out (Day and Perkins 1991).

Much of the craftsmanship and its relevant technology considered so far is in marked contrast to the most common of artefacts, pottery. Clay was used to make a variety of items ranging from loom-weights to the unique clay pot-lid in the form of a seated figure from Spong Hill (Hills 1980a; Hills, Penn and Rickett 1987: 80, Figure 82). It is most commonly found in the form of pottery vessels. Brisbane (1981) has suggested that there were three modes of production of pottery found in early Anglo-Saxon England: vessels for domestic use were made on the farm; specialised vessels were made for funerary use, both as a grave-good with inhumation burials and for containing cremated remains; and a relatively small quantity of imported wares. Very little research has been carried out on domestic wares and it remains far from clear to what extent domestic and funerary pottery production can be separated; where analyses have been possible they show that the types of clay fabrics used in a settlement and its adjacent cemetery are the same. The evidence at the settlement of West Stow, where stamped vessels of a type found in cremation cemeteries were present amongst other rubbish and which may have been made there, is ambiguous. The pottery was hand-modelled using the coil technique and then fired in a clamp, or bonfire. The decorated forms would have required considerably more modelling than the undecorated domestic wares whose very poor quality may suggest that wooden vessels were more frequently used than the archaeological record would suggest (Dixon 1994: 61).

The only known or suspected production sites are at Elsham in Lincolnshire, comprising concentrations of burnt material and sherds of pottery (which have not been excavated and which may be the remains of funeral pyres), the excavated kiln (?) at Cassington, Oxfordshire (Arthur and Jope 1963) and possibly Sutton Courtenay (Leeds 1936: 28). The settlement at West Stow has produced indirect evidence for manufacture (Figure 4.12) in the form of large quantities of pottery, antler pot dies and 'a reserved area of clay' (West 1985: 129), an area surrounded by a ditch presumably to keep straying animals away. The general absence of kilns has normally been accepted as negative evidence favouring the use of bonfires, or clamps, for firing pottery during the period.

Ceramic vessels were made in a variety of shapes with varying degrees and forms of decoration (Figure 4.13). A typology of the forms of cremation vessels was produced by Myres (1969, 1977) and a simplified version by Hurst (1976). Research on the shape of cremation vessels incorporating measurement indicates that a more logical method of sub-dividing the

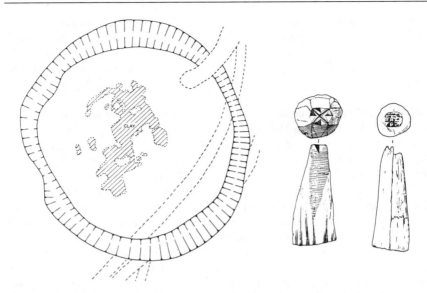

Figure 4.12 The evidence for pottery production, the enclosed clay reserve and bone pottery dies at West Stow, Suffolk (source: West 1985, Figures 235 and 254)

material is possible. Richards (1982) created a method of defining vessel shape using a fixed set of rules: the profile of vessels is recorded and normalised to a standard height, a parameter that does not appear to be relevant to the definition of forms. The plotting of frequency distributions of particular size ratios provides peaks that represent preferred forms. It has also been shown that particular shapes of cremation pottery tend to be correlated with particular grave-goods, with the sex of the individual contained in the vessel and with the decoration on the vessel (Richards 1987). Once again we find that choice was largely determined by social factors. Other typological systems lack such precision and, therefore, such correlations.

The decoration on pottery vessels is most frequently made by incised lines, wide or narrow, close-set or widely spaced, produced by small hand tools; in its most extreme form the surface can be corrugated. Much of the ceramic material in eastern England, less so in the south, is stamped: decorated by pressing a carved die or naturally occurring object into the surface. Few of these tools have been found; definite examples of dies are known from West Stow (Figure 4.12), Lackford and Little Eriswell (Suffolk), Shakenoak and Illington (Norfolk), mostly made of antler, but bone was also used (Briscoe 1981). Their rarity suggests that the majority were made of a less durable material such as wood or even a soft stone such as chalk. Alternatively if such dies were in use for more than one generation they might be expected

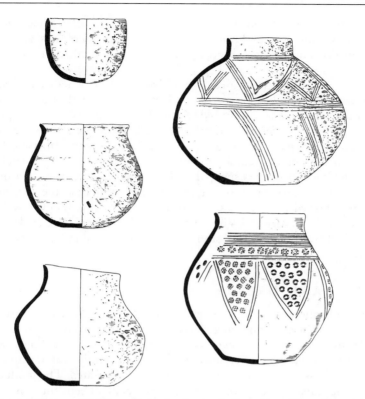

Figure 4.13 Examples of early Anglo-Saxon pottery from West Stow Heath, Suffolk (source: West 1985, Figures 273 and 274)

to have been made from a durable material and their rarity may be because they were destroyed when their use ceased. Linear decoration is often combined with bosses, where the walls of the pot are pushed up from inside into rounded or oval shapes.

The largest assemblage of domestic pottery, about 30,000 sherds, has been recovered at Mucking. It formed the basis for one of the most detailed studies so far undertaken (Hamerow 1993: 22–59). The surfaces of the vessels had been subjected to a variety of treatments including smoothing and burnishing, which increased their strength. Alternatively the surfaces were roughened by 'combing, finger-nail impression, pinching or the application of a coarse slip' (ibid.: 31) usually on the lower halves of the larger vessels, perhaps to assist in handling them. The analysis of the forms revealed that there were bowls, plates and jars with various sub-categories, with some types appearing throughout the history of the settlement, others being chronologically restricted. The percentage of decorated vessels varies only slightly from one settlement to another; at Mucking the figure was 5 per cent. While stamped decoration was increasing during the sixth century there was an overall decrease in decorated vessels through the sixth and seventh centuries (ibid.: 52).

A variety of tempers were used as additives to clays; whether the choice was conscious or not has yet to be studied, although it has already been observed that the same clay was used with different tempers in certain places. The most striking temper used was that of vegetable matter, known as grass- or chaff-tempering, perhaps added as a water-absorbing agent (Brisbane 1983: 254). Brown has argued that the material is animal dung, which would be in accordance with Brisbane's suggestion that domestic wares were a farmyard product (Brown 1976). Analysis of grass-tempered pottery at the settlements of Mucking showed that its frequency increased with time (Hamerow 1993: 31; Hamerow, Hollevoet and Vince 1994). Other tempers were chalk, lime-stone or shell, various localised stones such as flint, ground pottery (grog) and sand.

TEXTILES AND DRESS

In our consideration of technology and the production of particular artefacts we have largely been considering portable items that would have been of assistance to everyday life, some more so than others. One fundamental product that we have not examined is clothing, essential for warmth and protection, but also providing a surface that can be decorated. The production of textiles appears to have been a widespread craft. There must be some significance in the fact that it is the only craft for which there is considerable evidence. Both the tools used in its manufacture, such as combs, beaters and loomweights, and the finished products are well attested from both cemeteries and settlements. Hills (1981) has noted a correlation of combs with female cremations and other weaving equipment tends to be associated with female graves. If weaving was a predominantly female activity its visibility is in marked contrast to other manufacturing processes.

Combs, which may have had a variety of functions, are often found as grave-goods with cremations and often survive in sunken buildings associated with weaving equipment. They were often made from bone and antler, although wood may have been used more often than is now apparent because it rarely survives. Combs were made by cutting the tines on the edge, or edges if double-sided, of a flat sheet of bone. These were normally strength-ened by one or two ribs fixed along the edge or centre by iron rivets. Some of the more elaborate types have barred cases to carry the comb (Hills 1981). They were decorated, both before and after assembly, with incised lines, compass drawn circles and ring-and-dot motifs. They may be multi-purpose, for instance for combing hair as well as in the weaving process. It is generally believed that the tines are too close together to be used for carding wool, although some simpler combs that may be wool-combs are known. They may have had a function in aiding the picking out of broken threads on the loom. Nevertheless an assemblage of tools is often found together comprising shears, combs and spindle-whorls for spinning. Looms are most frequently indicated by clay loomweights (Figure 3.3), annular in form, for tensioning the warp threads on upright looms; they are occasionally found in rows in the base of sunken buildings where they may have fallen or been taken off the loom, or originally stacked in a column. Whether the length of such rows represents the width of the cloth has been debated. Parallel rows of clay rings found at Grimstone End (Suffolk) (Brown *et al.* 1957) were 2.4 m long and 0.22 m apart. A row of 43 found at Old Erringham (Sussex) was 1.5 m long; experiments have shown that 0.5 m of warp thread would require 14 loomweights; 1.5 m would therefore require 42 loomweights. A 'loom' found at Bourton-on-the-Water (Gloucestershire) (Dunning 1932) was represented by postholes 2.3 m apart, suggesting a maximum width of about 2 m of cloth. This type of evidence assumes greater importance when assessing the nature of early Anglo-Saxon dress. Looms such as these may have formed a part of every household.

Another weaving tool is the weaving batten, of bone or iron, used for beating up the weft. The iron examples are most commonly found in women's graves of the sixth century accompanied by a relatively large number of grave-goods; some are pattern-welded. Also used were pin beaters, long pieces of bone with a central swelling and pointed ends for beating down individual threads. Some of the best collections of these tools have been found in sunken buildings at Swindon (Wiltshire) accompanied by small bone pins and various iron instruments (B. Phillips, personal communication).

The textiles themselves are normally known from graves where they are preserved by corrosion from adjoining metal objects; wood and leather are often preserved in the same manner. The organic materials are visible as negative casts around the original structure that may be studied by scanning electron microscopy (Janaway 1985). The end result is an impression of the surface of the fabric, now disintegrated, maintained in the form of a metal compound resulting from the oxidisation of the adjacent object. Occasionally actual textile survives, adhered to metal. The majority of weaves preserved in these ways are plain, with a variety of twills, especially broken diamond twill; braids are also known (Crowfoot and Hawkes 1967). Little is known about textile dyeing.

Most of the textiles of which we have knowledge had been made up into clothing. It is possible to reconstruct some of the clothing in part through the textile remains in graves, but mostly using the position of dress-fasteners such as brooches and buckles (Cook 1974; Bell 1981; Owen-Crocker 1986). Some analysts have made considerable use of pictorial and literary as well as archaeological evidence from the Continent. It would be rash to assume automatically that Continental forms of dress were the same as styles used in early Anglo-Saxon England. A safer approach is to start with the evidence that is directly relevant. More work of this type could be carried out to isolate culturally determined variation in both dress and the manner in which artefacts were worn (Vierck 1978a, 1978b, 1978c).

Women's clothes show about eight variations in the position of dress-fasteners, with one, two or three brooches being worn in varying positions on the shoulders and chest, sometimes with sleeve-fasteners (frequently referred to as 'wrist clasps') particularly in eastern England (Figure 7.5). Men's dress-fastening is limited to buckles and sleeve-fasteners; three possible combinations are found. The principal problem in reconstructing clothing from this evidence is that the range of dress-fastenings may not only be dictated by dress; social identity and/or display may enter here. Similarly the dress-fasteners placed in a grave may not have been chosen purely because of their functional relationship to the garment being worn nor need the grave clothing bear a direct relationship to daily wear. The fact that many people were buried without durable dress-fasteners may imply that organic materials were often used, either on their own or in conjunction with metal fasteners; a few bone buttons are known.

Female costume comprised various combinations of a number of basic garments, a dress, undergarment, cloak and a veil. The dresses were secured, at either one or both shoulders, with brooches, pins or possibly stitches. They may have been open-fronted, the borders of the open seam either being fastened together or pinned back at the breast, again with brooches and pins. Such dresses may have been worn over a sleeved under-dress that generally received no fastenings although there are some exceptions that were secured at the wrist with a clasp that may carry evidence of braid (Crowfoot 1952). Some women wore a cloak fastened at the shoulder or breast, and some clothing gathered in at the waist with a girdle, usually secured with a buckle. Clearly the more elaborate the dress, the more fasteners required, although there is the danger here of a circular argument.

Wear on square-headed brooches has been examined by Leigh as a method of understanding how they were used to fasten clothing (1980: 487 ff., 1985). The majority of single brooches examined were found to be more abraded on the top left corner than the top right. A slightly larger percentage of pairs of brooches was more abraded on the top right than the top left. This may indicate that the brooches were consistently worn in a particular position, but not in the same way. Single brooches were generally worn with the headplates pointing to the left and pairs with their headplates pointing to the right, and parallel. Leigh argues that the wear arises more on the corner of the headplate because they were worn pointing downwards, and at a slight angle so that one corner was lower down. He suggests that they were worn for display only, rather than as a dress-fastening, being heavily abraded from contact with coarse outer clothing. However, even outer clothing must have required fastening and such wear could also have arisen if they were worn on undergarments in such a way as to come into contact with the inner face of the coarse outer garments; such extreme wear is perhaps more likely to have occurred in this way than on the outside.

Male dress presents a greater problem; sleeve-fasteners imply a sleeved upper garment, either inner or outer, and buckles suggest a belt, but there are difficulties in going beyond this. Buckles and strap-ends, for instance, need not be associated with clothing.

FUNCTION

Clothing may have been the principal use of textiles, just as the principal function of buckles, sleeve-fasteners, pins and brooches was to hold the clothing together. Such metalwork and fabrics may have been decorated in a way that conveyed meaning to the wearer and the viewer, but all of the artefacts whose technology we have considered had, first and foremost, a practical function to their owners. In certain instances these practical uses appear obvious to us, yet at times they are less so.

Vessels may have been used for preparing, consuming, carrying and storing liquids and solids, but each type may have had a specific function such as the use of open bowls as lamps. Glass vessels are normally interpreted as for drinking. Glass vessels also vary in size, but cone-beakers, generally *c.* 25 cm high and *c.* 9 cm diameter at the mouth, had a capacity of about 0.3 litres. The cone-beaker will not stand in an upright position, suggesting a degree of 'ceremony' involved with imbibing. 'Buckets' have a very similar capacity, one that seems too small for them to be practical for fetching liquids to the house or table. The majority of 'buckets' measure about 10 × 10 cm, with a capacity of about 0.7 litres. The various cups and horns in graves may also have been for the consumption of alcoholic liquid, including *beor*, *medu* and *win* (Fell 1975). The range of drink-associated items buried as grave-goods may be symbolic of an individual's identity in society in the same way that pieces of weaving equipment in durable materials are found in richly accompanied women's graves. Containers are strongly associated with richly accompanied male graves; did perforated spoons found in a few female graves symbolise a woman's role in preparing, controlling the supply of, or serving drink?

Durable containers for the bulk carrying and storage of liquids and solids are rare. The exceptions are the large metal cauldrons, dishes and buckets from rich seventh-century burials like that at Sutton Hoo mound I, whose function is perhaps more to do with feasting and largesse (Werner 1992). Larger vessels tend to be found with graves with an above average number of grave-goods, perhaps reflecting conspicuous consumption by leaders and symbolising a role in storage and distribution.

The function of early Anglo-Saxon pottery seems at first glance to be obvious. Much of it was used to contain cremations or as accessory vessels in inhumation graves; it is the pottery used in association with burial that has attracted the most attention. Very little research has been carried out on the functions of domestic pottery. The possible uses could be categorised as culinary, storage, cooking and serving, and non-culinary uses. As noted above it is far from clear whether vessels used in funerals could be drawn from the domestic stock or whether they were specially made. Cremation urns tend to have a greater volume than those accompanying inhumations, predominantly in southern England. This may imply that in cremating areas the vessels were made to a certain size for the specific function of containing the remains, whereas in areas practising inhumation there may not have been such specialised production, the vessels being drawn from the domestic stock. Vessels associated with inhumations are of similar size to those found on settlements. This may be because vessels buried with inhumations continued their domestic function by containing provisions for the dead person. Similarly animal bones are often found with cremated remains (Table 6.1; Figure 7.3). In that instance the urn has to contain the remains of the person and food and was therefore specially made, and made larger. Yet precisely what were the vessels found on settlements used for?

Published reports rarely comment on evidence for the function of domestic pottery, and unlike studies of later medieval pottery the presence or absence of sooting on the vessels' surfaces is not always commented on. Large domestic pots at West Stow had been given a thin coating of clay on the outside after they had been fired; this layer is usually slightly reddened as a result of partial firing (West 1985: 129). This may not be functional so much as a desire to have vessels of a particular colour. Leeds described coarse vessels, many tempered with organic material, found within sunken buildings at Sutton Courtenay as 'cooking pots'. These were associated with fire-reddened pebbles. While the association may not be relevant to the function of the pottery, he interpreted the stones as pot-boilers (Leeds 1936: 24). Hearths are a fairly common feature in a proportion of such buildings and Leeds also describes some pits as being for cooking. Sooting was noted on vessels at Bishopstone (Bell 1977: 229–33). However Hurst (1976: 292) has emphasised that such pottery 'presents a serious problem' for it is often so fragmentary or 'unstratified' as to make its study difficult; he also describes them as 'cooking pots'. They appear to range from small globular vessels to larger storage vessels, as found at Sutton Courtenay. The vessels from Mucking were categorised as bowls, plates and jars, yet despite having functional implications there was little analysis of use (Hamerow 1993: 37–44). Colander-type vessels with a few or numerous perforations are known from Mucking, West Stow and Sutton Courtenay (Hamerow 1993: 44; West 1985: Figure 152; Leeds 1927: 72–3) which may be associated with cheese production.

The discussion of early Anglo-Saxon pottery by Myres (1969) has little direct comment on the uses of pottery, except that many were used in mortuary rituals. Indirectly, the titles given to various types imply that distinctions were considered possible. All decorated wares were described as a subset of all cremation wares. Yet the undecorated vessels were given a variety of titles, despite the majority having also come from cemeteries; biconical and globular vessels were labelled 'urns', squat vessels as 'plain bowls', and a variety of shapes that could not be fitted easily into the typological scheme were labelled domestic wares, 'crude accessories', 'wide-mouthed cookpots' and 'cook-pots with lugs' (ibid.: 26–9, 148–70). Myres also emphasised the difficulties faced in categorising these wares because of their crude and formless nature. However, he noted that examples of his category of wide-mouthed cooking pots are often smoke-blackened on the outer surface. More direct indications of function come with small groups of vessels having three solid or horizontally pierced lugs for suspension by a cord or thong; these were designed primarily as household utensils. Horizontally pierced lugs on the rim as well as perforation in the necks of vessels are quite commonly found on settlements of the period, for instance Bishopstone (Bell 1977: 235) and Mucking (Jones and Jones 1975: 159; Hamerow 1993: 41–2).

We can but guess at the extent of the use of wood or leather containers for storage, cooking, serving, eating and drinking. Dixon (1994) has suggested that the reason that much domestic pottery is crudely made was that turned wooden vessels may have been preferred. The existence of small wooden vessels is demonstrated by those which were repaired, strengthened and decorated by metal parts, such as buckets, bottles, cups and bowls. If glass vessels were prestigious drinking vessels, one might expect their 'cheaper' equivalents to appear in the ceramic assemblage; true skeuomorphs are not present amongst the pottery, although there is a strong similarity between the turned wooden vessels with metal rims from the Sutton Hoo mound I ship burial and squat glass jars. Some domestic pottery has the same shape as turned wooden vessels. A rare glass vessel from Westgarth Gardens, Bury St Edmunds (Suffolk), was rightly described as 'bucket-shaped' (Harden 1978: 5) (Figure 4.11). In form there are similarities between certain glass bowls and plain ceramic bowls, but it is difficult to find ceramic equivalents of distinctive glass forms. This suggests that whatever significance the shape and function a particular vessel form might have had was also conveyed by the material used, and that there were rigid boundaries between them.

The practical function of certain artefacts is perhaps more obvious. Swords, spears and shields are taken to be offensive and defensive weapons of warfare, and there is nothing to suggest that they were used in any other than conventional modes (Alcock 1978; Davidson 1962; Swanton 1973, 1974; Dickinson and Härke 1992). As a grave-good the spear is most common, occurring in 80 per cent of weapon graves. Other offensive weapons such as swords, the single-edged seax, arrows and axes occurred in 10 per cent. The shield was the most common defensive weapon being found in 50 per cent of weapon graves whereas protective garments are very rare (Härke 1990, 1992b). Irrespective of the actual uses to which such weapons were put, their presence

Table 4.2 Types of artefacts, sub-divided by category, buried as grave-goods in early Anglo-Saxon inhumation cemeteries

	Miscellaneous					Weapons			Dress/ ornaments				Prestige/luxury						Tools				
	knife	buckle	strap-end	key	pottery	spear	shield	sword/seax	brooch	pin	bead	ring	glass	tweezers	bucket	purse	spoon	crystal ball	comb	spindle whorl	needle	brush	whetstone
Collingbourne Ducis	*	*	*	*	*	*	*	*	*	*	*	*	*		*				*	*	*	*	
Lyminge	*	*	*	*	*	*	*		*	*	*	*	*	*		*	*	*	*				
Spong Hill	*	*	*	*	*	*	*	*	*	*	*	*	*	*	*	*				*			
Alfriston	*	*	*	*	*	*	*	*	*	*	*	*	*	*	*	*	*					*	
Petersfinger	*	*		*	*	*	*	*	*	*	*	*	*	*	*	*					*	*	
Norton	*	*	*	*	*	*	*	*	*	*	*	*		*	*				*			*	
Polhill	*	*	*	*	*	*			*	*	*	*	*								*		*
Winnall II	*	*	*	*	*				*	*	*	*							*	*			

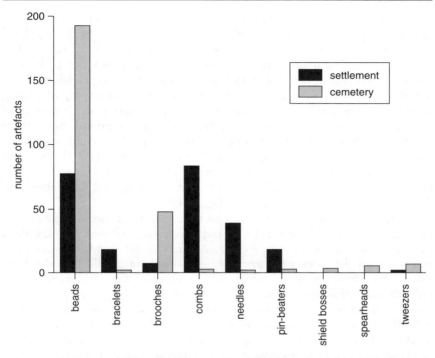

Figure 4.14 The numbers of various types of artefacts from the settlement of West Stow and the cemetery at West Stow Heath (source: Richards 1992, Figure 19)

in graves appears to reflect the status of the families to which the individuals belonged and it does not necessarily follow that such individuals were 'warriors' (ibid.).

The presence of the bones of wild animals on settlements, especially those of deer, points to hunting being practised, yet the means by which such animals were caught and killed is unclear. The frequency of weapon types in graves cannot be used to indicate the frequency of their use, but spears may have been used especially if there was a sporting element to hunting. Bows and arrows are very rare but would have been most suitable for hunting. Whether their rarity in graves can be explained in the same way as the rarity of tools associated with most crafts such as agriculture, carpentry, metal-working and textile production, that they had a high use-value and were not therefore disposed of in this manner, is debatable. Their frequency of burial is very different to items associated with dress (Table 4.2). The rarity of some classes of items in graves does raise questions about those types that are more common such as weaponry and items associated with dress.

The absence of brooches, or other dress-fasteners, in many female graves might lead to the conclusion that they were not necessary items, or that organic equivalents were also used. Despite their being one of the most common types of artefact in female graves, they may have been considered a personal luxury. Indeed all the grave-goods may be luxury items with a low use-value. The major exception is the ubiquitous iron knife, perhaps so common and such a personal item that it was felt to be expendable (Härke 1989). Knives were probably the most common tool in everyday life, being useful for numerous functions. However, as with weapons, the frequency of deposition and the combinations of items are dangerous grounds from which to draw conclusions about use and concepts of value. We should not assume that their values were, in any sense, equal. Richards' analysis (1992) of selected items found in the settlement and cemetery at West Stow demonstrates the difference between items deliberately selected for burial and those that were lost and not recovered in daily life (Figure 4.14).

There are some items whose functions have stimulated considerable debate, such as 'purse-mounts' (Brown 1977) and 'needle-cases' (Brown 1974). Others have provoked less comment, such as tweezers found in male graves. If it was accepted that they were primarily depilatory we should consider their role in the alteration of the physical appearance of men and women as a cultural trait. Although rather intangible, such a possibility serves to emphasise that there were various media available to express design and meaning as well as their more apparent manifestation in dress and the decoration of artefacts. It is difficult to gauge the extent to which cosmetics, leather-working, paint and carving were used, as surviving examples are rare or non-existent. We are forced to perceive early Anglo-Saxon society through those durable artefacts that have survived, whose functions and meanings are often poorly understood, and there is the danger that our image of the society is seriously distorted.

Chapter 5

Exchange

The exchange of raw materials and finished products in a society is an activity that is inextricably bound up with economic, social and political life. The nature of the movement of goods can only be understood if it is seen in relation to the complex and changing framework of society. In early Anglo-Saxon England small cohesive social units with low population densities and local leaders merged by peaceful and forceful means into larger political agglomerations. At the base of this structure was subsistence. Small, relatively isolated communities would have been extremely vulnerable if crops failed. In such circumstances, alliances with neighbouring groups would have assumed great importance when food was required in emergencies. Such alliances could have been established by such means as offers of reciprocity, payment through gifts of primitive valuables, or marriages between members of groups. In this way, alliance relations between descent groups would simultaneously have involved economic and social affairs and it would be entirely artificial to try and divorce them. Despite displaying a generalised and largely self-sufficient subsistence economy, precious metals and other valuable goods are known to have moved between such communities, thereby also having a role in the gradual blurring of regional identities. Thus there would have been a degree of craft specialisation at the local level.

The gradual development of cohesive political units with important leaders of lineages will have extended and strengthened this pattern. Exchange would have been an important factor in this general process of consolidation as control of luxury goods and raw materials would have enhanced the position of ruling families. Such leadership may be typified by superior access to ordinary goods and valuables as well as marriage partners through ceremonial forms of exchange. Goods may also have been acquired for the benefit of the élite sections of society by barter with neighbouring districts. Such goods could then be channelled through society, reinforcing the élite members' positions. This type of organisation may have been typical of the sixth century, at least before society became more politicised and commercially oriented. There were, therefore, both regional and inter-regional exchanges.

In support of this we should seek evidence for long-distance exchange as indication of political alliances and the growth of centralised political organisation. Bede's commentary on aspects of seventh-century English life reflects the nature and extent of the traffic of gifts, particularly between royalty and senior members of the Christian Church; they serve to remind us of some of the primitive valuables seen in the pagan graves. The items mentioned by Bede include clothing, gold ornament, a silver mirror, a gold and ivory comb, a horse, regalia, gifts as the price of peace, and gold and silver vessels (Colgrave and Mynors 1969: II 11; II 12; III 14; III 24; IV 1). The *Anglo-Saxon Chronicle* also mentions the giving of land and other gifts in return for peace; it should not be forgotten that land was probably the most important commodity of all.

The primitive valuables involved in such exchanges were neither money nor cash, but items that were often spent in political and social spheres of activity. They served to form alliances in peacetime and during war, as well as compensation for death, and bride wealth. In this way much of the movement of exotic items that can be traced archaeologically can be seen as part of a system of exchange in the formation of alliances. They were used by the heads of lineages for important political and social transactions, such as gifts to subordinates, alliances, marriages and funerals. In addition they fuelled the development of craft specialisation and exchange in an increasingly complex structure.

The seventh century sees the appearance of leadership by birth, perhaps resulting from a series of successful leaders from a single descent group. The Church was developing an administrative structure at the same time and may have influenced secular government. The development of complex administrative structures and institutions of political control was a crucial part of the centralisation of power and the control of trade should be seen as a part of this, even if the patterns of trade mirrored earlier ones. As such kingdom states were evolving, primitive money in the form of silver coinage appears. It was used for political obligations such as taxes and fines, for reward and increasingly for ordinary market exchange. Significantly, by the end of the period coinage as cash had appeared for commercial transactions. Such coinage was issued by rulers and may be viewed both as a measure of their power and prestige as well as an attempt to extend their influence. It is unclear which areas of the economy operated freely and which were under direct élite control and therefore where the dynamics of change originated, but it certainly seems that political and economic changes were closely allied.

The study of patterns of exchange requires information about sources of raw materials and the locations and organisation of manufacture and distribution. Direct information about some of these aspects is lacking; however, much can be inferred, particularly about places and modes of production. In the absence of data about production sites, studies inevitably fall back on the known distribution of the artefacts, representing their final place of use, usually as grave-goods. Distribution maps only inform us about consumption and cannot yet be demonstrated to be guides to places of production, or the means of dispersal.

OVERSEAS EXCHANGE

The occupants of the farms of early Anglo-Saxon England lived an essentially self-sufficient existence, and the farms were located to make maximum use of available resources amidst land most suitable for the form of agriculture practised. The majority of the items required on an everyday basis such as food, clothing, building materials, fuel and water, were either to be found locally or were produced on the farm. There is no evidence that such goods were moved any great distance from their place of manufacture and no reason why this should be necessary. However, some raw materials and goods, whether they fall into a utilitarian or luxury category, were not always available locally and these give us the clearest testimony of the extent of exchange in early Anglo-Saxon society. The actual mechanisms by which such goods were acquired, that is by some form of gift or an exchange involving barter, can only be inferred. It implies, however, that communities had an economic surplus to dispose of, be it scrap metal, agricultural produce, rare local resources or finished products. In addition to identifying the mechanisms for the movement of goods, there are difficulties in establishing the quantities involved, especially when considered in terms of their relative value. In the same way we are not able to talk of the actual volume of agricultural yields and the excess per capita from the farms although seventh-century law-codes indicate what was expected (Hodges 1982a: 136–41).

Indisputable evidence for the movement of goods is provided by commodities that came from the Continent, and at times originated from even further afield. Such articles will be discussed on the basis of their distribution patterns as they fall into two distinct groups. Some are densely concentrated in small areas, for instance the volume of amethyst beads, gold coin, garnet, rock crystal spheres and wheel-thrown pottery in Kent, which have Continental or Mediterranean sources. Others have a more widespread distribution in England, for instance amber, crystal beads and ivory rings, and are generally from north-west Europe. These commodities are arguably the primitive valuables of early Anglo-Saxon society, used to oil the wheels of social and political activities (Huggett 1988). The differences in their distribution speak volumes about the nature of the exchange and of relationships with the people in the places of origin.

Amber, a fossil tree resin, is commonly found in graves particularly in central and eastern England. It is found predominately in female graves, either rough or faceted and polished, pierced and worn as beads. The position of the beads in the grave normally suggests they were worn on a necklace, but a case can be made for some having been worn in the hair. Where found,

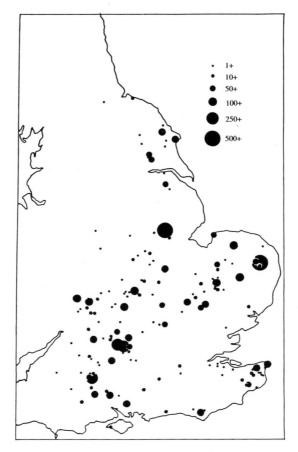

Figure 5.1 The distribution of amber beads in early Anglo-Saxon England
(source: Huggett 1988, Figure 1)

there are usually between one and twenty beads buried with an individual
but occasionally graves contain very large numbers; for example, grave 71 at
the cemetery of Long Wittenham I (Berkshire) contained 280 beads. The
largest quantity in a single cemetery, nearly 1,000 in total, is from Sleaford
(Lincolnshire). The majority of the beads are found in a band from
Lincolnshire and Norfolk to Wiltshire with cemeteries containing large
quantities at each end. To the north and south of this band amber is less
common. Throughout the area in which amber beads are found there appear
to be single, sometimes adjacent, cemeteries with relatively large numbers of
beads surrounded by cemeteries with lesser quantities (Figure 5.1). The
principal source of amber in Europe is the shores of the Baltic Sea, although

it is found elsewhere, for instance Romania and Sicily. Some amber can be found washed up on to the shores of East Anglia, but if this source was being used it does not appear to have resulted in high levels of consumption in that area. The marked differences between the distribution of Anglo-Saxon amber and that of the earlier British Bronze Age implies that neither distribution need be controlled in detail by the location of the source. Unfortunately no characterisation studies of early Anglo-Saxon amber have been made, but the Baltic Sea is believed to be the source (Beck 1970).

Another example of an imported good with a widespread distribution is ivory, which normally occurs as rings. The rings were used in a variety of ways: some were worn on the arm or wrist; others appear to have been the frames for the mouths of pouches that are often found to contain small metal items; a third use was as a girdle hanger. The evidence is frequently ambiguous because of the degree of preservation and the inadequacy of early reports. Over seventy examples are known, varying in size from 9 cm to 15 cm diameter, averaging 10 cm. The largest numbers occur in Lincolnshire, Cambridgeshire and Norfolk with a thin spread south-westwards and an isolated peak in Kent (Figure 5.2). The highest number, eleven, is from the cemetery of Illington. The source of the ivory is difficult to determine, and the question of whether the material derives from elephant or walrus has not been resolved. The interpretation of some examples that have been studied is that they were rings cut from the upper part of an elephant's tusk with the pulp cavity forming the natural ring (Myres and Green 1973: 100–3). This is also the conclusion resulting from more detailed analysis of cremated ivory rings from Spong Hill (Bond 1994b); it is suggested that some pieces appear more like contemporary than fossil elephant ivory. However, others appear to be made up in regular jointed sections which do not conform to the natural lines of cleavage. This suggests the use of smaller pieces of ivory, possibly fragments of elephant tusk, or the smaller walrus tusk, or even the tusks of wild boar, that were occasionally pierced and threaded on necklaces. If the source of the ivory was elephant (MacGregor 1985), Indian or African, a larger number might be expected in Kent which appears to have had a dominance over many of the goods imported from the Continent and the Mediterranean. The easterly distribution, implying importation from Scandinavia, might point towards walrus. Walruses were quite commonly encountered in the Shetland Islands and the coasts of Scandinavia until quite recently. It has been suggested that after AD 700 until the eleventh century 60 per cent of ivory was derived from walrus, much of it coming from Scandinavia (Beckwith 1972).

Rock crystal was used for beads and was made into spheres mounted in metal cages, but the distributions are different. The crystal beads, sometimes described as spindle whorls, are pierced, sometimes smoothed and slightly domed, or faceted. They are found in graves concentrated in central and eastern England (Figure 5.3), the largest number being from Sleaford where

Figure 5.2 The distribution of ivory rings in early Anglo-Saxon England
(source: Huggett 1988, Figure 3)

there are approximately twenty-five from five graves, although absolute numbers were not reported. The greatest number from a single grave is twelve, from Chatham Lines, Barrow II (Kent). The balls only occur in graves singly, normally accompanying the richly furnished graves of a small number of women, in eight cases associated with silver spoons, which are often perforated, both lying between the knees. The balls are normally spheroid and enclosed in a cage consisting of either a cross-shaped piece of sheet metal, often silver, or two metal bands. These are wrapped around the ball and fastened at the top with a collar through which passed a wire ring for suspension from the belt or wrist. About thirty examples are known, 75 per cent of them from Kent, especially at Bifrons and Chatham Lines with four each.

Figure 5.3 The distribution of rock crystal beads in early Anglo-Saxon England (source: Huggett 1988, Figure 4)

Outside Kent they occur at Chessell Down (Isle of Wight) and, rarely, in the Midlands (Figure 5. 4). Sources of adequate rock crystal for the manufacture of beads are widespread in England and Europe, but as the spheres require large crystals it may be possible to narrow down the range of sources. Germany, Switzerland and Scotland may be suggested. That more than one source for the crystal was involved is suggested by the differing distributions and the fact that few cemeteries contain both beads and spheres. Only Faversham, Bifrons and Chatham Lines and Kempston (Bedfordshire) fall into this category. The beads are more common than the spheres in a ratio of about 3:1. The crystal beads and spheres are probably the only objects made of one material and which have different distributions. They highlight

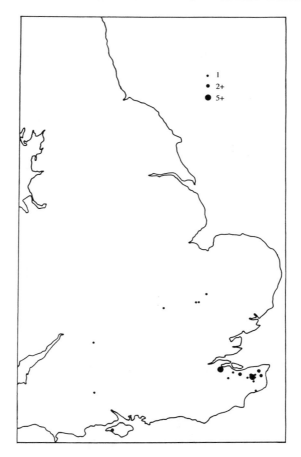

Figure 5.4 The distribution of crystal spheres in early Anglo-Saxon England (source: Huggett 1988, Figure 5)

the division between the localised and widespread types of distribution pattern. In addition to the crystal spheres there is a wide variety of goods that also have a localised distribution, particularly in Kent.

Considerable quantities of gold were utilised in particular areas of England, for instance Kent and the upper Thames valley, which gives ample testimony to the relationship between trade and the advancement of political élites and centralised political power. It is found in the form of coin imported from the Continent and in jewellery. Analysis of both the coin and jewellery appeared to show that the gradual debasement of the coin was matched by the quality of the gold in the jewellery, which was used to suggest that the coin was the source of the jeweller's raw material (Hawkes, Merrick and

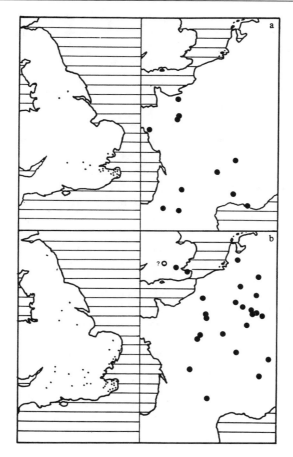

Figure 5.5 The distribution of unmounted gold coin in the British Isles (small dots) and the Continental sources (large dots): a = AD 595–625; b = AD 625–71. In the earlier phase the coin is concentrated in Kent, but later they have a more widespread distribution. The location of the mints supplying the coin shifts northwards through time (data: Rigold 1975)

Metcalf 1966). Equally it could indicate that the source of the gold for the coin and the jewellery was the same. Kent was the major producer and consumer of gold jewellery and it is not surprising to find also that the greatest number of coins is found there, often mounted on suspension loops and worn as necklaces. Outside Kent precious metals are used very sparingly, usually as thin coatings, and a range of other methods was adopted to colour the surfaces of objects (Mortimer 1991a: 167).

The greatest concentration of gold is found in Kent (Figure 5.5) although there are localised peaks caused by major single finds such as the Crondall hoard in Hampshire, the contents of the purse from mound I at Sutton Hoo and the possible hoard at Kingston-on-Thames (Surrey) (Rigold 1975). Coins earlier than AD 625 are mainly found in Kent and the upper Thames valley; after that date they are found spread over a wider area as far afield as Ireland, Scotland, Derbyshire and Yorkshire, although they remain concentrated in south-east England. This change in distribution appears to be a reflection of the changes in the mints from which they were drawn. Prior to AD 625 the sources are southern Frankia, Lyon, Provencal, Vienne, Marseilles and Arles, whereas afterwards the mints from which the coins were derived are mainly in the Meuse and Moselle regions, such as Limoges and Paris (Rigold 1975; Grierson and Blackburn 1986). This also has implications for political as well as economic structures at this time (Wood 1991). It may be no coincidence that the period in which this shift in distribution occurred was also the time when the devaluation of the gold had become serious.

The coins are found in graves, hoards, re-used in jewellery, and as 'casual' finds (which were not necessarily 'casual' losses), the last category being the most numerous. The more obvious uses to which the coin was put, the contexts in which they are found and their distribution has led to a general belief that they were not used as currency in commercial transactions; rather, they were valued as bullion. The near absence of true hoards (deposits of coin or other metalwork in the ground not associated with burial) in early Anglo-Saxon England until the seventh century may be taken as an important indication of the role of hoarding in other societies and of the economic organisation of this period. Such gold is an important development in its use as primitive money, the first uniform commodity used in the payment of taxes and fines. In this way it is also an important indication of the growing powers and sophistication of leaders and kingdom states. In the seventh century gold coin was actually minted in England at London and Canterbury. This may be the clearest evidence of the change from the imported gold coin acting as a valuable to being used as money. Near the end of the period gold coin may have been used in commercial transactions, but the dwindling supply of gold in western Europe caused a switch to silver as the principal precious metal. The silver coinage, *sceattas*, of the late seventh century took over the developing role of gold coin and may be the first true cash in England for commercial transactions. This may only be a change in the precious metal brought about by necessity, and silver coinage may also have continued the earlier function of the gold coinage, as bullion.

It is difficult to understand the function of gold in early Anglo-Saxon society in much greater detail. Certainly gold, as bullion, is a practical method of storing wealth. From c. AD 620 there were rare English imitations of Frankish coin, but despite any possible tendency for this coin to become currency, it would still have found its greatest use in high-value transactions and storage. Once a surplus had been converted to gold it could be used, for instance, to reward, and to supply jewellers with the necessary raw material to produce lavish items of jewellery; it has even been suggested that Scandinavian decorated gold pendants, *bracteates*, may have been a source of bullion like the later coins (Hawkes and Pollard 1981; Gaimster 1992). They also are found most commonly in Kentish graves.

Most knowledge of the earliest Anglo-Saxon gold coins comes from the hoard found at Crondall. It is notably the first post-Roman coin hoard known in England and may in itself signify a change in the economy. One coin bears the mint name DOROVERNIS CIVITAS, Canterbury, and another gives the mint name LONDVINIV around a cross; the obverse shows a priestly head. These 'thirds' of a Merovingian solidus fall within the period *c.* AD 604–16 and *c.* AD 675. There are also two series of coins in which a secular character is explicit, one bearing the name AVDVARLD REGES, and another showing a diademmed portrait with 'sceptre' (Figure 7.12) and a reverse with the moneyer's name WITMEN around a cross. Audvarld may be Eadbald, King of Kent 616–40, but whether or not this is the case, the coins point to a royal and ecclesiastical responsibility for their production.

Gold allowed the easy storage of wealth because of the high ratio of value to bulk, and its being minted by royal and ecclesiastical courts may reflect the need to administer justice, maintain officials and finance commerce, and goes hand-in-hand with the development of written law and taxation; in the oldest Kentish laws, fines were listed in gold 'shillings' and in silver. By the end of the seventh century, possibly *c.* AD 675, a shortage of gold forced a change to silver coins. Their initial frequency in Kent points to Kentish supremacy in this type of exchange and, perhaps, the direction in which commerce was moving when the change was necessary.

Grierson (1961) has suggested that seventh-century coins have a social rather than a commercial significance. This may in part be true, but it ignores the mechanisms by which gold was obtained, assessed and utilised. It must be seen against the social background of early Anglo-Saxon society in the seventh century. This was a society with true leaders of kingdoms within which commercial activities were becoming more institutionalised. Society had changed from the earlier structure where primitive valuables were of greater importance.

The clearest testimony to the level of exchange being carried on between England and the Continent, especially in transactions involving gold, is the existence of sets of balances often accompanied by weights (Scull 1990). Ten complete balances are known from sixth- and seventh-century graves, mostly in Kent but also from the upper Thames valley (Figure 5.6). Eight of them were accompanied by sets of weights. There are also five cases of detached balance pans from graves. These small copper alloy balances had an inverted T-shaped beam supported from its centre by a suspension arm. The pans were suspended from the ends of the beam. The weights were custom-made or ground down Roman coins; two appear to be actual Byzantine weights,

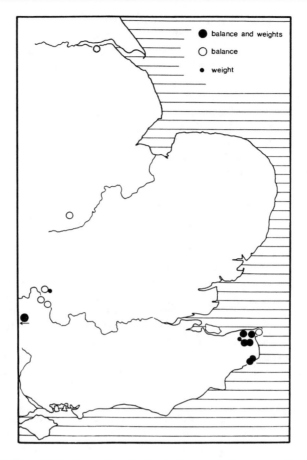

Figure 5.6 The distribution of early Anglo-Saxon balances and weights
(source: Scull 1990, Figure 9)

or imitations, indicating the extent of exchange networks at this time in
Europe (Figure 5.7).

The metrology of six of the sets of weights has been analysed (Scull 1990:
187–96). Those from Dover, Gilton, Osengell and Sarre (Kent) and
Watchfield (Oxfordshire) are based on two common standards that are close
to the weight-standards of two contemporary gold coinages, the Byzantine
tremisses of *c.* 1.52 g and the Merovingian tremisses of *c.* 1.33 g. The objects
associated with the balance from Barton-on-Humber (Lincolnshire) do not
appear to be a coherent set of weights and may have belonged to a jeweller.
Few of the examples of balances outside Kent are complete although this
may be due to their having had an entirely different use prior to burial. They

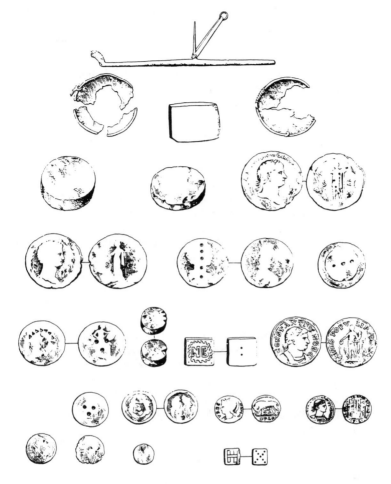

Figure 5.7 An early Anglo-Saxon set of balance, touchstone and weights from Gilton, Kent (source: Smith 1856)

are strongly associated with male burials. While there is no coherent pattern in the additional grave-goods deposited, the presence of balances and weights may reflect the identity of such individuals as bullion traders who might also have been high-ranking officials. Some were reported as being found with touchstones (Figure 5.7), used for assessing the purity of gold (Moore and Oddy 1985) although this would not preclude their use for weighing other high-value materials. It does emphasise that it was not only the quantity of precious material that was being assessed to standards but also, at least in terms of the gold coin and uncoined bullion, its quality. It may also be significant that most of the balances date to the period when the debasement of the gold coinage was at its most serious.

The number of balance-sets from Kent and the upper Thames valley emphasises that these areas were the major importers of bullion and this is mirrored in their having strong evidence for exchange links with the Continent. The upper Thames valley may have been acquiring these goods from Kent, emphasising that there was an inter-regional and international dimension to the trade over which Kent had a near monopoly, albeit a temporary one. The context for this exchange may have been ruling élites through which such goods were channelled, perhaps using officials whose trading equipment was sensitive to the standards used in the larger European dimension and which may also have been used for the internal regulation of justice and taxation. At an international level such trade may have symbolised any real or manufactured sense of dominance, for instance in the relationship between Kent and the Merovingian kingdoms (Wood 1992, 1994). Kent was obviously well placed to exploit such trading possibilities with the Continent, even if this did depend on cross-Channel dynastic ties, and the need to regularise transactions brought about the development of commercial centres on the Wantsum Channel and the River Stour (Hodges 1982a). Clearly such political structures were developing elsewhere and Kent was gradually eclipsed.

Another imported luxury item that is also very strongly represented in Kent is amethyst, usually polished pear or droplet shaped beads, pierced down their length. Most have been found in graves, especially at Faversham which accounts for about two-thirds of all such beads found in England (Figure 5.8). Their ultimate origin was the east Mediterranean, reflecting the complexity of the long-distance ties in Europe of which England was on the edge. If the majority were being imported into Kent very few were allowed to pass further which may indicate that they contributed, during the time of their currency, to the symbolisation of a Kentish identity. There are rarely more than two in a grave, the largest number from a single grave being the seventeen examples from a grave at Breach Down (Kent). They, like most beads, are usually found in female graves, strung with others in a necklace or used as pendants mounted in metal loops. Some may have been worn as earrings.

The vast majority of the pottery used in England for both domestic and funerary purposes was hand-made locally. However, some wheel-thrown pottery was imported from the Continent and is found in contexts dated after AD 625, mostly in east Kent (Figure 5.9) with a scatter around the Thames estuary and along the east coast to Suffolk (Evison 1979b). It is grouped into five general types: bottles, jugs, biconical and globular bowls, and shouldered jars, the total number being about 130; the cemetery at St Peter's, Broadstairs (Kent), produced twenty-six alone. Most are deposited as grave-goods in inhumation graves, often showing signs of extensive use with

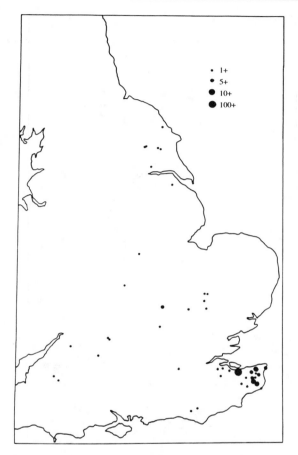

Figure 5.8 The distribution of amethyst beads in early Anglo-Saxon England (source: Huggett 1988, Figure 2)

damage repair. Bottles make up 51 per cent of the total, all but three being from Kent, the important exceptions being from the seventh-century rich graves of Asthall and Sutton Hoo. The high incidence of vessels compared with dishes may, as Evison suggests (ibid.), imply that they arrived as containers of oil or wine; the crude workmanship of some examples may emphasise that the contents were more important than the packaging, even though the vessels, whether full or empty, might have aptly symbolised an individual's status and identity at death.

This pottery is a rare instance of an import that is found more often in male graves (46 per cent) than female (27 per cent); bowls and jugs are more common in female graves. This may reflect different roles amongst men and

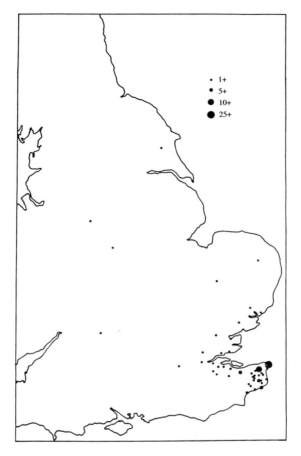

Figure 5.9 The distribution of wheel-thrown vessels in early Anglo-Saxon England (source: Huggett 1988, Figure 8)

women in the preparation, serving and consumption of food. In the light of the apparent division between Kent and the rest of England in terms of some luxury imports, it is interesting that Evison (ibid.) observed that the wheel-thrown vessels found outside Kent, and which are widely scattered, had originated from different and often distinct parts of north-west Europe. This emphasises that not all luxury goods came exclusively through Kent and that political alliances were at least as important as geographical location; the prerequisite social cohesion and political complexity were developing in all parts of England even if at different rates.

A similar pattern is found with imported bronze vessels (Richards 1986). Most of the Coptic vessels found in Kent are types which Werner (1957,

1961) has shown to have been common on the Continent, but outside Kent there are a larger number of rarities. Examples of a type belonging to a general class of the later sixth and seventh centuries on the Continent, with drop-handles and tripod rings, are known from the Kent sites of Coombe, Gilton, Faversham, Sarre and Ash. Three-legged Coptic forms are known only from seventh-century contexts, often richly accompanied burials in barrows such as Sutton Hoo, Taplow, Asthall and Cuddesdon (Oxfordshire). Byzantine vessels in contexts dated to the second half of the sixth century are known from the Isle of Wight (Arnold 1982a), presumably reflecting a short-lived period of regional hegemony with strong contacts with Kent. A similar example is known from Bromeswell, Norfolk (Carver 1992a: Pl. 1).

Kent also appears to have been a major importer of garnet, although the actual amount that has been recovered has not been quantified. Large quantities were brought to Kent from the sixth century onwards, with the jewellery contained in mound I Sutton Hoo creating a notable seventh-century peak. Used as an embellishment to ornate metalwork, the garnet may have originated from any of the main world sources – Egypt, Britain, Turkey, Scandinavia, Ceylon and many parts of Europe. One analysis has pointed to Bohemia as a source in that instance (Roosens and Thomas-Goorieckx 1970). A similar study of the garnets used in the jewellery found at Sutton Hoo has suggested that the source was similar to that which the Frankish world drew on, but was different to that used in Gotland and south Russia. No light was thrown on the mechanisms of exchange, except that the assemblages of garnet on a number of the Sutton Hoo pieces were distinct (Bimson, La Neice and Leese 1982). In a grave in the cemetery at Buckland, Dover, a woman was buried with a bag at her hip that contained seven loose garnets. Much of the inspiration for the use of garnet in England was derived from Frankia. Its use in England in particular places for varying time-periods symbolised not merely membership of a particular status group within a given region but also involvement with élite groups on the Continent.

Alongside these luxuries we may consider a wide range of other imports, especially the numerous Frankish imports such as ornaments and weapons that were buried as grave-goods especially in Kent with lesser numbers filtering through to other areas. As a whole they indicate contacts with the kingdoms of Neustria in north-west France and with the Austrasian Franks in the Rhineland. The sheer quantity of such imports might preclude transmission to England purely as part of social and political alliances but if material exchange was taking place with the Continent it has to be noted that durable items of English manufacture are particularly rare on the Continent.

There are other potential imports that are less apparent; mercury, for instance, was used to gild at least some of the metalwork in England at this time (Oddy 1980). The major sources of mercury in Europe are Italy, Yugoslavia and Spain. Exchange in such a commodity with Spain may explain

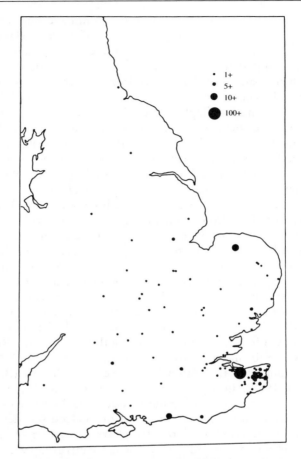

Figure 5.10 The distribution of glass vessels in early Anglo-Saxon England
(source: Huggett 1988, Figure 7)

the amount of Kentish metalwork in the Bordeaux region of south-west France (Leeds 1953), as at Herpes-en-Charente, the Frankish interest in the area expressed by the campaigns of Clovis from the late fifth century onwards (James 1977), and the Merovingian efforts to ally themselves with the Visigoths through marriage (Wood 1994: 169–75).

The majority of the observable luxury goods considered so far have a restricted distribution but there are two examples with a more widespread distribution: glass vessels and cowrie shells. Glass vessels appear in a variety of forms in graves and were classified by Harden (1956b) into eleven types divided into three chronological groups, which he later reviewed and extended (Harden 1978) (Figure 4.11). These are concentrated in Kent with 65 per cent of the total (25 per cent at Faversham alone). Over the rest of England the distribution is thinner (Figure 5.10). The strong similarities between English glassware and that in Belgium, northern France and the Rhineland, especially the area around Trier where Carolingian glass factories are known, has suggested that the majority of glassware in England was imported. However, some types, the squat jars, bag beakers, pouch bottles and cone beakers (Evison 1972) are rare on the Continent and may well have been made in England; Harden (1956b: 146–7) suggested that the Faversham area was a strong contender for the centre of this production but scientific analysis has been unable to confirm this. We may see here not only ties with the Continent, perhaps emulation of Frankish culture, but also an example of one English region manufacturing goods used, in part, to bolster links with, and dominance over, other regions. If the distributions do indicate such relationships it is notable that in the sixth century Kentish contacts were sporadic and general whereas in the seventh century they were especially with the upper Thames valley and East Anglia. It must be noted that glass vessels are one of the few Germanic artefact types to occur in western and northern Britain in large quantities (Alcock 1992), larger than in the majority of pagan Anglo-Saxon cemeteries. The possible complexity of these ties is well illustrated by the rare deep blue squat latticed jars of early seventh-century date which in England often occur in pairs and are strongly associated with high-status burials (Figure 5.11). The jars are common in Kent and are also known in Norway, eastern England, the upper Thames valley and south Wales (Campbell 1989). It is noteworthy that while some metalwork and glass was transported to western Britain, distinctive types of metalwork, such as cloisonné garnet inlaid jewellery, were not. Similarly Mediterranean and French imported pottery and enamelled penannular brooches do not appear to have been moved eastwards. Some items were identifiers and could not be exchanged, others were not and had no such restriction placed upon them.

Cowrie shells originate in the Indian Ocean and the Middle East and are occasionally found in late sixth- and seventh-century graves, most frequently in Cambridgeshire and Kent (Figure 5.12). They were often accompanied in graves by other unworn 'trinkets' and either placed in a wooden box at the foot of the grave, or were worn as pendants. Unfortunately there have rarely been precise identifications although two are stated to be of Middle Eastern origin, the *Cypraea Arabica* from Sarre and a tiger cowrie from Haslingfield (Cambridgeshire), whose source is the Red Sea. Another example, found amongst cremated bone in an urn from the cemetery at Girton (Cambridgeshire), has also been identified as *Cypraea tigris* (Arnold and Wilkinson 1984: 26). Some may be from the Indian Ocean.

More light can be thrown on the mechanisms for the dispersal of such imported goods by a detailed examination of their distributions (Huggett 1988). The varied nature of the materials transported to particular parts of

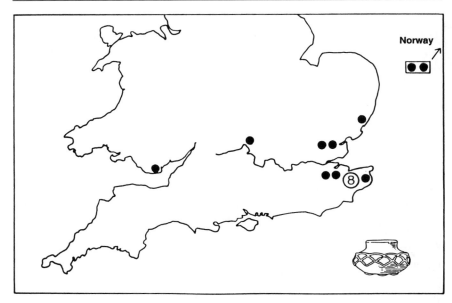

Figure 5.11 The distribution of blue squat latticed glass jars in England and Wales (source: Campbell 1989)

England in the sixth and seventh centuries is mirrored by the patterns of dispersal revealed by plotting fall-off curves. The Kentish concentration of items likely to have come via the Merovingian kingdoms, amethyst, glass (Figure 5.13B) and wheel-thrown pottery, all have a pronounced peak and fall-off. The pattern emphasises the manner in which dominant lineages, in these cases in Kent, were the focus for their importation, consumption and redistribution on a small scale. Not surprisingly those cemeteries that display high quantities of such imports are also those with graves that might be identified with members of such ruling families. There are two concentrations of such luxury goods, at Faversham in west Kent, and at Dover in east Kent, indicating that there may have been two centres of power. When such items are found outside Kent they tend to be restricted to high-status graves, both of the sixth and the seventh centuries.

These distributions are in marked contrast to those with, ultimately, a northern and Baltic Sea origin, especially amber (Figure 5.13A) and crystal beads and ivory. The centres of highest consumption are some distance from Kent where the quantities are relatively small. Their distributions show pronounced concentrations with a smaller number of secondary, yet significant, clusters of smaller size over a wide geographical range; the greatest quantities are found at Sleaford and Lackford. This suggests that in the Midlands and East Anglia goods were being acquired directly from different

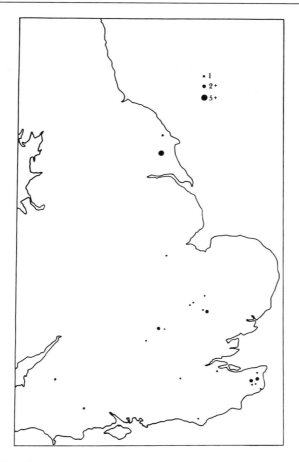

Figure 5.12 The distribution of cowrie shells in early Anglo-Saxon England
(source: Huggett 1988, Figure 6)

sources than those in Kent but in a less monopolistic manner suggesting a
great deal more redistribution.

Within both distribution patterns it is found that it is nearly always the
same cemeteries that contain relatively large quantities of the imported goods.
The pattern is unaffected by proximity to coastline. Such cemeteries may
therefore have been used by dominant lineages within regions. The distributions are revealing both about the circulation of goods within England and
the links with the areas from which they were derived. The wheel-thrown
vessels in Kent were derived from northern France while those elsewhere in
England, particularly in East Anglia, were from the Rhineland. This supports
the view that by the end of the sixth century England was involved with

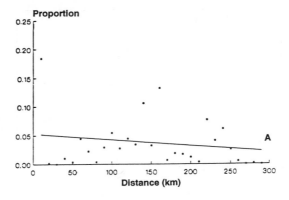

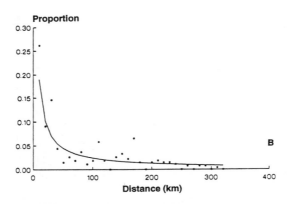

Figure 5.13 Frequency curves for (A) amber beads and (B) glass vessels (source: Huggett 1988, Figures 9 and 10)

two developing exchange networks in Neustria and Austrasia (Hodges 1982a: 35–6). Similarly ivory rings are concentrated in East Anglia and the Rhineland. It is unclear whether ivory rings in Kent were derived from reciprocal relationships with East Anglia or directly from a Continental source. There is clear evidence in other media for contacts between Scandinavia and East Anglia and Kent of an exclusive nature, for instance sleeve clasps, D-bracteates and relief brooches.

Goods imported from the Continent may then have become powerful social tools by their redistribution through the social system, and in this way they form part of the subject of internal exchange. The study of the distribution of exotic imported goods has extended as far as noting that there are two basic patterns to their distribution, apparently depending on their sources, and that particular areas or individual cemeteries have disproportionately high quantities of some of these goods. The fall-off curves (Figure 5.13) suggest that the redistribution of such goods was controlled, but there has been little research carried out to determine the patterns of dispersal in any more detail. The amber bead is an example of such an imported commodity that is found in very large quantities at some cemeteries often with relatively low proportions amongst surrounding communities (Figure 5.1). It would be useful to know whether there are any similarities in the graves with and without amber in each type of cemetery as it may help us to understand whether such goods are being handed down through society and something of the controls on access to them.

Examples of cemeteries with large quantities of amber are Sleaford and in the Thames valley Long Wittenham I. At Sleaford a higher proportion of graves with amber beads contained small-long brooches and pendants than those without amber beads, the latter being more strongly characterised by the presence of cruciform brooches. The graves lacking amber beads also had smaller numbers of disc brooches, earrings, bracelets and bags, implying that the differential access to amber also extended to other objects. At Long Wittenham I the presence of amber beads makes little difference to the nature of the brooches accompanying the graves, but those graves with such beads had significantly higher quantities of rings, coins, pins and toilet implements.

The theories expounded for the contexts of dispersal for such raw materials and objects find support in written sources in those societies that can be considered literate at this time. The visibility of the materials of exchange is dependent on a variety of filters as are the written sources, which are much concerned with the interaction between royal personages and the early church. Late seventh-century Kentish law-codes indicate a royal involvement in the control of mercantile activity through a *praefectus*. In exchange for royal protection, foreigners paid tolls and rents; kings thereby not only controlled but also profited from trade that may earlier have been under aristocratic control (Sawyer 1978: 156–8; Astill 1985: 221). Law-codes may only be institutionalising what had previously been common practice. The Kentish laws of Wihtraed *c.* AD 695 instructed travellers from afar or foreigners to shout or blow a horn before leaving a road, to avoid being treated as a thief or worse. A late seventh-century law of Wessex provided that the king should receive a large part of the *wergeld* of any stranger 'who came across the frontier'. It is notable that there is no mention of the regulation of prices or of a method of arbitration in the event of a dispute. Hints of this are first found in the Wessex King Ine's laws of *c.* 694 that stipulated that traders were to make their transactions before witnesses or the king's reeve. The protection afforded to foreigners presumably applied to all, whatever the purpose of their journey, but Ine's laws imply a need to promulgate conditions for peaceful trade.

Royal interest is emphasised by the close relationship between royal vills and possible points of entry. Sarre, like Dover, has a large proportion of wheel-thrown vessels and is closely associated with Sturry; Hodges has suggested that Kent's trade with Neustria was channelled between Quentovic and Sarre (1982a, 1982b; Astill 1985: 221). Notably a large number of the earliest silver sceattas, the coins that replaced the gold issues more common earlier in the seventh century, are concentrated in east Kent around the Wantsum Channel (Grierson and Blackburn 1986). Like the River Solent, the Wantsum enjoyed a double tide and provided a natural, sheltered harbour, although later silting makes present appearances deceptive. Such early manufacturing and trading centres, or emporia, may have been established purely for the profit of the king and the servicing of his estates. However, the status of those working in such centres is far from clear. The earliest indication of the existence of such commercial centres is in AD 675 in relation to Fordwich (Kent); Fordwich is higher up the River Stour and about 5 km from Canterbury which was by that time an established royal and ecclesiastical centre. Toll charters were issued for Kent settlements such as Sarre and Dover in AD 761 and 696 × 716 respectively. Kent is not of course unique and each of the major kingdoms appears to have had such trading centres by the eighth century (Hodges 1982a; Biddle 1976; Astill 1985). Even an inland centre such as Northampton was a royal centre that was also described as a trading centre. All such evidence emphasises a royal desire to institutionalise the extraction of income from commercial activity that may have been taking place, in whatever form, much earlier. An obvious source of tension may have arisen where landlocked kingdoms wished also to be involved in the international exchange and all that it implied but were denied by the controls imposed by kingdoms enjoying a coastline.

Early Anglo-Saxon kings were closely involved with the establishment and control of ports-of-trade and profited from the commercial activity. Such control and profit required the centralisation of activities that were not necessarily new but that may previously have been more dispersed. Royal households would have been the principal consumers of luxury goods some of which may have been exchanged as gifts between leaders. One possible context for the exchange of gifts might have been royal marriages. A number of marriages between leading Anglo-Saxons and Frankish royalty and aristocracy are recorded, not least that of King Aethelberht of Kent to Charibert I's daughter, Bertha. Their son Eadbald married Emma the Frankish, aristocratic daughter of the Neustrian *maior* Erchinoald and there are strong grounds for accepting a link between the East Anglian royal dynasty and the Merovingians in the seventh century; two East Anglian princesses were abbesses in Frankish nunneries (Wood 1994: 176–9). Such dynastic alliances created an appropriate climate for the exchange of goods between aristocratic families both between England and the Continent and between areas within England, such as Kent and the upper Thames valley (Scull 1990: 200). The archaeological evidence is that most areas of England enjoyed contacts with various parts of Europe and not even Kent's connections were limited to

Merovingia although that was undoubtedly a very strong axis. The written sources make it clear that at least some Franks were settled in Kent. In the 550s the Merovingians claimed overlordship of southern England and Clovis claimed to be able to uphold the rights of Franks in English courts (Wood 1994: 176).

Exchanges between kingdoms need not always have been in durable and observable goods which may account for the difficulty in identifying goods moving from England to the Continent in similar quantities to goods being brought to England. In the search for foreign exports many commentators place a great deal of emphasis on textiles, stimulated by a limited amount of written evidence recording gifts and the exchange of textiles in the eighth century. Certainly textiles were produced in England on a widespread basis although the only instance of textiles with a known or suspected origin are braids brocaded with gold strips (Crowfoot and Hawkes 1967). These were used as woven decorations on head-dresses and the borders of garments. They are found in richly accompanied graves of women during the second half of the sixth and the early seventh centuries, especially in Kent, and are also found in similar contexts on the Continent. Some of the Continental examples are made in the same tradition as the English ones. A headband from Cologne, St Severinus, grave 73, is very similar in design to one from Chessell Down, grave 45, and those from Saint-Denis, Paris, grave 9, and Planig, Rheinhessen, Germany, are similar to some Kentish braids; they are, however, made of silk and no silk has yet been identified in an Anglo-Saxon grave. Silk is categorised as a luxury import into western Europe and, it is assumed, arrived as ready-made lengths of braid. The woollen tablet weaves of England, which were relatively crude in the sixth century but which were improving in quality thereafter, may be another product. The very close similarity between examples on each side of the English Channel at least indicates that they should be viewed as part of the network indicated by other goods and written evidence. They may even indicate that the networks of connections were more widespread than the written sources suggest. For instance, braids from Chessell Down have been compared with examples from Envermeu and Herpes-en-Charente in France, the latter producing additional Anglo-Saxon objects matched in both Kent and the Isle of Wight. Such connections may reflect the complex political relationships, reflected in both marriage alliances and warring, between the Merovingians and Aquitaine, Gascony and the Visigoths.

The evidence of overseas exchange is the easiest to observe in the archaeological record, although much more research is required to work out the details. Also, analysis of goods or materials that are not apparently part of the exchange of luxuries might reveal the true depth of these activities. The identification of regions involved in overseas exchanges is important in beginning to isolate centres of production that will in all likelihood be involved with internal exchange also.

INTERNAL EXCHANGE

The explanations for international exchange, however much driven by need, may also apply to exchange between the developing kingdoms within England, both in redistributing goods acquired through international networks as well as those produced locally. Behind such production must have been the supply of raw materials that, again, may have been supplied from the Continent or may be of insular origin.

There are a number of classes of object made in England which can be shown to have regional and/or local distributions. In the absence of direct evidence for the place of manufacture, or at best the source of the raw materials, there has been a degree of reticence about interpreting the distribution of goods. The majority of the evidence for such a study are the grave-goods found in cemeteries, although the growing number of excavated settlements are slowly extending our knowledge. Nevertheless, we remain largely ignorant about the manufacture of the items from such evidence as the tools that were used and industrial debris.

The written sources are almost silent about the subject of internal exchange, just as the meagre details of the overseas movement of goods come nowhere near to matching the volume of the goods themselves. What we do learn from them is that there was a trade in slaves in early Anglo-Saxon England that also had an international dimension. As a class of people, slaves are mentioned in the laws of Wihtraed, *c.* AD 695, and Bede mentions the intention of a Mercian to sell a Northumbrian slave to a Frisian merchant in London in AD 679. Wilfrid is claimed to have baptised 250 slaves, women and men, at Selsey (Sussex) and there is the celebrated case of 'Angles' from Deira, an area approximating to the historic counties of Yorkshire, being sold in the market-place of Rome *c.* AD 700 (Colgrave and Mynors 1969: IV 22; II 1; IV 13). People such as these may have been enslaved as a result of capture in war or through failure to meet obligations. Presumably slavery is what is meant, in part, when the *Anglo-Saxon Chronicle* records the capture of villages and booty as a result of war. The scale of the practice, which was by no means new, is unclear (Davies 1982: 66; Sawyer 1978: 173) and slavery is difficult to determine through archaeological evidence (Pelteret 1981). For a more detailed and broader perspective on internal exchange the archaeological evidence is of paramount importance, even if little research has yet been carried out. An understanding of the supply of raw materials and finished products often relies on measures of similarity. It should not be assumed that similarity is only the result of production methods and economic activity as social factors clearly played a major role; all are intimately interrelated.

Traditionally decorated artefacts of the period have been studied using art-historical techniques. As well as understanding the evolution of styles such studies also measure the degree of similarity between examples. There is however considerable distance between the measurement of similarity and the isolation of the factors determining the distribution of types. Characterisation studies of clay, glass, metal and stone are beginning to have an impact on the subject by demonstrating the similarity of raw materials in groups of artefacts and, at best, their actual source. In addition, decorated metalwork and pottery can be studied by the measurement of elements in designs to determine which objects may have been made at the same source, or at least using the same tools, at times possibly by the same person. In this way the results of characterisation studies can be corroborated by alternative, and independent, measures of similarity.

Technical difficulties have not encouraged the widespread analysis of the composition of metal artefacts. For instance, the analysis of the metal alloys used in a series of silver brooches from Howletts and Chessell Down indicates strong similarities in their alloys. The interpretation is obstructed by the possibility of segregation of the minerals in the artefacts during burial, thus normalising the results. Nevertheless, there would appear to be an optimum recipe, especially in the silver and copper content used to manufacture the brooches found in each cemetery, suggesting some sort of connection. The sources of silver used at this time are unclear despite the quantities used. Without knowing the actual source of the metal it is difficult to proceed further, except by detailed analysis of the decoration (Leigh 1980: 185 ff., Table 9, App. 2).

Analysis of the metal content of Kentish gold bracteates presents similar problems (Hawkes and Pollard 1981). Results are available from the examination of the bracteates themselves and from their suspension loops, thus making comparison possible. Further scope for comparison is provided by groups of bracteates found in the same grave and cemetery, and especially between die-linked specimens. Some of the die-linked examples have similar metal compositions, while others do not, and the loop occasionally differs from the bracteate itself. There is actually a wide variety of permutations represented by the data which may suggest that the re-working of the bracteates and their loops, both together and separately, was common. It also emphasises that contemporaneity need not be demonstrated by two objects having the same metal composition, nor by them having the same decoration. Alternatively, the metal alloys from which the bracteates and their loops were made need not always be from the same source. Clearly this is a case where the factors determining the shape of the archaeological record are very complex (Arnold 1991). Indeed analysis of cruciform brooches in East Anglia has revealed that recycling of metal alloys was common but it is difficult to calculate the amount of fresh metal that was available (Mortimer 1991a). The earliest brooches from different parts of western Europe reveal less variation in the alloys than with later examples. The rarity of some brooch types in particular areas may be the result of recycling old-fashioned types.

The ability to recycle metals is fortunately not a property that applies to clay and stone, but they have their own limitations. Petrological studies of stone are constrained by the difficulties of distinguishing the actual source of the material from the basic choice of parent material and that which is glacially derived. In the absence of widespread sampling of clays uncertainty will remain as to whether all of the potential sources of a particular clay have been located. The studies that have been undertaken on early Anglo-Saxon pottery emphasise that, unlike the more exotic materials discussed above, it rarely travelled far from a clay source to the point of consumption, regardless of whether it was for funerary or domestic purposes, or both, although some classes of funerary pottery may have been transported further.

A study of undecorated pottery from settlements in Northamptonshire suggested that there was a limited number of fabric groups, each originating from sources up to 50 miles (80 km) from the place of discovery (Walker 1978), although a lack of detailed knowledge about the area's drift geology led the author to have serious doubts about the results. Similar inclusions were found in pottery within the cemetery at Great Chesterford, although such material is present in the local drift clay. All of the pottery found at Great Chesterford and divided into five fabric types could have been made from local sources (Williams 1994). Grain size and heavy mineral analysis of selected sherds of pottery from stamp-linked groups excavated at the predominantly cremation cemetery at Spong Hill indicated that there was a minimum of ten clay sources, possibly relating to the settlements using the cemetery. In one case there was a unique relationship between a fabric and a stamp-linked group (Brisbane 1980, 1994).

A long-held belief has been that decorated cremation pottery, at least, was a product of specialist workshops that traded their wares. Much of the more recent research indicates that this is an inappropriate model for the context of manufacture and the mechanism of dispersal of such pottery which appears to have been more complex than was previously thought.

The greatest scope for study exists with cremation pottery. It is highly decorated and presents a greater number of variables for study, thereby reducing the range of possible interpretations of the patterns produced by analysis. A study of cremation urns, grouped on a stylistic basis as being the products of the 'Sancton-Baston' potter or workshop, incorporating the analysis of fabrics and measurement of all of the stamp impressions, produced a complex pattern (Figures 5.14 and 5.15) (Arnold 1983). Vessels from the cemeteries in north-east England, Baston, Elsham and Sancton were found to have fabrics specific to the respective cemeteries, although they had been decorated using the same set of dies. This would suggest that the dies, rather than the clay or the finished vessels, had been transported up to 160 km. We have already discussed (p. 63) the question of fuel used in cremations that, at least for the larger cremation cemeteries, argues that the cremating may be more likely to have occurred at home than at the cemetery. Some cremation urns contain the bones of more than one individual which may be the result of using common pyre sites. In the Midlands and

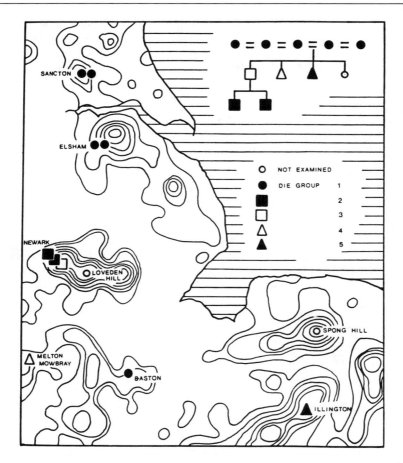

Figure 5.14 The distribution of Sancton-Baston die-groups and the suggested sequence of production

East Anglia individual examples of the vessels from cemeteries were also made with a separate clay and also a specific set of dies. One exception was at Newark (Nottinghamshire), where two die-sets and two clay sources were in use, but these were not mutually exclusive. Ten additional examples from Spong Hill add to the complexity of the pattern (Hills, Penn and Rickett 1994, Table 9).

The Sancton-Baston cremation pottery has been viewed as the products of individual potters or workshops (Myres 1969, 1977). However, the fact that in the detailed study it was found that five sets of dies were cut to produce a minimum of nine vessels suggests a different mode of production. It is possible that the decoration of the pottery had a totemic significance to

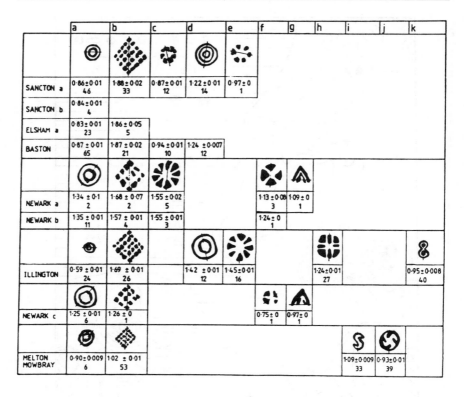

	a	b	c	d	e	f	g	h	i	j	k
SANCTON a	0·86±0·01 46	1·88±0·02 33	0·87±0·01 12	1·22±0·01 14	0·97±0 1						
SANCTON b	0·84±0·01 4										
ELSHAM a	0·83±0·01 23	1·86±0·05 5									
BASTON	0·87±0·01 65	1·87±0·02 21	0·94±0·01 10	1·24±0·007 12							
NEWARK a	1·34±0·1 2	1·68±0·07 2	1·55±0·02 5			1·13±0·08 3	1·09±0 1				
NEWARK b	1·35±0·01 11	1·57±0·01 4	1·55±0·01 3			1·24±0 1					
ILLINGTON	0·59±0·01 24	1·69±0·01 26		1·42±0·01 12	1·45±0·01 16				1·24±0·01 27		0·95±0·008 40
NEWARK c	1·25±0·01 6	1·26±0 1				0·75±0 1	0·97±0 1				
MELTON MOWBRAY	0·90±0·009 6	1·02±0·01 53							1·09±0·009 33	0·93±0·01 39	

Figure 5.15 The combinations of dies used to decorate Sancton-Baston urns

individual families. Additions to the range of stamps (Figure 5.15) may reflect exogamous marriages in successive generations, with family sets of dies being cut in each, with a merging of 'heraldry'. The new examples from Spong Hill appear to support this interpretation, adding another tier to the group. If such an interpretation was accepted the stamps can be viewed as more than decoration as they become symbols conveying information about family and, at least in the case of the less common designs, it may be possible to determine details regarding families' histories. This may also be the strongest indication we have that in some areas there were lineages owning not only, perhaps, real property, but also such intangible property as magic crests and names. People's dependence on their lineage in such a system would be comprehensive as there would be no other means of livelihood and protection. The strength of the connection between cremation urns and the deceased was very strong and there appears to have been 'a collective conception of the urn form that was appropriate for the burial of a person of a particular age, sex, ethnic, totemic, or other social grouping' (Richards 1982: 43).

Another, but much larger, group of vessels of late sixth-century date, which have been assigned to a potter or workshop is known collectively as the Illington-Lackford group, after the two principal cemeteries in Norfolk and Suffolk where they have been found. Petrological analysis by Andrew Russel (1984) revealed that they were made from twenty fabrics, and undecorated vessels are found in the same fabrics. The sheer volume of material, about 200 vessels from about twelve locations, one being the settlement of West Stow in Suffolk, might seem to argue strongly that the products are from a single workshop. Yet the twenty clay sources point to something more complex again.

The presence of antler stamps and clay dumps at West Stow (Figure 4.12) indicates that decorated pottery was made there (West 1985: 129). The same stamp designs are represented on vessels from there and the cemetery at Illington. The limited number of urns per fabric may reflect, Russel suggests, a number of pottery-making occasions or different potters, perhaps even the maintenance of a clay-pit or different years of pottery-making. There are hints that certain sets of dies were used to decorate pots made from specific fabrics, while some were retained for a later occasion and occur again on another fabric; this may represent lineage-specific clay sources and the inheritance of dies. The Illington-Lackford type of pottery occurs in 4 per cent of cemeteries and 15 per cent of settlements in East Anglia, which might suggest that it was being used in domestic as well as funerary contexts; equally this may simply indicate that all pottery was made in the domestic environment. It is estimated that undecorated pottery made from the same fabrics outnumbers the decorated Illington-Lackford pots by 15:1. Two basic fabric types were used, silty and sandy. Most of the former occurs at Illington, whilst others were 'traded' further afield into neighbouring valleys. The change from a silty to a sandy fabric may also reflect a change of production centre. This may be mirrored in a change in the style of decoration in this pottery group.

The metrical analysis of the stamps (Arnold 1988b) supports some of these conclusions but reveals additional problems. The group as a whole can be divided into two, a southern and a northern sub-group, the two being linked by two common stamp designs. The use of the dies in each group was very different. In the southern group the die-sets, whose range is limited, remained together to be used to decorate a relatively large number of vessels. In the northern group die-sets were more frequently changed, although a single die may have been retained for the manufacture of a number of vessels, but fewer than in the southern group. The analysis suggested that the southern group with its limited innovation in the range of designs, was the product of a limited number of individuals and were made to a different set of criteria to the northern group, which displays an impractical complexity. The pattern is very different from that of the Sancton-Baston group and if the southern group was produced on commercial lines the northern one was not (Table 5.1). It is interesting that the burial rite of early Anglo-Saxon cremation may

Table 5.1 Numbers of dies, stamp designs and vessels of the Sancton-Baston group and from Illington and Lackford

Site		Dies	Stamp designs	Vessels
Sancton-Baston	no.	24	35	9
	average			
	per vessel	2.6	3.8	
Illington	no.	37	69	31
(northern group)	average			
	per vessel	1.1	2.2	
Lackford	no.	17	37	16
(southern group)	average			
	per vessel	1.0	2.3	
Combined Illington	no.	54	106	47
& Lackford	average			
	per vessel	1.1	2.2	

seem relatively uniform, yet the modes of production and the symbolism the decoration conveyed varied considerably between regions.

The results of the study of early Anglo-Saxon pottery have as yet hardly come near the commercially based model envisaged by Myres, with specialists producing for a consumer market; social explanations appear to be more appropriate for similarities between vessels, and their movement. Analysis of ceramic material from cremation and inhumation cemeteries on the Isle of Wight is also revealing. Cremation urns, which also may be early in the cemeteries' histories, were made from local clay sources. More unusual forms of pottery, however, were made from sources foreign to the island and were found as grave-goods with inhumations; they are types most commonly found in Kent. This might be used as an example of commercial exchange. However, other links between the island and Kent in a limited amount of metalwork, dress and burial form might indicate a family connection. Gift exchange within a social framework seems a more probable explanation than commercial exchange (Arnold 1981a, 1981b, 1982a).

Very little pottery from settlements has been examined in this manner although Brisbane (1981) has proposed a model for various modes of production that may be appropriate for such pottery: domestic wares were produced on the farm from clays available in the immediate vicinity; funerary wares were manufactured from a variety of local clay sources, although the basis for their selection and use is unclear (p. 128); and imported wares. Petrological analyses that have been carried out support the model to some extent, especially for the production of domestic pottery; much of it is grass-tempered which Brown (1976) suggests represents an equal mixture of clay and horse manure. When fired the organic components are burnt out leaving a porous fabric. This practice made the clay into a more workable material, improved the firing qualities as well as making economic use of materials readily available on the farm (Hamerow, Hollevoet and Vince 1994). Such grass-tempered vessels have open-mouthed, simple, rounded forms, whereas 'funerary' wares are larger and have more restricted mouths although there is some ambiguity at West Stow as to whether decorated pottery served domestic as well as funerary functions. The evidence currently suggests that the factors controlling the dispersal of similarly decorated pottery related more to the social system than to purely commercial factors, even if economic considerations controlled the distance travelled to a chosen clay source. Russel (1984) suggests that some sporadic longer-distance movements of the Illington-Lackford group of pots are related to exchange between social groups. It has been noted that societies living in areas where resources are rare or absent may compensate by the production of pottery for exchange with neighbouring groups better endowed with the necessary resources (D.E. Arnold 1985). The basic problem here remains one of the identification of the sources of the raw materials used during the period.

Characterisation studies have also been undertaken on early Anglo-Saxon stone artefacts. These allow an understanding of the range over which materials were gathered for use on the farm, reflecting the extent of human interaction and movement. They also allow us to see whether stone with special properties was transported over greater distances. At the farmstead excavated at Walton (Farley 1976), the occupants had acquired a rotary quern of a stone comparable with greensands in Buckinghamshire and Bedfordshire, probably from the Leighton Buzzard area c. 16 km distant. This stone had not apparently been transported over any great distance. In contrast, the whetstone, used for sharpening metal tools and weapons and found on settlements and cemeteries, seems on occasion to have been transported further; an example excavated at the settlement of Old Down Farm was a glauconitic limestone from Northamptonshire (Davies 1980). A survey of early Anglo-Saxon whetstones showed that a number were made of a sand-silt graywacké that has its source in the north-west Pennines, the Lake District and south-west Scotland. They are assumed to have been quarried there and not removed from the glacial drift. Amongst this group are the large decorated examples from Loveden Hill (Lincolnshire) and Sutton Hoo mound I, which are considered to be symbolic and ceremonial. The majority of the examples of this stone type have been found in eastern England (Figure 5.16). In the south a different range of stone sources was used; whetstones of Kentish ragstone have been found in Suffolk, Oxfordshire and Kent (Evison 1975). An example of Devonian sandstone originating in the Bristol area has been excavated in Berkshire and examples of metamorphic rock from the Ardennes-Rhineland area, or the Boulonnais in Normandy, are known in Kent and Essex.

The problem, as with the provenancing of clays, is in determining whether the movement of the material is due to natural or human action. The

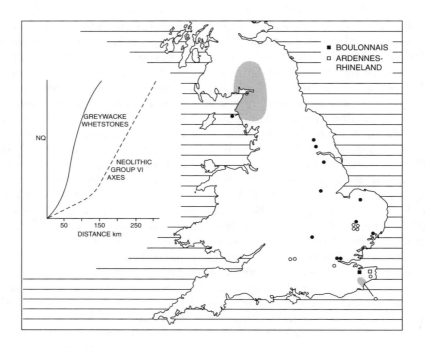

Figure 5.16 The distribution of early Anglo-Saxon whetstones and fall-off curves for greywacké whetstones and Group VI neolithic axes (data: Evison 1975)

whetstones have been accepted as evidence of trade from their quarry sites as opposed to random stones selected from glacially deposited material. One group of whetstones are of a stone from south-west Scotland or north-west England. They are found in eastern England (Figure 5.16) although their distribution does not simply reflect that of cemeteries. It is possible that they were brought the 400 km from the parent rock and there is other evidence of contact between the areas. Settlements in south-west Scotland were re-working Anglo-Saxon bronze scrap and perhaps glass; the fragmentary whetstone with a facing human head from Collin, Dumfriesshire (Laing 1975: 39, Figure 7), and Irish examples, are stylistically related to the examples from Loveden Hill and Sutton Hoo. The strong British element in some of the metalwork from Sutton Hoo might also be seen in this light (Brenan 1991; Ryan 1992; O'Brien 1993). Alternatively the stone to make the whetstones may have been taken from the glacial drift and stone of this type is found in the drift deposits of eastern England (Penny 1974: 248).

The pattern of distribution of the whetstones is similar to that of Neolithic Group VI axes from the same area (Figure 5.16). While some of the stone for making such axes was derived from the parent rock others may be from drift deposits. It is therefore difficult to determine precisely the actual source of stone in each case.

The same problem exists with touchstones, or more accurately basanite or lydite, which is a flinty jaspar or finely crystalline quartzite, black or dark grey in colour, used to test gold–silver alloys for their gold content (Figure 5.7). Rubbing the alloy on the stone produces a streak whose colour determines the gold content to an accuracy of one part in one hundred. A study has determined the petrology of two examples from seventh-century graves at Kingston and Osengell in Kent (Moore and Oddy 1985), both bearing gold streaks on their surfaces. One was a siltstone whose provenance is given as south-west England, and the other a tuff, from Wales or Cumbria.

The most common items found in early Anglo-Saxon graves are those made of metal, especially iron, copper-alloy, silver and gold. The volume of the evidence is, unfortunately, not matched by our understanding of the organisation of production which is essential if we are to address the matter of its dispersal. The smith obviously needed fuel and metal to carry out the work but we do not know the extent to which the smith was dependent on local resources as opposed to trade, nor the size and structure of the industry. It is possible to characterise metals, be they copper-alloy (Mortimer 1991b), iron, lead, silver or gold, but the interpretation of the results presents many problems. It is also very difficult to use the particular form of the artefact, or the style of decoration, when present, to determine the mechanisms involved in their production and dispersal; the factors determining similarity between artefacts beyond learned tradition and functionality are barely understood. 'Style-zones' may be identified, but the roles played by the craftspeople and the consumer (if such a model is correct) in the generation of such patterns is unclear. Much of the evidence that exists suggests that a social model is more appropriate than a commercial one. In order to understand the problems of studying the distribution of types of metalwork it is necessary to consider a variety of aspects of their production. Discussion of some of these aspects here might seem to repeat the technological details in the preceding chapter but the two are inextricably linked.

The sources of metal used are very difficult to determine. We do not know whether the ores were extracted and smelted by the smith, or purchased from others. The supply of metal may not have been a problem if scrap was plentiful and if there was a continuous recycling of the raw materials. The problem is knowing how this would effect the smith's relationship with the supplier, who may have been the customer.

The smith is elusive in the archaeological record but there are references to such metalworkers in the early law-codes, which in itself may emphasise their standing in society. In Aethelberht's laws the king's smith was protected by a special *wergeld*, called a *leodgeld*, amounting to 100 Kentish shillings, which would be paid for causing the smith's death (Loyn 1962: 103). In King Ine's laws the smith was rated as the equal of a reeve and a child's nurse, who, being servants, could be taken with a *gesithcund* man, an aristocrat, if he moved to a different area (ibid.: 104).

The earliest record of post-Roman iron extraction in England is found in a charter of AD 689 in which the monks of Canterbury were granted the right to mine ore at Lympne, Kent (O'Niell 1967: 189). Silver must have come from silver-bearing lead and copper ores but while there is no evidence of mining lead in England until the late Saxon period, there is growing evidence from Wales for the extraction and processing of lead, copper and iron at this time (Arnold forthcoming). Importation to England seems the most likely answer for many of these metals, but the existence of scrap in the forms of late Roman silver coinage, plate and, increasingly, Germanic silver may easily have satisfied the demand.

Metal analyses of silver-alloy brooches reported by Leigh (1980: 185 ff.) suggest that the silver used was moderately pure and was mixed with a copper-based alloy, possibly of Roman origin. Pairs of brooches often have similar values of silver, but some reveal significant differences in copper values indicating they were not made from the same batch of metal. Analytical research carried out on copper-alloys (Manser 1977: 22–3; Brownsword and Hines 1993) indicates a very wide range of composition, matched by the range found in Roman copper-alloys, which suggests extensive recycling. Even when the form and decoration of two brooches are very similar their alloys may be significantly different. Scrap metal may have been a valued commodity and it is occasionally found in bags accompanying skeletons (Myres 1978), although such collections may equally have had an amuletic purpose (Meaney 1981: 249–62). Analyses of cruciform, saucer and great square-headed brooches suggest that the majority were made from recycled metal, although with a preference for a low lead content (Brownsword and Hines 1993; Mortimer 1990; Dickinson 1993a). The earliest great square-headed brooches in East Anglia have stylistic parallels with Scandinavia where they would have been made of relatively pure silver, but those in East Anglia are of debased silver suggesting the metal was not as available there at that time (Brownsword and Hines 1993). Analysis of alloys, therefore, is of technological importance but because of the sources of metals used fails to assist in understanding dispersal.

Few craft activities of the early Anglo-Saxon period have left any archaeological traces except in their finished products, and metalworking is notable for its near absence thereby denying us the benefit of at least knowing where items were made. The limited evidence for manufacturing metal objects has to be seen in the perspective of the many thousands of pieces of metalwork which have been cast in moulds. Only the settlement at Mucking has produced direct evidence, with pieces of a two-piece mould for casting a great square-headed brooch (Jones 1975, 1980; Hamerow 1993) (Figure 5.17). Indirect evidence for the methods of manufacture might be drawn from two failed castings from the upper Thames valley (Dickinson 1982: n. 4), a pendant from Woodeaton (Oxfordshire) (Vierck 1967: 111–13) and a saucer brooch, now lost, from Cassington (Arthur and Jope 1963: 3). Metalworking is also indicated by crucibles found at Walton, Sarre, Portchester (Hampshire) and Sutton Courtenay but these do not significantly improve our understanding of the organisation of such industry. A die for impressing sheet metal with Style II ornament was found at Barton-on-Humber with a balance (Capelle and Vierck 1971) and other dies are known from Salmonby (Lincolnshire), two from Suffolk and there is an example from Salisbury (Wiltshire) (ibid.), all of seventh-century date. Three lead-alloy models for making bow-brooches are known from East Anglia (Mortimer 1994) and a jeweller's hammer from Soham (Cambridgeshire). The sum total of data connected with metalworking is hardly a representative guide to such industry or exchange. On the Continent the incidence of metalworking tools in graves is much higher (Wilson 1976b). It is possible that the rarity of this type of evidence in England is an important clue, that is, while some metalworking took place in the domestic environment, the majority did not.

The absence of information concerning metalworking requires explanation. Itinerant manufacturers have been argued for on the basis of the use of metal models for the production of two-piece clay moulds (Werner 1970; Capelle and Vierck 1971). Hines also views travelling metalworkers as the most suitable explanation for the dispersal of ornamental metalwork (Hines 1984). With such equipment, jewellers would be able to replicate a series of similar designs from a single model. However, it is suggested that much of the detailed ornament was added either to a consumable model, or the mould on each occasion. Their rarity might suggest that they were deliberately destroyed, whether as part of the manufacturing process or for other reasons. In complete contrast, however, is the evidence for a large and centralised metalworking industry at Helgö in Sweden (Holmqvist 1961, 1964, 1970, 1972, 1975). While evidence of metalworking in domestic contexts is rare so too is its representation in funerary contexts, emphasising perhaps how the craft may have been seen as external to normal domestic life and ritual. The absence of metalworking tools from graves may actually point more to the decisions that lie behind the choice of grave-goods to be interred with the dead. Tools generally are rare; from a practical point of view they have a very high use-value and may not have been used as grave-goods for this reason. However, this does not explain the rarity of evidence from domestic contexts.

In regions where there is a very distinctive form of metalwork, such as the disc brooches of Kent (Avent 1975; Leigh 1984b), the distribution might be suitable for analysis as the problems concerning the measurement of

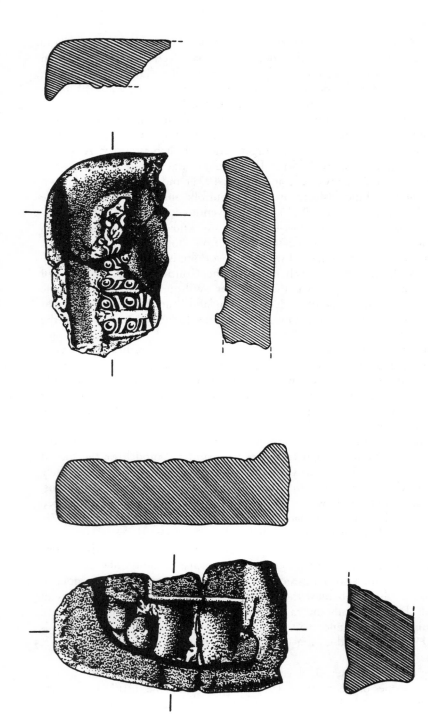

Figure 5.17 Mould fragments for the manufacture of a Group III square-headed brooch from Mucking, Essex (source: Hamerow 1993, Figure 141)

similarity are less important. However, the very fact that the extent of replication is greater with certain classes of metalwork in one region than those in another may be the result of differences in the organisation of their manufacture, even if the actual system is unknown. The manufacture of disc brooches was a complex procedure requiring the procurement of a wide variety of raw materials and their processing before the brooch could be made. Few of these brooches are found outside Kent, in keeping with the observed pattern of distribution of imported luxury goods; where they do occur in other regions they frequently accompany other items that might be labelled 'Kentish'. Within Kent the largest number of examples has been found at Faversham, with the second and third largest peaks in the Wantsum Channel and River Stour area, and the coastal region of east Kent around Dover.

This distribution pattern may be compared with that of a similar brooch type found commonly in the upper Thames valley, the cast saucer brooch. In her study of the type Dickinson (1993a) concluded that, while the methods by which the brooches themselves were made are tolerably clear, without evidence from production sites it will remain difficult to distinguish between itinerant and workshop production. In an earlier (1982) study of pairs of brooches there appeared to be indications of a shift during the sixth century to centralised production on the basis of increasing standardisation of designs. A study of square-headed brooches came to a similar conclusion (Hines 1984: 180); they could be divided into three phases on the basis of their distribution: general, localised and, finally, more numerous and widespread. Such a change may also have social implications: the rise of individuals having the ability to employ a craftsperson, who then benefited from the arrangement personally and who could distribute the products to the surrounding region. Certainly there is a change from a limited range of simple motifs in ornament to a 'varied production of complex and compound motifs' (Dickinson 1982: 36). Both examples serve to emphasise that earlier sixth-century distributions are localised and may, therefore, have been confined to lineages. Gradually the pattern changed until we may see the growth of greater commercialism. By that time the symbols in ornament had less meaning in terms of personal identity as social networks were supplanted by larger political groupings in which traditional symbols were superseded; regional designs continued to evolve but the goods were distributed in an entirely different manner. The change may not, therefore, be the result of developments in the organisation of manufacture so much as the evolution in the meanings that such brooches conveyed and, in turn, access to the goods and their distribution. Earlier brooches may have served to identify social groupings which may eventually have required less emphasis with the growth of political structures (Fisher 1988). When the control over the manufacture of, and access to, such metalwork was more flexible the jeweller may have been freer to use more efficient methods, replicating designs with a freer hand in ornament variation. Such

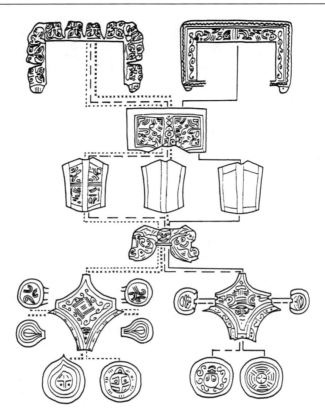

Figure 5.18 The relationship between the decorative elements of four Group III square-headed brooches from Chessel Down (Isle of Wight), Paglesham (Essex), Linton Heath (Cambs) and Tuddenham (Suffolk)

observations, however, still do not explain who made decisions about the choice of ornament nor do they explain the absence from settlements of evidence for actual manufacture.

A study of a small series of sixth-century, square-headed, brooches showed how the various brooches could be placed into a sequence resulting from the interchange of parts of the decoration on them (Figure 5.18). It could be shown that the relationship between the brooches deserved more attention than simply considering them as a 'stylistic group', but exactly how or why the interchange of decorative elements was carried out is more difficult to understand; the moulds for casting the brooches may have been made with models constituting separate elements of the decoration of the brooches, or entirely remodelled each time a brooch was made, with variations. A parallel could be drawn between the choice of designs for dies on the Sancton-Baston cremation pottery and on brooches such as these: certain elements remain constant. This may signify membership of some larger group. Elements that regularly changed may represent membership of a sub-group requiring more frequent variation as sub-groups merged, for instance through marriage. Irrespective of the actual method of replication, the series is found spread across southern and eastern England from the Isle of Wight to Suffolk. This may indicate the extent of social interconnectedness whether at the level of the manufacturer, the client or the wearer (Arnold 1980; Hines 1984).

Linked pieces of ornamental metalwork also serve to emphasise the extent of the movement of people and, therefore, of contact. Hines has extended understanding of such relationships in a thorough review of square-headed brooches in England (1984). While the research was primarily designed to explore the origins and chronology of types, the resulting groupings are based on similarity of design elements. A variety of patterns is apparent in these groupings. There are small ones such as Group VI concentrated in the valley of the Warwickshire Avon, and Group XV in Cambridgeshire, Suffolk and the Midlands. There are also larger groups that reveal connections between distinct areas, for instance Group I in Kent, Sussex, Surrey and the upper Thames valley, and further north Group XVI in East Anglia, Leicestershire and Nottinghamshire (Figure 5.19).

Hines divided the brooches into three overlapping chronological phases that reflect developments in the manufacture and use of such brooches. The first phase is marked by about nine brooches that are 'distinctly individualist' and dated c. 500–20. Larger groups of brooches characterise the second, overlapping phase of c. 510–50, which can be viewed as attempts 'to reproduce the same recognisable prototype', thereby playing down the change that actually occurs. In the final phase, c. 530–70, the majority of the brooches are found in a small number of groups characterised as being 'mass produced' reproductions of a single type. These characteristics are couched in terms of the evolution of commerce when the changes may be socially driven. Geographically in the first phase the brooches tend not to cluster in any particular region and are found dispersed over much of England. In the second phase they tend to be more regional, although they are still dispersed over considerable distances, up to 200 km apart. In the third phase the area of dispersal is larger and the distribution more dense (Figure 5.19).

Similar patterns are discernible with other brooch types although there has been less detailed research. Types of florid cruciform brooch in the Midlands and East Anglia, for instance types 'c', 'd', and 'g' surveyed by Leeds and Pocock (1971), have distinctly regional distributions similar to the phase 2 of Hines. Certain types of cast and applied saucer brooches also reveal the same distribution patterns.

Some of the most detailed studies have been carried out by Leigh (1980) on sixth-century square-headed brooches from Kent. The study was geared towards isolating the products of specific workshops or craftworkers. This

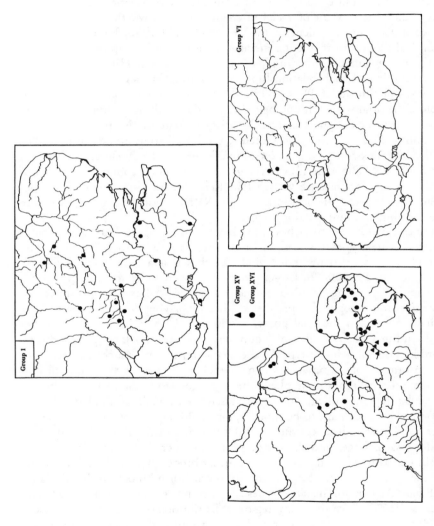

Figure 5.19 The contrasting distributions of groups of square-headed brooches (source: Hines 1984, Maps 3.1, 3.3 and 3.6)

Table 5.2 Analyses of a trio of square-headed brooches from Chessell Down, Isle of Wight

Brooch	*45 ix*	*45 x*	*45 xi*
line spacing on foils (mm)	3.19	2.81	2.83
% silver	91.4	92.0	91.0
% copper	5.7	5.9	7.0
% zinc	1.0	0.8	0.8
% gold	0.6	0.6	0.6
% lead	1.3	0.7	0.6

Source: Avent and Leigh 1977; Leigh 1980

was achieved by examining brooches that are pairs and, more rarely, trios (Figure 5.20), those not paired but which are very similar and those which are of different design but which share the same characteristics. By this method it was possible to isolate the features that give the groups cohesion. One group, represented by nearly 30 brooches mostly from Kent, was characterised by the care and precision of the design and layout, the notched ridge making up the designs, the well-made and neat niello bands and garnet inlaid cells, and the carefully carved animal and geometric ornament, with sharp tops to the ridges. Some minor differences, such as the angles at which the tools had been applied to surfaces, might indicate the hands of separate jewellers (ibid.: 75). Some of the problems posed by such metalwork are exemplified by a trio of square-headed brooches that belong to the corpus of material studied by Leigh, although found outside Kent at the cemetery of Chessell Down (Arnold 1982a: 27–8). They are silver gilt brooches with garnet inlays (Figure 5.20). One is different from the others in that it is a less accomplished piece suggesting that a pair and a single brooch were made on separate occasions. The line spacing on the foils beneath the garnets tends to support this but the metal analysis presents an ambiguous picture (Table 5.2); the differences, however, are not statistically significant. To place these brooches into their social context we would need to know more about where the pair and the single brooch were made, in what sequence, why they were made, who they were made for and why these Kentish brooches may have been exported to the Isle of Wight.

The principal conclusion of Leigh's research was that all three of the series of square-headed brooches that were isolated (two of silver and one of copper-alloy), the majority of keystone garnet inlaid disc brooches (of silver), and at least some of the garnet inlaid buckle plates (some silver and some copper-alloy), are the products of a single workshop made over three generations. Alternatively they may be the product of close copying in different workshops by people trained by one jeweller. Certainly the work of individual people can be detected on certain examples. It should be noted that this grouping of sixth-century metalwork includes nearly all of the

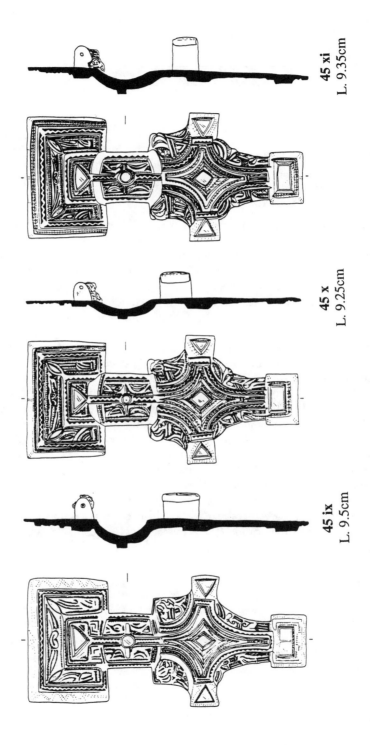

Figure 5.20 A trio of square-headed brooches from Chessel Down, Isle of Wight

45 ix
L. 9.5cm

45 x
L. 9.25cm

45 xi
L. 9.35cm

known examples, and only gives rise to the question of how similar items have to be for us to be able to determine where they lie on a scale ranging from individual jeweller to the learned traditions of a single society. However, as the conclusions are based on the minutiae of the production process it seems likely that Leigh has come closest to identifying the work of individuals.

The identification of apparent patterning amongst groups and sub-groups of types of ornamental metalwork can easily induce an unjustified sense of satisfaction. It is a far cry from actually understanding the patterns, and at present we can only really raise possibilities. When such replication and variation are found we should ask what were the factors controlling the results? Are such objects the product of itinerant jewellers who produced objects to order? Was the jeweller free to determine the design? Does the choice represent a particular person's or group's identity? Is the movement of such metalwork carried out by the manufacturer or by the consumer, for instance as gifts or the movement of people in marriage? It is noticeable that the dies for decorating the surface of pottery are as rare as the tools required for producing ornamental metalwork. It may be of use to compare the regional groupings of brooch types with those areas that were high consumers of imported luxury goods; while such a correlation would tell us nothing about the mode of production of the brooches, it might provide some articulation to the distribution maps. Problems such as these extend even to the more commonplace types of metalwork in which the lack of replication might lead to the suggestion that everyday items were produced locally as required; but were such technical skills possessed by someone on every farm or hamlet, at only a few locations, or were the metalworkers or jewellers mobile specialists?

Most ornamental metalwork has only been studied from a typological standpoint on the basis of form and decoration. This allows estimation of chronology and the identification of regional types, but it says little about the organisation of manufacture and dispersal. The absence of exact replication with most brooch types strongly suggests that each brooch, or each pair, was manufactured as required, thereby offering an opportunity to innovate that was frequently taken. This brings us no nearer an understanding of what or who determined the form of the decoration. The distribution of stylistic groups may reflect the beneficence of wealthy individuals, the region of activity of a metalworker, or the distribution of associated groups of people (or other exchange networks), who wore such items, in part, as an indicator of their identity.

When such a high proportion of metalwork is associated with women it would be helpful to examine types connected with men, for instance weaponry, to redress the imbalance. However, the very nature of weaponry does not lend itself so readily to such analysis. A limited number of swords are very individualistic, but shield bosses conform to a relatively limited range of designs that appear to change slowly through time (Dickinson and Härke 1992). Spearheads were made in a wide range of identifiable forms, most having broad geographical distributions (Swanton 1974). The principal problem is that each iron object was a unique forging.

Another means by which light may be shed on the problems concerning the modes of production and dispersal of metalwork would be to consider very distinctive examples. Their very individuality might imply the hand of a single jeweller. It is easy to see why it is the more unusual types of artefact that are used for this type of research. For instance, there is a group of bronze-bound wooden vessels whose binding hoops were decorated with a distinctive repoussé ornament and which are found distributed over central southern England (Arnold 1982a; Davies 1984). Similarly, there are pieces of metalwork decorated with enamel that are found in the Lark valley in Cambridgeshire (Brown 1981a; Scull 1985).

The close association between exotic metalwork and élite members of society is particularly apparent in the seventh century when the development of a distinctive style of animal ornament, Style II, occurs. The most ornate and rich pieces are strongly associated with richly furnished graves in Kent, at Sutton Hoo, Cuddesdon and Broomfield (Essex) and Taplow. As Speake has observed 'Patronage to support and pay a goldsmith or craftsman who utilised such expensive materials as gold, silver and garnet, could only be given by the "top people" in Anglo-Saxon society' (1980: 39). While there are less accomplished versions of the elaborate examples in a given region, as in Kent, the virtuosity of the buckle, shoulder-clasps and purse from mound I at Sutton Hoo inevitably led Speake to talk of a Sutton Hoo master craftsperson and a workshop; later pieces may have been produced by workers trained there. The style as a whole points to the continuing exchange of ideas between England and the Continent and also to how at this social level in the first half of the seventh century the paramount members of society employed their own metalworkers to produce exotic display items demonstrating their success in leadership and exchange in acquiring the necessary raw materials.

The time and expense involved in manufacturing pieces of metalwork may reflect on the social standing of their users, and this must be borne in mind when considering the controls over their distribution patterns. If only the more labour-intensive, individualistic forms are considered, not the more common varieties, the result will be a marked bias in our view of the economics of metalworking and of the period as a whole. Indirectly this problem may reveal something of the organisation of craft activities in early Anglo-Saxon England.

Throughout the early Anglo-Saxon period the basis of the economy was the products of the land and the efforts of those who farmed it. For many, life remained at a self-sufficient level in which food was produced with little need to create a surplus; materials were found locally. There may not have been any need to generate an agricultural surplus if Roman metal artefacts provided a source of scrap. But as the demands grew, to enable some members of society to enjoy the products of long-distance exchange, gift exchange and the use of fine goods produced by specialist craftworkers, a surplus had to be produced. To achieve this surplus the necessary infrastructure in terms of the control of people and land had to be in place. At all times goods were being imported; in much of England the distribution patterns imply unequal access to such goods, the quantities falling off rapidly beyond the point of greatest consumption. The exception is Kent, which not only imported a particular range of materials from the Continent, but also maintained a near monopoly over those goods. The overseas economy of Kent was the most developed in early Anglo-Saxon England and it was so strong that Kent might have been viewed as part of the Continent at this time. Other regions also enjoyed imported goods, exploiting additional parts of Europe even if they were linked together in a more extensive network within England than was Kent. The observables, the exotic items of gold, amber, shell, garnet, pottery (and what it contained, for instance, wine), glass, mercury, ivory, may give us a distorted image of the nature of exchange, but there is no reason for rejecting the acceptance of the pattern at face-value. It is considerably harder to characterise the form of exchange at a local level, although we may hypothesise about its nature on the basis of the organisation viewed through alternative forms of evidence.

The archaeological evidence is a kaleidoscope of numerous activities operating on various levels and spheres that differ from one area to the next through time. The data would fit a picture of an agrarian society capable of producing a surplus within a relatively simple economy. With varying degrees of restriction people had access to the products of specialist manufacturers, sometimes using imported raw materials, as well as imported goods. The economy may, therefore, be characterised as operating on a number of levels: subsistence, production, and exchange operating at a local, regional and inter-regional level.

This structure may be viewed in terms of the evolution of the early Anglo-Saxon kingdoms through 'peer competition and competitive exclusion' (Scull 1993: 73–4) as corporate groups made or strengthened relationships by the action of exchanging goods, and of corporate leaders acquiring valuable objects and forging relationships. Through competition, emulation and restriction their position and power were enhanced and the material means were provided to set in motion communal activities. As these activities became more intense a greater demand would have been placed on those who made it possible, the food-producers, who would have been under increasing pressure to maximise output. Such an evolutionary model is valid in as far as it is possible to see that the volume of exotic raw materials was increasing with time as leaders increasingly desired appropriate symbols of power. Alliance networks changed with events over time and the role of exchange in the making and breaking of such alliances would have been crucial. Much production and exchange were clearly socially embedded but the increasingly institutionalised political structure would in time lead to greater commercialism.

Chapter 6

The topography of belief

In the absence of contemporary, or near contemporary, written evidence we have no direct source for the study of 'pagan' Anglo-Saxon beliefs. Even the details of early Christian worship are obscure (Owen 1981). The mainte-nance of the secular structure of society is aided by ritual and the symbolic content of material aspects of ritual certainly fall within the scope of archae-ological research. Within one symbolic form may be condensed numerous aspects or meanings of the world, such as the unity and continuity of social groups, primary and associational, domestic and political. There is a strong symbolic content in the grave-goods buried with the deceased that reflect a hierarchy of identities on either side of the boundary between life and death. It is more difficult to distinguish between social custom and religion, espe-cially when considering burial. This is because a funeral is largely the response of grieving friends and relatives rather than a religious ceremony despite the fact that religious beliefs may impinge on aspects of the procedure. Detailed studies of aspects of burials regularly find an association between the choice of the burial form and a social factor. Inevitably the most detailed studies of 'paganism' (Wilson 1992) draw much of their data from burial rites but there is a danger in ascribing anything we do not understand to ritual and of imposing on the early Anglo-Saxons a pattern of belief that is ultimately based on our, predominantly, Christian models. The ways in which indi-viduals and communities perceived, explained and constructed their worlds will have impinged on all aspects of everyday life and any attempt to separate 'ritual' as a distinct set of symbolic actions may, in this context, be inap-propriate. However, there may be certain ways in which religious beliefs can be isolated.

The evidence for paganism contained in place-names may indicate places of contemporary worship (Gelling 1978: 158–61). However, there is no strong evidence that pagan religious practices took place at specified places and there is, at present, no unambiguous archaeological evidence that such places formed a part of their beliefs; some may have no religious significance at all (Blair 1995; Meaney 1995). The place-name elements that have been considered at length by many writers are normally divided into two groups: those containing the name of a god such as Thunor in *Thunreslau* (Essex), and those which may mean a sacred place (Wilson 1985, 1992). Consideration of their distribution must be tempered by the knowledge that later events have robbed us of early place-name forms in some regions especially in north-east England. Both types, however, are evenly distributed from the Humber to the south coast, although Norfolk is notably blank (Gelling 1978, Figure 11). Whether there is a relationship between the locations of names indicative of a sacred place and topography, especially prehistoric and Roman route ways, is problematic. The case is weakened by the absence of any consideration of the possible coincidence of topographic factors determining the position of the roads and of other archaeological features that may be contemporary with paganism of this type. Wilson has observed that there is a noticeable difference in the location of names with *hearg*, and of those with *wēoh* and *wig*. The former tend to be on high ground not close to such roads, the latter on low ground and close to old routes. It is argued that *hearg* names represent tribal cult centres, whereas *wēoh* names were roadside shrines.

There are no known buildings that may be definitely linked with such names. The only building that has been interpreted as a place of pagan worship is building D2 at Yeavering (Hope-Taylor 1977). The first timber building was left standing when enclosed by a larger structure that may be Christian. The nine successive deposits of ox skulls heaped against a wall led to the suggestion of sacrifice and feasting. At Yeavering there were also nearby burials but the many excavations of cemeteries have failed to produce buildings and there is therefore insufficient evidence for claiming an association between burials and shrines. Alternatively we might perceive the link between *hearg* names and buildings as inappropriate and place more emphasis on the similarity in location of those place-names and the large cremation cemeteries of midland and eastern England that may well have acted as cult centres. A few cemeteries produce structures associated with individual burials, both inhumations and cremations (p.156), but they provide a focus to a grave and need not be communal shrines. It may also be wrong to think of ritual activity as occurring at specialised sites rather than being part of everyday life. For instance, a pit was dug adjacent to a house door at Cowdery's Down (Figure 6.1) the bottom of which was filled with clay and covered with cobbles, above which was placed the body of an adult cow; there was nothing to indicate this was a rubbish pit, although butchery had started before the body was placed there (Millett and James 1983: 218–21). In comparison there are cases of the burial of horses, partially cremated, and dogs from the cemetery at Great Chesterford (Evison 1994), possibly associated with, but in some cases stratigraphically later than, particular human burials. Examples of this type of activity are however rare. The incidence of pits is variable on early Anglo-Saxon settlements but when they do occur their function can be obscure, as is the case with some from Mucking (Hamerow 1993: 20, Figure 179).

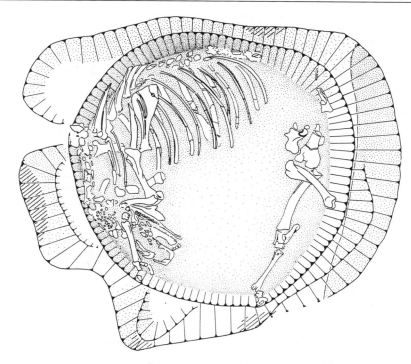

Figure 6.1 Plan of a cow-burial at the settlement of Cowdery's Down, Hampshire (source: Millett and James 1983, Figure 50)

The existence and nature of possible shrines remain intangible at present although there may be other ways by which we may gain some insight into the pagan Anglo-Saxon belief system, for instance, runic inscriptions, the decoration on artefacts and cemeteries. In each case there are difficulties in separating possible religious beliefs from other factors.

Runes and the runic alphabet are interpreted as being connected with magic (Page 1973a, 1995). The greatest problem arises with the interpretation of the inscriptions for there is 'no recorded context of thought to help us understand an inscription' (ibid. 1973a: 12). Runic letters and inscriptions have been identified on a number of objects of metal, ceramic and bone found in early Anglo-Saxon cemeteries (Figure 6.2). Examples include that carved on the astragalus of a deer found in a cremation urn at Caistor-by-Norwich (Page 1973b), or the h-rune on a sixth-century brooch from Wakerley. There are examples of the t-rune on weaponry, for instance, a sword-pommel from Gilton and a spear-blade from Holborough (Kent) which may refer to Tiw as a war god; it also occurs on some cremation urns from Caistor-by-Norwich (Norfolk) (Figure 6.3) and Loveden Hill. Other

Figure 6.2 The distribution of runic and rune-like inscriptions in early Anglo-Saxon England (source: Page 1973a, Figure 6 with additions)

stamped decoration such as swastikas and *wyrms* on cremation urns seems particularly symbolic, 'often representing powerful evocations to specific gods' (Richards 1992: 142). An urn from Sancton (Figure 6.8) decorated with a swastika contained a whetstone and may be connected with Thunor, the god of thunder and the forge (Reynolds 1980; Timby 1993). Few of the runic inscriptions on early Anglo-Saxon objects have been interpreted. Some were put on to the object at the manufacturing stage, such as those on a cremation urn from Loveden Hill and on the Holborough spearhead which is inlaid in a contrasting metal. Others were probably added some time after manufacture such as the sword scabbard mount (Figure 6.3) and Byzantine pail from Chessell Down (Arnold 1982a).

The occurrence of such inscriptions is rare, which may imply that the right or ability to produce and own an object bearing runic letters was limited to a small group in a society that was otherwise illiterate. However, there may have been many others on organic materials, such as the Caistor-by-Norwich astragalus, which have perished. We do not need to assume that the owner of a runic inscription understood it, but their apparent rarity does suggest some form of exclusion. Similarly, on some portable objects, such as

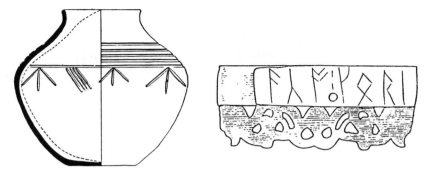

Figure 6.3 Examples of runic and rune-like inscriptions on a cremation urn from Caistor-by-Norwich, Norfolk (source: Myres and Green 1973, Figure 15) and on the rear of a silver scabbard mount from Chessel Down, Isle of Wight

the Chessell Down scabbard fitting, the inscription would not have been visible under normal circumstances. The geographic distribution is also uneven, there being concentrations in Kent, the Isle of Wight and the region around the Wash from the River Humber to Norfolk. The remainder of the country is without examples in the period up to *c.* AD 650, but it cannot be said that they were runeless regions. The use of runes did not die out after that date and they occur in comparatively large numbers on Christian artefacts, especially in the north of England.

The feeling of secrecy and exclusivity that is conveyed by runic letters and inscriptions is also to be found in the early Anglo-Saxon interest in riddles. These have been noted in the decoration of some metalwork, especially brooches. The whole basis of the type of decoration common in the sixth century, Style I (Salin 1904), was the production of visual riddles. At their simplest they are reversible human and animal faces. On bracteates, meta-morphoses are depicted which may have been intended to have a mythical or religious symbolism. Leigh (1980) suggests that dancing and acrobatic figures emphasise that some type of shaman ritual and belief may be implied (Figure 6.4). Profile masks are so commonly depicted wearing head-dresses, often a feather in a head-band, that they cannot be described as abstract. Such iconological elements must be seen with technological and artistic factors that are combined in determining the outcome of Style I art.

The artistic and iconological elements of Style I are seen at their best on square-headed brooches, although they also occur less commonly on such objects as sword-fittings, buckle plates, saucer brooches, clasps and drinking horn mounts; the potential symbolism of a wider range of artefacts has been explored by Meaney (1981). The 'chip-carved' Style I ornament is three-dimensional with exciting interplay of design. The shape of square-headed brooches cannot be functional, but there is a consistency of shape suggesting

Figure 6.4 Examples of human–animal representations on early Anglo-Saxon brooches (source: Leigh 1990, Figure 8)

that it satisfied both artistic and iconological requirements; the rectangular head-plate and rhomboidal foot allowed the exciting mixture of symmetry and asymmetry. Each area is laterally symmetrical providing room for the pairing of animals or other motifs in mirror images suitable for any narrative or iconographic scheme concerned with such pairs of creatures. The varying pattern of upraised bands created a variety of fields for such designs. Leigh believes that such brooches were modelled in wax, an ideal 'medium for the communication or representation of iconological ideas, even if, at present, we are ill-equipped fully to appreciate these intentions' (1980: 428).

A primary requirement in such decorative schemes appears to have been that of ambiguities (Leigh 1984a, 1990). An animal had to be interpretable as human; for instance when an animal mask is inverted or turned through 90° it becomes a human mask and vice versa (Figure 6.4). By these tricks the designs are full of visual surprises. In addition, the fragmentation of forms permitted disguise and deception as originally pointed out by Bakka (1958: 5). As with the runes we may well ask what proportion of society could understand such decoration, noting that the metalwork with this degree of decoration is relatively rare. In later Germanic mythology smiths are depicted as the repositories of wisdom, masters of runes and of magic songs (Turville Petrie 1964: 233). Leigh suggests that the Style I art is a facet of Anglo-Saxon society seen previously only in poetry; the decoration can be viewed as graphic poetry based on metaphor and alliteration, often in the form of riddles (1984a, 1990).

The chronologically overlapping and succeeding decorative system, Style II, also contains a variety of combinations of animals and humans, especially the boar, bird and serpent (Speake 1980: 76–92). The written evidence concerned with Germanic myth and belief, and certain artefacts, indicates that such animals had particular associations; the boar, for instance, may have had associations with kingship, although the situation is complicated by each possibly having multiple symbolic associations and being used for both magical and decorative reasons.

Many of the animals depicted cannot be identified but the symbolic significance of animals has been explored (Hicks 1993) and their association with burials discussed (Richards 1992: 137–41). The greatest difference in the incidence of animals at settlements and cremation cemeteries is with cattle and horses (Table 6.1). Cattle are the most common animal represented on settlements but are rare in cremation burials, whereas horses are rare on settlements but are the second most common animal in cremations. Dog and bear are represented in cremations, the latter as claws probably resulting from the cremating of skins. Animal bones do occur in inhumation burials but they are rarely reported. At Great Chesterford there were burials of horses and dogs (Evison 1994). Additional evidence (p.186) indicates that particular species were linked to the age and sex of the deceased (Figure 7.3) even if they were also part of a funeral feast. For instance, horses, which may have been associated with mobility and wealth, are associated with adult males, not children; they occur also on metalwork, such as brooches and shields, and cremation urns. Cattle bones, especially the heads of oxen have, as we have seen, occasionally been found in quantity as individual deposits and are found with inhumation burials, often at the feet. Oxen may well have been used for sacrifices (Richards 1992: 141).

A funeral is as much a social event as a religious one and the precise form of the burial may be influenced as much by one as the other. Most modern studies of the variables associated with early Anglo-Saxon burials conclude that the particular choice has most to do with the individual being buried as mediated through those responsible for the funeral. The only overriding

Table 6.1 Proportions of animals from settlements and in cremation burials

%	cattle	sheep/goat	pig	horse	deer	bird	dog	bear
6 settlements average	40	34	16	2.5	1	5		
3 cremation cemeteries average	11	30	12	34	1	3	4	1

Source: Richards 1992: 138; Bond 1993, 1994a

constant is the choice of the type of burial, inhumation or cremation. There are a large number of other variables such as the choice and position of the grave-goods, body position, funerary urn decoration and shape, orientation, the grave construction and associated structures and there must surely have been other ceremonies associated with the funeral that have left no trace. In any description of burials there is a danger of understating what appears commonplace and of giving too much emphasis to the unusual. For instance, most inhumation graves were not accompanied by grave-goods and they therefore receive less attention than those that were. Whatever the major factors involved in determining the form of the burial, people believed there was an appropriate form of burial for each individual, irrespective of what it signified. By this means the burial rites reiterated contemporary society through the medium of ideological or religious ideas. The absence of recognisable, communal places of worship might suggest that religion was a personal activity, but at death individuals were buried in communal cemeteries, sacred places that would have had a powerful significance to the communities that used them.

Modern methods of archaeological excavation have encouraged the study of whole cemeteries and associated structures, such as buildings and markers, whereas in the past there was a tendency to focus on the graves alone. The growing number of known structures in cemeteries suggests they may have been more common than is apparent. Aerial photography of the cemetery of Updown (Kent) suggests the cemetery was bounded by a ditch for much of its life, perhaps spilling outside when it was believed to be fully used. At Bishopstone the focus of the cemetery was a prehistoric barrow beside which were a number of postholes some of which assumed a trapezoidal shape. Measuring about 6.15 × 2.50 m it had a large posthole in the centre (Bell 1977: 195). A variety of structures have now been identified in cemeteries – for instance, individual timber grave markers, fenced areas as if demarcating family plots, and four-post structures, particularly around cremation burials, which have been interpreted as houses of the dead (Down and Welch 1990) (Figure 6.5). Round and rectangular ditched enclosures around graves may have served a similar purpose (Hogarth 1973) and possible reconstructions have been considered (Hedges and Buckley 1985). The majority of the cemetery features associated with graves appear to represent grave markers and enclosures for the continued veneration of the dead (Figure 6.6). The majority of graves, however, do not appear to have had any structural features associated with them although they would have been visible as graves for some time after the funeral.

Although there is a wide variety of structural evidence it unfortunately rarely allows reconstruction and some imagination is required to put superstructures into the surviving foundations. The graves themselves vary in their shape, being sub-rectangular or more ovoid, but rarely in the past were details of the shape in three dimensions recorded. Sockets are found, usually in

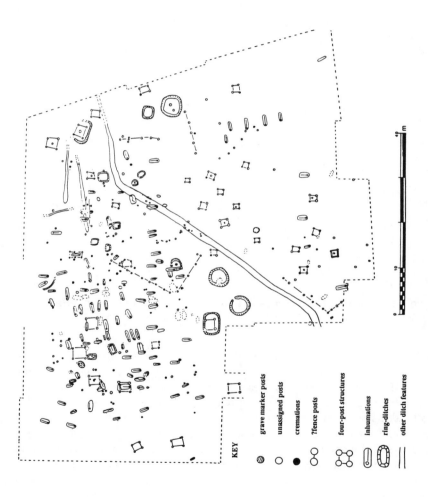

KEY

grave marker posts
unassigned posts
cremations
?fence posts
four-post structures
inhumations
ring-ditches
other ditch features

Figure 6.5 Plan of the cemetery at Apple Down, Sussex (source: Down and Welch 1990, Figure 24)

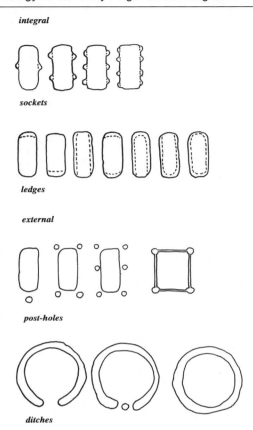

Figure 6.6 Structural features associated with burials in early Anglo-Saxon cemeteries (source: Hogarth 1973, Figures 7 and 8 with additions)

opposing pairs on each of the long sides of the grave in varying combinations, two to eight in number; their shapes suggest use for vertical and horizontal timbers. In a few examples from east Kent the sockets were angled as though the graves had been covered with a pitched structure with the surfaces angled at 30°. Posts set in a four-post array may be found 1 m from the edge of the grave. Sometimes they are misaligned suggesting that they may be associated with the grave but are not strictly contemporary. Ledges may be found around all or part of the mouth of the grave-pit; some may be intended to support lids to the graves, or they may be a slightly more complex way of achieving the same result as with sockets but using a ground plate rather than earth-fast timbers; sockets and ledges are also found together.

Individual sockets for free-standing posts have been located at some cemeteries, and they may also occur with other structures such as ditches and kerb-slots. Ditches, 6 to 7 m diameter around a grave, may have a causeway, sometimes containing a relatively large posthole, or may be a complete ring. Their vertical sides suggest they are not purely quarries for a barrow mound, and the evidence of holes for upright timbers suggests a fence. The cemetery at St Peter's, Broadstairs, produced an example with a rectangular slot in which had stood sandstone slabs, forming a kerb, acting either as a boundary or to retain soil on a platform. One would need to know the original depth that such slabs were inserted into the ground to be able to determine whether they could retain soil; certainly the penannular ditched structures imply an 'entrance' through the fence that would obviate a soil filling although, as suggested for the Orsett (Essex) cemetery (Hedges and Buckley 1985), there may have been a low mound over the grave. Four-post arrangements connected by horizontal timbers, and ditches, are also found around cremated burials, sometimes together. Individual posts at the foot of the grave, or in such a gap, may be grave markers whether plain or marked in some way.

As many of these marked graves were aligned east to west and had no grave-goods there has been a tendency to view them as emanating from a Christian context and dating to the seventh and eighth centuries; other examples are known from Ireland, Wales, Scotland and the Continent, some dated to the early sixth century (Brassil *et al.* 1991). It is difficult to dis-entangle the questions of cultural affinity with the practical response to the varying needs of construction, protection and veneration of a grave. In Kent such graves tend to lie near the edges of cemeteries, which is therefore taken to indicate a late date as though the cemetery spread outwards from an original nucleus. A problem is that the presence of such a ditch need not imply that there was a barrow. However, the wide spacing of some graves in cemeteries suggests the existence of barrows, albeit without other structural evidence.

Occasionally the excavation of cemeteries reveals preserved examples of more complex graves. An annular ditch at Spong Hill contained a wooden lined grave of great complexity that appeared to have been robbed in antiq-uity. The floor was planked and the walls, probably also built of horizontal planks, had regular corners although there was no trace of nails or clamps; traces of a lid were located. Such timber chambered graves with lavish and varied grave-goods are known elsewhere in England and on the Continent (Hills 1977; Hills, Penn and Rickett 1984) and it is argued that this kind of grave befitted a person of high rank. Other forms of more elaborate burial include the use of coffins, bed-burial (Figures 4.5 and 7.11) (Speake 1989) and the ultimate expression in the form of boat burials known from Sutton Hoo (Figures 4.3 and 7.10) and Snape.

The two basic forms of burial in early Anglo-Saxon England were inhu-mation and cremation (Figures 3.9, 6.7 and 6.8). Both forms may occur in cemeteries in varying proportions, but the basis for the choice is not known.

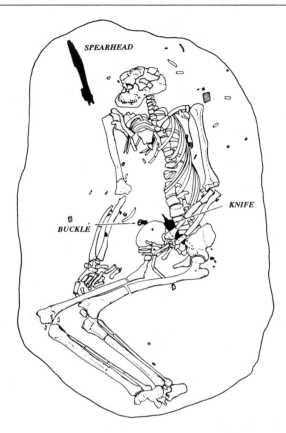

Figure 6.7 An inhumation burial from the early Anglo-Saxon cemetery at Sancton, Humberside (source: Timby 1993, Figure 49)

Inhumation and cremation appear to have been practised simultaneously by some communities, whereas in others there may be a shift in emphasis with time, with inhumations being more strongly represented latterly. Timber structures are more commonly found associated with inhumation burials which is seemingly the more common burial rite in early Anglo-Saxon England. The bodies are normally on their backs, extended or lightly flexed, and most frequently without grave-goods. There are rare elaborations on this form with bodies covered with stones, accompanied by charcoal or with evidence for burning. Where grave-goods do occur they may be personal items that, at least in life, would be attached to clothing or carried on the person such as knives, jewellery, actual dress items, for instance strap-ends, buckles, pins, with additional items such as weaponry and vessels of various materials. There was a degree of regularity about the position of the artefacts

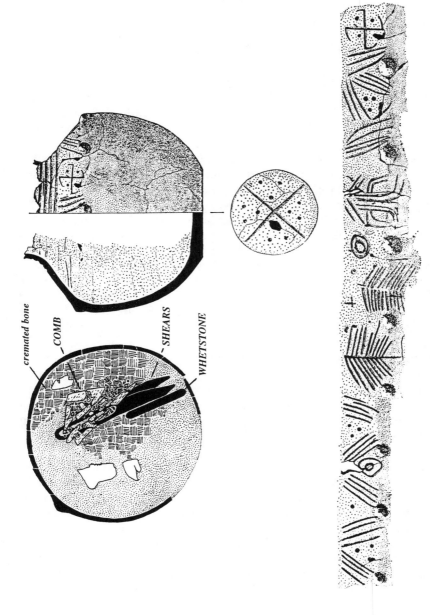

Figure 6.8 A cremation burial from Sancton, Humberside (source: Reynolds 1980)

in the graves, especially within individual cemeteries, as though such positions were considered most appropriate.

The orientation of inhumation graves lends itself to analysis which has led to a variety of conclusions (Rahtz 1978). The majority of graves are aligned roughly west–east with the head to the west, and south–north with the head to the south, although other variants are found, if rarely. The choice of grave orientation has been seen as having an ethnic connotation distinguishing between natives and migrants (Faull 1977) although this interpretation breaks down when comparison is made with Continental practice. Some analyses have started with the premise that the grave-digger would align the grave on the position of the sunrise resulting in seasonal variation in grave-alignment (Hawkes 1977). At Norton (Cleveland) the predominantly N–S graves could be viewed as aligned on the probable site of a prehistoric barrow (Sherlock and Welch 1992: 14–15). The choice may also be linked with the identity of the individual; in relation to a cemetery at Alton (Hampshire) Evison showed that while the majority of the community were buried west–east and south–north the other directions were the graves of sub-adults, non-local women and women buried without grave-goods (1988: 38–41).

Re-use of prehistoric barrows is found in most areas of England, for both inhumations and cremations, but the frequency of primary barrow burial is less clear. Later agricultural activity can easily remove low barrows, but the existence of various sized barrows over graves is attested in many counties. Such elaborate forms of burial occur towards the end of the pagan period, at first as a component of a cemetery, or as a wholly barrow cemetery and later with often lavish, 'isolated' barrow burials. Many are known from old excavations but some have been re-assessed (Dickinson 1992; Speake 1989; Carver 1992a; Collis 1983), although their isolation may be more apparent than real. It may be argued that elaborate and visible forms of burial occur at times when individuals are asserting their power roles and at times of stress in society, although the nature of the stress during the phases of barrow building is unlikely to be the same. Stress may be caused during earlier periods by the effects of migration and colonisation or by the turbulent political and economic state of affairs in later phases. On the other hand Shephard (1979) has suggested that isolated barrows of the early seventh century onwards symbolised a stability in the social system through the emergence of paramount rank, and that the earlier barrow cemeteries reflect a system regulated by a higher degree of organisation than the flat-grave cemeteries. An alternative view is that such monumental graves were a direct confrontation with churches as a place of burial, extending to a physical juxtaposition in the case of Taplow, where the barrow is within the church-yard. In this way such barrows 'articulated the opposition of pagans to a changing ideological world and promoted their own interests by actively using the past' in referring back to the long tradition of barrow building (van de Noort 1993).

Cemeteries in which cremation was the predominant rite are located in eastern and midland England. The evidence suggests that cremating took place on the ground with the fuel heaped over the body (Wells 1960; McKinley 1994a, 1994b) and if personal items are present some may have been included in the pyre, others may not. Some of the cremated remains were placed on or below the ground surface. Burial in a plain or often lavishly decorated vessel is the most commonly observed practice. Some were covered with stones or even small cairns. The objects accompanying cremations may be burial items such as jewellery, playing pieces or toilet sets and miniature versions of household items, such as combs and shears. Wells also noted that animal bones often accompany cremated remains and more systematic study has supported his conclusions (Richards 1987, 1992); not only was the frequency of particular species different from those found on settlements (Table 6.1) but there were also appropriate species for persons of a particular age and sex (Figure 7.3). Some urns have a hole deliberately made in them, in rare instances fitted with a piece of glass although it is unclear what this signifies. If inhumations, especially when accompanied, were taken to indicate a belief in an after-life then cremation may suggest a different belief. It is possible that both have more to do with 'killing' an identity than with any other belief.

Beneath the basic distinctions in burial rite a considerable amount of variability is found, about which there has been little detailed research. It would actually require all of the funerary evidence to be placed on a database for this to be possible although some specialised research of this type has been carried out with cemeteries within regions (Huggett 1995), with a sample of graves of one burial rite (Richards 1987) and with graves with weapons (Härke 1992b). One problem that is frequently encountered with the data is the extent to which the variability is determined by ritual and belief rather than other factors. On the Isle of Wight, for instance, the largest cemeteries (Figure 6.9) occur at the lower altitudes, whereas the re-use of prehistoric burial mounds occurs at heights greater than 100 m; the latter observation may be governed by the distribution of the prehistoric barrows, the former need not be, but neither need be a response to ritual. A pattern of this type may reflect changes or variability in the settlement pattern. Some, but few, of the possible permutations do not occur. It may be true that cremations and barrow burials only occur at higher altitudes or it is equally possible that later land-use has removed the visible traces of barrows, primary or secondary, on low-lying ground.

A great deal is learned about Anglo-Saxon society (Chapter 7) and about belief when the many variables are correlated enabling patterning to be observed. Some graves are very unusual because of the cause of death, the grave-goods or the position of the body. Such graves inevitably generate more comment than the vast mass of graves that in a variety of ways might be seen as 'conforming' to a limited range of norms. Such unusual graves present

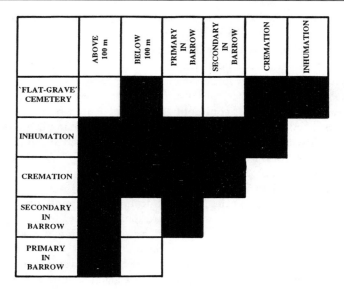

Figure 6.9 Matrix indicating correlations between cemetery location and mortuary data on the Isle of Wight. Positive correlations are shown in black

their own problems of interpretation because it is not always clear whether they are different because of the cause of death, which may be the result of punishment, sacrifice or belief, or because the person was unusual. Such causes are in any case not mutually exclusive. There is little direct evidence regarding attitudes to crime and punishment in pre-Christian England, but the attempts of the early Christian kings, from Aethelberht onwards, to replace the blood feud with a system of financial compensation suggest that previously crimes were avenged with violence.

There are many examples of skeletons buried either without the head or with the decapitated head placed elsewhere in the grave, a trait that has tended to be taken to indicate human sacrifice or capital punishment although interpretation is very difficult (Davidson 1992). A group of graves to the east of the burial mounds at Sutton Hoo may be the victims of sacrifice in the seventh and eighth centuries (Carver 1992a: 353–5). They were characterised by unusual body position, being prone, kneeling, flexed and extended, some having had their wrists and ankles tied, some beheaded or the neck broken. Carver has suggested that the graves represent human sacrifices in a ritual area contemporary with the mounds.

Other graves are thought to belong to individuals who were buried alive. At Sewerby (Yorkshire) the burial of a contorted elderly woman above another burial suggested an execution for, perhaps, witchcraft (Hirst 1985, 1993). At Worthy Park (Hampshire) one grave was of a woman lying on her back, her face crushed against the side of the grave, arms bent behind the chest, knees bent to the left with the feet together. The unaccompanied 16-year-old in another grave was in a similar position and osteological examination suggested that she had been raped (Hawkes and Wells 1975).

There are a number of graves of women buried with, amongst other items, miniature buckets, or bucket pendants, which may have been contained in leather bags. One example from Bidford-on-Avon that has been discussed in detail (Dickinson 1993b) was accompanied by a bag at the hip containing rings, an antler cone and a metal stud. Such graves may be those of women with special powers in 'beneficent magic, healing, protecting and divining the future' (Dickinson 1993b: 52; Meaney 1981: 249–62). If that is true such graves not only provide us with an unusual identity but also inform us of the nature of belief.

Another means by which pagan Anglo-Saxon beliefs might be identified and better understood is by determining those aspects that were transferred to a Christian milieu following the conversion and those that became redundant. Unfortunately this suggestion is tinged with optimism; it is, for instance, arguably impossible to distinguish a pagan from a Christian grave, it is difficult even to define the contemporary Christian 'norm', and even when a grave might be ascribed to one of those notional categories it tells us little about the actual beliefs held by the interred person or the mourners. Much of our knowledge of the conversion of England is contained within Bede's *Ecclesiastical History of the English People* and the *Anglo-Saxon Chronicle*, in which the progress of missionaries and the conversion of leaders is documented, however accurately. The written sources provide the only framework for the conversion to Christianity and dependence on it is a cause for concern. It is difficult for archaeology to provide such a framework when it is unclear which material correlates are relevant. The missionaries appear to have followed a policy of converting the head of a socio-political group which was often effective and may have been carried out in the hope of freedom and material benefit. How long it took the remainder of the population to convert is less clear. There quickly developed a juxtaposition of the earthly with the spiritual lord from which much else flowed. In the absence of a concept of the Church, the newly converted may have seen themselves as a spiritual family with a heavenly lord; in this way the conversion operated through existing political and social frameworks with an earthly world mirroring the heavenly (Gilchrist and Morris 1993: 113). Religious milieu developed close to royal palaces. London was a bishop's see from AD 604 and Kentish kings had a hall there by AD 675 (Biddle 1976: 116). Paulinus was bishop of York in 627 and it was also a royal and mercantile centre (Addyman 1977: 500). The same pattern is found at Canterbury, Winchester, Hereford and Worcester.

The Church became involved in trade and exchange, even minting coin. The very nature of kingship may have changed as a result of the introduction of new models following the conversion along with changes in attitudes to wealth and ownership. Such massive developments may lie behind changes in cemeteries and settlements as well as the appearance of emporia. If we understood the nature of early Christian communities we might learn more about the structure of earlier Anglo-Saxon society. There may have been a tension between pagans and newly converted Christians illustrated by the competitive monumentality in the juxtaposition of pagan burial mounds and early churches (van de Noort 1993), but in reality we do not know how long it took for the conversion to Christianity to have an effect on burial practice; hence a statement was being made but there are a number of alternatives for what that statement actually was. Bede tells us of the burial of royalty in major churches in the seventh century such as that of King Aethelberht and Queen Bertha in the church of SS Peter and Paul in Canterbury. No such grave has been excavated intact under anything approaching controlled archaeological conditions.

Attempts have been made to chart the conversion to Christianity through late, or 'Final Phase', cemeteries, but the problem is that graves without grave-goods oriented west–east, and which might be accepted as Christian after a notional date in the seventh century, are also known before that date (Boddington 1990; Geake 1992: 84–5). The reduction in the number of grave-goods during the seventh century might be seen as the result of Christian influences but given that the reduction does not appear to be uniform (Härke 1992a) there must be other factors in operation. The question of the development of churchyard burial is therefore very difficult as factors that applied to the definition of Christian burial often apply equally to pagan ones, and elements of pagan ritual may have persisted many generations after a nominal conversion to Christianity.

It is suggested that in England during the late seventh and early eighth centuries, cemeteries were abandoned in favour of new sites and that such secondary, and possibly Christian, cemeteries were subsequently abandoned in preference for a graveyard that would lie within a Christian community (Hyslop 1963; Meaney and Hawkes 1970). Whether the mobility of the cemeteries was matched by that of the settlements, or whether a Christian village with its churchyard might be expected to overlie its pagan predecessor, is rarely discussed although Baldwin Brown argued that the graveyard would owe its existence to the presence of a secular church (1903: 262–3). The archaeological evidence suggests that the majority of pagan cemeteries were adjacent to their settlements, although artefacts deemed to be suitable to a pre-Christian context have been recovered within churchyards and later villages, albeit relatively rarely. It is also apparent that pagan cemeteries are more stable, locationally, than the nuclei of their contemporary settlements. A change in the location of a cemetery might, therefore, indicate a change in attitude to the distance that was deemed appropriate between settlement and cemetery. The number of possible permutations between pagan cemetery,

Christian cemetery and churchyard on the one hand, and 'pagan' and Christian settlements on the other is quite large. The present weakness of the argument is that cemeteries are being linked to belief which in turn is linked to settlement pattern when in most cases only the locations of the cemeteries are known.

It should be noted that the basis for distinguishing between a pagan and a Christian cemetery is merely the presence and absence of grave-goods. This distinction gives rise to many problems; unaccompanied graves in cemeteries where grave-goods are present are interpreted as the pagan 'poor', slaves or other persona, whereas graves in cemeteries with no grave-goods are Christian (identity indeterminable) and graves within graveyards, even with grave-goods, are Christian. Such assumptions may greatly mislead and the dangers are the same as those that arise when using the orientation of graves as a guide to belief, as pointed out by Rahtz (1978).

Christian influence might be seen in a limited number of grave-goods in seventh-century cemeteries. Overt Christian symbolism is seen in crosses such as the gold pectoral cross from Desborough (Northamptonshire). Crosses of varying sizes and degrees of elaboration are known from Durham to Kent (Åberg 1926; Meaney and Hawkes 1970: 54–5) although their overall number is small. That from Winster Common (Derbyshire) is an equal-armed pendant with a central garnet. The arms are decorated with rows of filigree in scroll patterns. A cross from Wilton (Wiltshire) is also decorated with filigree. Others reflect the jewellery traditions of East Anglia and Kent in their use of garnet-filled cloisons, such as the cross of St Cuthbert (d. 687) found among other relics in his coffin at Durham. There is also Christian symbolism on some of the grave-goods of Sutton Hoo mound I, for instance the two silver spoons inscribed with the name of the Apostle Paul (Figure 6.10), possibly baptismal spoons, and the five pairs of silver

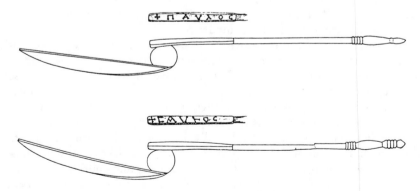

Figure 6.10 Pair of silver spoons from Sutton Hoo mound I (source: Werner 1992, Figure 2B)

dishes which may be connected with a Eucharist meal (Werner 1992). As well as the influence of Christianity (irrespective of the beliefs of the owners of such objects), we are witnessing the connections between secular kingdoms extending to the Church. Royal patronage now includes the Church and patterns of emulation and competition developed within it.

The process of conversion should not automatically be expected to reveal itself in the material manifestation of religious activity. The subject should not be treated as though a limited number of models are favourable when the factors determining the location of pre-Christian and Christian cemeteries and settlements will be varied and numerous (Morris 1983). Despite this, the study of the latest 'pagan' Anglo-Saxon graves and cemeteries has introduced a seemingly strong argument regarding the conversion to Christianity. The example of Sancton is instructive (Faull 1976). A large downland cremation cemetery (Figure 6.11) was in use there during the fifth and sixth centuries (Myres and Southern 1973; Timby 1993). Its size, like that of a number of cremation cemeteries in eastern and midland England, suggests that it was a centralised crematorium serving a wide geographical area. In the sixth century a smaller and predominantly inhumation cemetery came into existence close to the present village in the valley bottom and which Faull suggests was for the 'local Sancton settlement'. This second cemetery, Sancton II, is adjacent to the medieval churchyard, which might suggest that one was a continuation of the other. In neither case is the location of the contemporary settlement known. Another example is Barton-on-Humber where a seventh-century pagan cemetery might be seen as having been replaced by a cemetery that stood outside an enclosure 300 m away in the middle-Saxon period. In the tenth century a church was built inside that cemetery (Rodwell 1984: 17–18). We may note that, again, the location of the settlement contemporary with the seventh-century cemetery is not known. The limited study of middle-Saxon settlements, and especially the manner in which beliefs about nucleation and stability of settlement have come under attack (Foard 1978; Taylor 1977, 1978; Hamerow 1991), should encourage caution in the search for uniform models.

'Double cemeteries' are those where an earlier one, often large and with greater numbers of grave-goods, overlaps with or is superseded by a nearby smaller example [why smaller?] with fewer grave-goods (examples discussed by Morris 1983: 54 ff.; Boddington 1990; Geake 1992). There are problems with the study of this configuration: there is for instance uncertainty about whether such changing patterns reflect belief and/or an ongoing shift, failure or multiplication of settlements. Equally it is generally assumed that the reduction in the volume of grave-goods is largely a factor of a wholesale change in religious beliefs, whereas social and economic considerations may be as pertinent (Arnold 1982b). Warnings about relying too heavily on belief and ignoring the relationship between belief and material culture have been given by Morris (1983: 54):

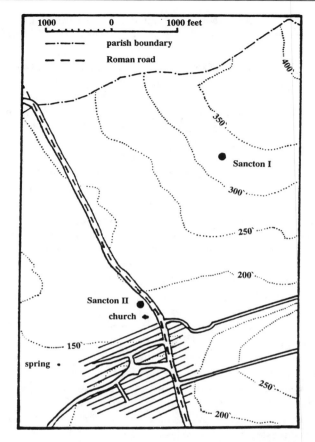

Figure 6.11 The spatial relationship between Anglo-Saxon cemeteries at Sancton, Humberside (source: Faull 1977, Figure 1)

There is virtually no archaeological evidence to confirm that cemeteries like Winnall II [Hampshire] or Polhill [Kent] were being operated under Christian influence, or that the material culture displayed within them was in any way due to the impact of Christian ideas.

Obviously what is not in doubt is that the conversion to Christianity did eventually take place, but the process and its material correlates are far from clear. Morris (ibid.: 59–62), concerned about the dangers of seeking all-embracing explanations, has listed those medieval churchyards that appear to be located wholly or partly over pagan cemeteries. While the number may be larger than the examples of so-called 'Final Phase' cemeteries, it still needs to be demonstrated that this coincidence is significant in terms of the conversion and is not a factor of statistical probability given changing settlement location preferences and the multiplication of settlement *loci* (ibid.: 62).

The difficulties in determining the nature of pagan Anglo-Saxon belief systems is the same as with overtly Christian evidence; it is because there is always a wide range of factors determining the form of religious activity and belief, especially when it may not be appropriate to divorce them so forcefully from domestic life, that doubt can always be cast on our conclusions. There is no evidence that the Christian Church continued to function in south-east England beyond the period AD 425–50, at least not in a form that we can recognise or one that later commentators would have wished to have recognised. It remains a possibility that throughout the sixth century some interest in cult sites was maintained, or that they remained sufficiently identifiable, to act as foci for later churches (Rodwell 1984).

At the time of Augustine's mission to England in AD 597 British churches already existed. Nearly 100 seventh-century churches are known, mostly from written evidence, and therefore the number of complete plans is very small, among them being those at Yeavering (Hope-Taylor 1977) and Winchester (Kjølbye-Biddle 1986) (Figure 6.12). The first church at Winchester, later called the Old Minster, was built for King Cenwalh of Wessex in *c.* 648 and comprised a nave 22 m in length with adjoining *porticus* to the north, south and east. The timber structure at Yeavering had a rectangular plan with an entrance in each wall and an annexe added to the west wall. The building stood within a cemetery and close to the fence around a Christian graveyard. Such evidence is rare because the robust continuity of Christian sites 'militates against chances of excavation' (Thomas 1986: 123).

The important early churches were sited in a limited range of locations. They have been listed by Morris (1983: 40). Ease of communication may have been an important consideration and, even allowing for bias in the written sources, it appears that many churches were established either at centres of royal authority or in juxtaposition to them. Canterbury, for example, was a royal *civitas* in Bede's eyes. It appears to have been the usual practice to found churches at royal centres in the seventh and eighth centuries and this led to the pattern of minsters at royal *tun*. Such developments aimed to coalesce royal and ecclesiastical authority in a physical form possibly because the pattern of secular power was rarely static. By 601 Gregory had decided to designate London and York as the metropolitan sees of Britain. Re-use of Roman churches is known in Canterbury and has been argued for at London (Rodwell 1993), perhaps as part of a religious complex associated with a royal palace.

As power was often divided between various members of a royal family, acting as sub-kings to an overlord, there was considerable scope for the proliferation of churches. To some extent the distribution of churches in the seventh century may reflect the centres of spiritual and secular power and

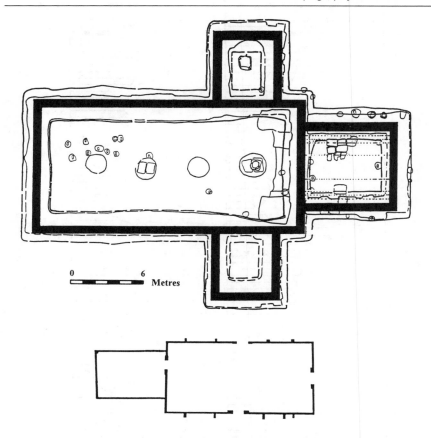

Figure 6.12 Plans of the stone Old Minster, Winchester, Hampshire (reconstructed) (source: Kjølbye-Biddle 1986, Figure 136) and of the putative timber
church at Yeavering, Northumberland (source: Hope-Taylor 1977)

wealth (Figure 6.13). The early dioceses reflected kingdoms and kingship and
their centres were generally areas of concentrations of pagan Anglo-Saxon
cemeteries as might be expected. The fact that a majority of churches were
established in former Roman towns suggests a greater concern for 'pastoral
and political factors' (Biddle 1976: 119) than for concern with the past.

The connection between Christianity and kingship is hardly surprising
when missionaries and bishops could only operate with the support of secular
leaders. It was the royalty and nobility who provided the land and resources
necessary for the erection and maintenance of ecclesiastical centres. Thus
Morris suggests that 'the mechanisms that enabled the spread and consolidation of Christianity in the 7th century were basically political' (1983: 46),
and he cites numerous examples and the various forms which this associa-

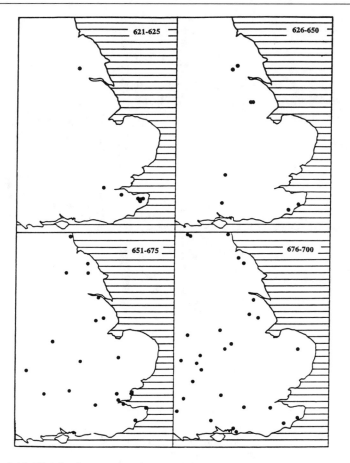

Figure 6.13 Distribution maps of seventh-century English church foundations in four chronological phases (data: Morris 1983)

tion could take. Naturally this begs the question of why secular leaders were prepared to accept the new religion. Were they already sympathetic? Were they swayed by the power of the argument? Was there a material benefit in acceptance?

Little recorded building took place in England prior to AD 650 (Figure 6.13) and that which did is confined to Kent, with lesser efforts in East Anglia and Wessex. There was a short and premature flurry of activity in Deira in the 620s, and in Northumbria there was an almost continuous building programme from the middle of the century. It was in the 670s and 680s that most church building activity was taking place, possibly during a period of relative peace and stability after the turbulence that had characterised the preceding decades. The turbulence took the form of warfare between kingdoms, normally aimed at the acquisition of territory. In the middle years of the seventh century Northumbria is recorded as having fought seven wars while playing a major role, according to Bede, in the process of conversion. The lull in warfare during the second half of the seventh century provided an environment in which nine sees could be founded in twenty-five years, compared with seven during the previous fifty years, many of them in areas of Mercia or Mercian political influence. Mercia also led the field in the establishment of monastic sites.

The important aspect is the manner in which the protection of people's souls and the spread of Christian belief went hand-in-hand with commerce and administration. Some centres may have earlier, albeit presently obscure, origins given the sixth-century burials in Northampton, Worcester and St Paul-in-the-Bail, Lincoln. While the important royal and ecclesiastical centres, and what may be subordinate royal seats, played a major role in founding a structure for Christian worship, we know far less about its organisation and, indeed, about the buildings themselves. About ninety churches are known from this formative period, but few have been excavated by archaeologists. The putative church at Yeavering (Figure 6.12) could easily be translated to a rural settlement and look at home because its plan is very similar to that of domestic buildings. An unexcavated rectangular timber building with what may be an eastern 'apse' stands at the centre of a small enclosure on the edge of a settlement at Foxley, Wiltshire (Figure 8.4); it is only the rounded end of its 'annex' that distinguishes it from other buildings there (Hinchliffe 1986). The same layout is to be found at St Paul-in-the-Bail, but there remains doubt about the dating of the first two phases. There remain many questions about the origins of church form in England but the similarity between 'halls' with rectangular annexes and a simple church with chancel cannot be a coincidence. Similarly it required only a slight transformation to convert a rectangular domestic building into what may be a church with an eastern apse (Figures 3.6, 6.12, 8.4). The evidence we have warns of the difficulties in identifying early timber churches, in particular distinguishing them from domestic structures.

The dates given in the written sources for the first conversion of kingdoms, ignoring the possibilities of biased reporting and the relapses into paganism, offer an indication of the topography of the conversion of England. The known foundation dates of seventh-century churches in England, when plotted in twenty-five-year periods (Figure 6.13), show a pattern of early churches in Kent followed by a rapid extension along the east coast. During the period AD 651–75 there was a multiplication of churches in these areas, as well as a gradual expansion westwards.

Competition between kings will have influenced their willingness to embrace Christianity. While some may have resisted and gained support and other advantages for their conservative beliefs, patronage of the Church

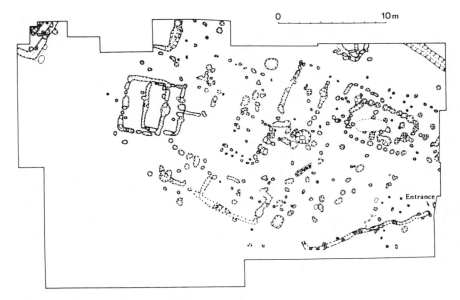

Figure 6.14 Plan of part of the monastery at Hartlepool, Cleveland (source: Daniels 1988, Figure 2)

became entwined with the structures of secular life. This is clearly reflected in the foundation of monasteries which were signals both of some kings' imperial ambitions as well as those of the Church; the flag may well follow trade but in these circumstances the Church often intervened, being intimately involved in the minting of coin in the seventh century and the development of emporia (Webb 1975). We know of the existence of a number of monasteries but, like the churches, few have been investigated (Cramp 1976). Burgh Castle was an Irish missionary station (Johnson *et al.* 1983), Whitby was a double house for men and women and Monkwearmouth and Jarrow were set up in the Northumbrian kingdom using glaziers and masons brought from Gaul. It is the Northumbrian monasteries that have received the most archaeological attention. Hartlepool was founded in the 640s and excavations have revealed a layout of small timber buildings (Figure 6.14) that would not have looked out of place on a rural farm (Daniels 1988); indeed, we might ask on what basis they can be said to be part of a monastery. Whitby was founded in 657 and while the excavated remains are confused (Johnson 1993) there is a strong possibility that the stone buildings were preceded by timber ones as at Hartlepool. Work on Wearmouth was begun in 674 by a Northumbrian aristocrat, Benedict Biscop, and Jarrow was founded in 681. Both benefited from donations of land from King Ecgfrith.

It may be relatively easy to carry out an investigation of churches as build-ings, but whether we consider paganism or Christianity, it is harder to see the workings and activities of such religions. It is also difficult to determine the effects of Christianity on people and to appreciate the extent to which pre-Christian beliefs remained popular during the seventh century and later. It is one thing to view the conversion of royalty and the construction of churches, but an altogether different matter to view the religious activity of the remainder of the population. The written sources cannot be accepted uncritically as there was more in the activity of missionaries than the mere saving of souls. The archaeological evidence suggests a very close alliance between secular and ecclesiastical power and that as a popular religion Christianity, in the form envisaged by contemporary written sources, may have taken many years to develop.

Chapter 7

Mighty kinfolk

IDENTITY AND STATUS

A man's status in English society has always depended primarily on his own consciousness; for the English are not a methodical or logical nation – they perceive and accept facts without anxiously inquiring into their reasons or meanings. Whatever is apt to raise a man's self-consciousness – be it birth, rank, wealth, intellect, daring or achievements – will add to his stature; but it has to be translated into the truest expression of one's sub-conscious self-evaluation: uncontending ease, the unbought grace of life.

(Namier 1930: 15)

Archaeologists' attempts to explore social identity through archaeological evidence may seem crude in comparison with the depths of investigation of modern sociologists and anthropologists. This is in part because the very nature of the evidence limits the questions that can be asked. However, the sophistication of the theory and the methods used is increasing and holds great promise.

The subject of the social organisation of human communities began to be studied in detail by archaeologists from the beginning of the 1970s. Much of that early research was carried out using prehistoric data, but the rich data from the early Anglo-Saxon period has encouraged wide-ranging investigation at both a theoretical and a practical level. This has grown considerably in its sophistication aided by the availability of high quality, accessible data, and the increasing use of computers to manipulate that data. Historians of the Anglo-Saxon period have also tackled the subject and, given that among the principal sources are the earliest law-codes and regnal lists, have been predominantly concerned with the origins of institutions. For the archaeologist, interest has been in the social organisation of society at all levels, the expression of individual identity, how individuals may have formed a hierarchy, the structure of communities and the formation of the kingdoms.

The social structure of early Anglo-Saxon England is a subject that was originally confined to historians and social anthropologists. They depended on limited amounts of written evidence, particularly the laws and the charters, which are frequently difficult to reconcile with each other (Chadwick 1905; Seebohm 1911; Bullough 1965). Information regarding early Anglo-Saxon social structure has often been extrapolated from these documents that all tend to belong to the latter half of the period or even later. The view has been expressed that the task is made more difficult because much of the earlier structure of society may have been suppressed by the power of later lordship and Christian kingship (Loyn 1974: 209). From the later laws it emerges that there were a number of classes of person, ranging from the slave (*theow*) to the governor of the shire (*ealdorman*), and including unfree or half-free cottagers (the *ceorl*), freedmen occupying farms and rent-paying tenants (*gafolgelda*), and also the free farmer (*frigman*) and landed nobleman (*gesith*). It is notable that in this hierarchical representation of society distinctions were sometimes made in terms of property holding and at other times status was reflected in the fines paid by each class for specific crimes. Hence it belongs to a period when systems for the ownership of land with fixed boundaries had been established, something that, as we have seen, occurred late in the period under consideration. The written evidence provides one of the major hypotheses derived from the written sources that may be testable by archaeology, but it must be tested using appropriate data.

Studies of kinship in Anglo-Saxon society using the written sources (Lancaster 1958; Loyn 1974) suggest that society was seen as being descended from a common ancestor and was non-unilineal. The limits of the kin group are not given in the sources, probably because it was common knowledge and unquestionably adhered to. It is not possible to discern the patterns of residence, but there are hints of a predominantly virilocal system. Anglo-Saxon poetry suggests that emotional identification with the kin was very close. The system, however, was by no means rigid and the circle of effective kin small. A lack of descent groups is thought to be probable despite the patrilateral bias.

The laws, charters and poetry allow such generalisations to be made. Yet they remain very distant from the nature of the archaeological data for the period, notably the settlements and cemeteries. During the period prior to the laws being written down, the greatest resource must be the 26,000-plus Anglo-Saxon graves that have been excavated. These may be examined through their orientation, the character of the grave and the interment. Much of the early work assumed a direct relationship between the relative wealth of the grave-goods and the status of certain individuals, a theory that was then applied more rigorously to a larger sample of graves and incorporating a broader spectrum of variables. More recently the emphasis has moved towards defining the manner in which the identity of individuals was expressed after a person's death and how such individuals may have fitted into a hierarchy of identities. A number of writers have attempted to integrate the written and archaeological data. Alcock (1981) has compared the range of grave-goods in Northumbrian male graves with a three-fold division of society based on the documentary evidence for noble-warriors (*thegns*), free warriors (*ceorls*) and the unfree. The graves were graded into three classes on the basis of their weaponry and then each 'class' was labelled. As we have seen, the written sources suggest that early Anglo-Saxon society was more complex than this. The method overlooked the potential for greater subtlety in the other grave-goods present, ignored the role of age and assumed contemporaneity in the two sources of data. Similar approaches have been taken by Hawkes (1982) and Welch (1992).

The earliest approaches to variation in early Anglo-Saxon grave form were ethno-historical (Leeds 1913: 26) and while individual variables such as grave orientation have been considered (Russell 1976; Faull 1977: 5–8; Wells and Green 1973; Hawkes 1977; Rahtz 1978) it is classes of object that aroused most comment (see for instance: Davidson 1962: 9–11; Chadwick 1958: 32; Hawkes 1973: 145). Such a statement as 'a very rich grave may give an idea of the social structure . . . of a particular person' (Wilson 1976a: 3), while not necessarily false, serves to emphasise how status was being defined on the basis of the quantity and quality of grave-goods rather than the particular combination, and also demonstrates how such observations tended to be limited to those graves with status-related grave-goods overlooking the majority of graves that either had no grave-goods or were not especially rich. This was a logical step forward after many years of treating graves as sources for the study of particular types of grave-good or, at best, the study of noteworthy associations of artefacts in individual graves, or 'grave-groups'. During the 1970s the principle that the quantity of grave-goods reflected an individual's relative status was applied to larger samples of graves, albeit with the same shortcomings (Arnold 1980). The use of the computer in cemetery studies made it possible to examine larger samples of graves and a larger number of variables and hence it has become possible to be more certain about common identities within regions. Hence it remains difficult to determine the significance of the identities defined by archaeologists. They may signify the identity of the person during their lifetime (e.g. age, sex, gender, family, region, role). Alternatively the identity may have been given to the person after death for more emotional reasons by mourners. Similarly there are problems in applying labels to such identities and in defining the relationship between particular identities.

The form of a burial may reflect a person's life, their relationship to other people, the perceptions of mourners and ritual in varying degrees and combinations. It is difficult to determine which is most relevant. It is therefore most appropriate to examine cemeteries as an expression of how society perceived itself rather than precisely how it was. It is the psyche of the society that is perhaps most reflected through the patterns of behaviour of those responsible for funerals.

The problems of using burials to reconstruct social organisation extends beyond those of mortuary ritual. As Richards has observed if 'material culture does not merely passively reflect social relations, but is actively used to articulate them, a simple relationship between artefacts and social status is denied', and therefore 'we cannot assume that status is directly mirrored in the wealth of grave-goods, and by assigning "wealth scores" to artefacts arrive at the hierarchical structure of society' (1984: 42). It will remain difficult to demonstrate, except in unusual cases, that the form of a grave does reflect social identity, but the study of large numbers of graves does allow recurring combinations of grave-goods to be highlighted and examined for their possible significance.

Early Anglo-Saxon society, like any human society, was made up of individuals between whom there were varying real and perceived relationships, both within the family and outside it. The basis for defining individual identity may have been drawn from many possible factors, some of which may not be visible. Indeed, while individuals are visible any sense of self is obscured except in as much as physical attributes of the individual were acknowledged by society. Such individuals would have had membership of a variety of groups, a strong sense of identity arising from the lineage group, and perhaps a weaker sense of identity with the region or tribe and eventually the kingdom. At all levels there would have been a hierarchy of individuals based on degrees of power. Scull (1993) has modelled the dynamics of descent within a settlement and the manner in which such settlements may have become associated with larger territorial and political units (Figure 7.1) albeit from an evolutionary perspective. Descent groups within settlements acquired senior status by economic superiority, ultimately based on agricultural surplus, and marriage. This would gradually be projected outwards amongst groups of settlements to create local socio-political groups under the leadership of the most dominant descent group, and finally the process of fusion would extend to formal administrative units, or kingdoms. Social identities would have operated at different levels and would have had to adapt to the growth of the entities to which an individual belonged.

Such levels of membership may also be encoded within the design and decoration of ornamental metalwork. By this method the combination of elements could say much about the person depending on how close the viewer was. For example, at a distance it would be possible to identify the shape of a brooch, closer the generalities of the decoration would be apparent, and closer still – when the viewer had entered the wearer's personal space – the details (Figure 7.2). Each level of detail may have informed about the tribal, regional and family origins of the individual. The movement of such female associated items would have been increased through marriage in a patrilocal structure. In a similar way Norwegian women continue to have a set of silver jewellery and traditional costume made for their marriage that symbolises, at least, which area of the country they come from. Women may have been married to distant groups in forging alliances resulting in the occasional movement of ornamental metalwork some distance from the regions

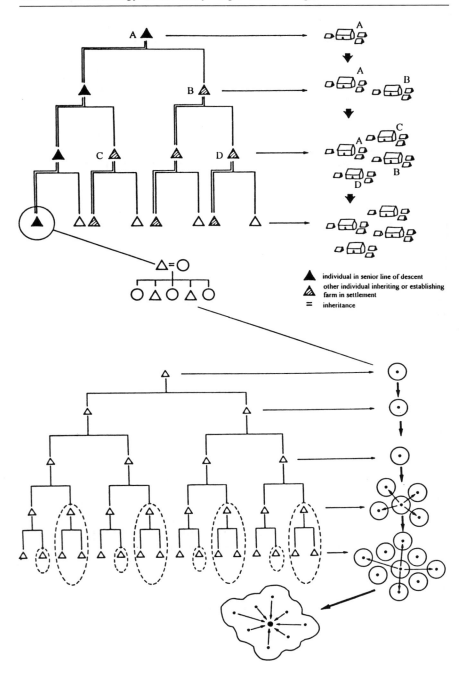

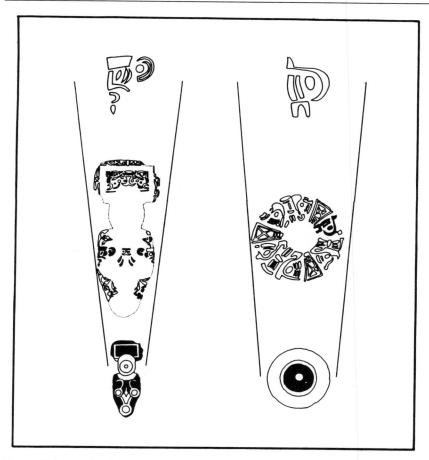

Figure 7.2 Levels of information conveyed by brooches with distance

where it is most commonly found, the core area of a social grouping. Depending on the rules governing such customs some identities may have been exported in marriage while other individuals may have had to adopt an identity appropriate to their new locality.

Figure 7.1 (left) Model of the relationship between descent and structure on a rural settlement and its potential role in the development of political units (source: Scull 1993, Figures 2 and 4). A dominant family remains pre-eminent as the kin-group and settlement expands. In time that élite family takes its place in a network of such families who compete for control of neighbouring territories and their populations

Studies of the inhumation and cremation graves within Anglo-Saxon cemeteries have demonstrated in a variety of ways the manner in which identity, at a variety of levels, may be symbolised. Despite the very large number of excavated graves, much of the data was collected in the last century and either classes of data are missing or the samples are too small for significant relationships to be demonstrated. There is no standard method of analysing cemetery data and while the various methods that have been used produce patterns their significance and interpretation present problems. Few of the techniques could be considered neutral.

THE INDIVIDUAL

That there were preferred combinations of grave-goods is not in doubt and has been known for some time. The study of eight predominantly inhumation cemeteries in southern England using a monothetic divisive technique (Arnold 1980), a measure of the gregariousness of types of grave-good, clearly revealed that there is some significance to grave-good combinations both within cemeteries and over larger regions. Very common objects such as knives and buckles were omitted as they cause a high number of small subdivisions, although this should in no way imply that they are insignificant. Table 7.1 summarises the results of the analysis of four cemeteries.

The technique divides the individuals into principal clusters based on their sex. A number of combinations comprising up to two artefacts are found to be common to a number of the cemeteries. Where unique combinations are found it is usually the result of particular types of grave-goods being found commonly at only one of the four cemeteries, particularly with female graves; pins at Long Wittenham and tweezers at Chessell Down are cases in point. This emphasises how there is more variety in female possessions than male. Tweezers at Chessell Down are most strongly associated with females, yet at Long Wittenham they are accompanied by spears, not usually associated with women. Keys, beads and brooches are as strongly associated with females as weaponry is with males. There are certain combinations that are peculiar to Sarre and Chessell Down, hinting at connections between these, relatively, distant locations.

The strong association between particular grave-goods and the individual's sex has been demonstrated statistically in a study based on twelve cemeteries in the southern Midlands (Huggett 1992). The analysis of the cemetery at Abingdon, Berkshire (Huggett 1995), showed that spears and beads were the most diagnostic artefacts although it was found that on occasion single grave-goods that had strong links with one sex were buried with a member of the opposite sex, albeit in small numbers. Cluster analysis of the graves generated a number of groups whose membership was largely single-sex. Similar success in distinguishing the sex of individuals through grave-goods was had with a cemetery at Sleaford (Brenan 1985).

Table 7.1 Comparison of monothetic divisive groupings of grave-goods in four early Anglo-Saxon cemeteries (upper, female; lower, male)

Object combination	Sarre, Kent	Long Wittenham, Berkshire	Alfriston, Sussex	Chessell Down, Isle of Wight
brooch	*	*	*	*
beads	*	*	*	*
beads/brooch	*	*	*	*
pin	*	*		
key	*		*	
beads/pin	*	*		
brooch/key		*	*	
brooch/pin		*	*	
brooch/beads/pin		*		*
beads/key/brooch	*	*		
brooch/beads/chatelaine			*	
brooch/beads/pin/tweezers				*
beads/chatelaine			*	
tweezers				*
brooch/tweezers				*
brooch/ball/spoon				*
beads/key	*			
sword	*	*	*	*
spear/shield	*	*	*	*
spear	*	*	*	*
shield	*		*	*
shield/sword	*		*	
shield/spear/sword	*			*
shield/spear/sword/bucket	*			*
spear/shield/bucket		*		*
spear/sword			*	*
spear/tweezers		*		
spear/key		*		
shield/sword/bucket			*	
spear/bucket			*	
spear/pottery			*	
spear/brooch	*			
shield/beads	*			
pottery			*	

The sex of the individual is the first-order factor determining such choices, although this hardly informs about the relations between the sexes or such things as the division of labour (Brush 1988). Age is the second factor. Certain grave-goods are found to have been appropriate for individuals of a particular sex and who had passed a certain age, although the types vary on a regional and cemetery basis. At Holywell Row (Table 7.2) four classes of object were found only with females, irrespective of their age, whereas with

Table 7.2 Relationship between attributes of graves at Holywell Row, Suffolk

Object/Skeletal Position	Sex	Age
brooch	F	NS
implement-holder	F	NS
beads	F	NS
sleeve-fastener	F	NS
knife	NS	ADULT/CHILD
belt	M>F	NS
vessel	M>F	NS
spear	M	ADULT/CHILD
shield	M	ADULT
extended skeleton	NS	ADULT/CHILD
flexed skeleton	F>M	CHILD/ADULT

Note: M = male, F = female, NS = not significant
Source: Pader 1980

males only the shield and spear were linked with men; only the shield was found specifically with one age group. Knives were found with men and women, especially with adults. Either there was the least restriction in the selection of grave-goods for women or there was a wider variety of types to choose from. The flexed skeleton position was primarily a female attribute.

At the cemetery of Westgarth Gardens, Bury St Edmunds, the choice of artefacts was more strongly constrained by the age of the individuals. Particular objects and skeletal position were both strongly associated with age and/or sex. In addition, spatial position within the cemetery was found to account for the presence or absence of certain grave-goods and their position within the grave was linked to skeletal position. Comparison of female graves in two areas of the cemetery showed clear differences (Table 7.3). Similar differences were found with the male graves; in one area knives and buckles were always on the left and all other grave-goods at the head, usually to the left. Elsewhere in the cemetery spears were found on the right and shield bosses by the feet or on the chest.

Table 7.3 Differences in the position of grave-goods in female graves in the cemetery of Westgarth Gardens, Bury St Edmunds, Suffolk

Sector	Knife and implement-holder	Shoulder ornament	Sleeve-fastener
1	right	left and right or just left	flexed – yes extended – no
2	left	left, right and centre	no

Source: Pader 1980

The patterns observed in these Suffolk cemeteries suggest that there 'is a closer relationship between females and children than between adult males and either adult females or children' (Pader 1980: 155). As young children had items that they must have been given, it seems more likely that they indicate ascribed status. Pader feels that it could also indicate achieved status. It was suggested that the burial programme related to an 'attitude' towards children as a group and did not necessarily represent the distribution of their own power or wealth so much as reflect the adult situation. The most obvious conclusion that emerges from the study, and all others, is that the sex of the individual is strongly reflected in the accompanying grave-goods, when they are present. Furthermore, females were often buried with a greater number of grave-goods which represents another means by which the 'principles governing the different social positions of males and females are emphasised' (ibid.: 156). In Huggett's study of the cemetery at Abingdon cluster analysis produced groups that were either adult, of mixed ages, or infants. The position of the body in the grave did not appear to be age-related (Huggett 1995). At Norton (Sherlock and Welch 1992) the number of objects placed in the graves clearly discriminated against the young (Figure 7.7).

Analysis of age-related features may be distorted because of the rarity of infant burial in cemeteries (Crawford 1993). The evidence suggests that infants were treated differently from adults by either not being included in the adult cemetery and being disposed of in an archaeologically invisible manner, or perhaps being buried in a casual manner, for instance in a shallow grave. It is possible that infanticide was practised but there is nothing to suggest that this was determined by the sex of the individual. When infants are included in the cemetery they tend either to be buried with adults or their grave is in some way unusual. This was achieved by using a different orientation, burial under a small cairn or burial with amuletic grave-goods. As some adults are buried in the same manner, Crawford suggests that the choice of grave-form has more to do with the manner of death than with an age-related ritual. One indication of attitudes towards children is revealed by the fact that adult males who were at death accorded the rite of weapon burial had above average stature, possibly because of a better diet. Yet this appears to be contradicted by the incidence of hypoplasia, a tooth defect caused by starvation or illness, which was the same in those with weapon burials as those without (Härke 1990: 38). Perhaps this warns against simplification of the complex inter-relationship between specific and general factors. The high mortality rate amongst children may have given rise to considerable superstition.

The analysis and comparison of two cremation cemeteries in eastern England, Spong Hill and Elsham (Richards 1984, 1987), revealed similar patterns albeit through different media. The factors that can be considered are urn size, shape and decoration, as well as the grave-goods and the sex and age of the individual where that can be ascertained. Choices were clearly being

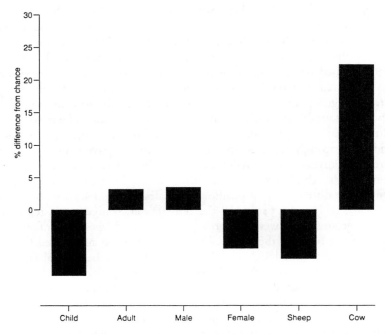

Figure 7.3 The relationship between plastic decoration on cremation urns and other factors. The bar-chart indicates the percentage difference from chance for age, sex, cows and sheep (source: Richards 1992, Figure 23)

made to create appropriate funerals for particular identity groups and some were more heavily symbolised than others. At each cemetery, groups marked by the presence of toilet sets and 'male' groups were distinguished both in the form and decoration of the urns. However, only a few types of urn decoration indicate 'femaleness', which is never reflected in urn form. The female grave-goods are the direct equivalent of those found in inhumations. However, toilet sets and the male grave-goods found in cremations occur less frequently in inhumations, and the male symbolism was more highly developed in the elaboration of pot form and decoration. These basic social identities were treated differently in cremations; it may be that the obvious difficulties of incorporating large and heavy weaponry in men's cremation urns resulted in over-compensation in other areas where symbolism was possible. In the same way, the lower degree of distinctiveness in female urns may be the result of the symbolism being overt in the grave-goods.

In a selected analysis Richards examined the significance of cremation pottery shape. Certain decorative motifs were found to be more appropriate to certain shapes, at times running counter to the supposed chronology. Similarly, certain grave-goods are found more commonly in certain shaped

Figure 7.4 Comparison of decoration on cremation urns and annular brooches from Spong Hill, Norfolk (sources: Hills and Rickett 1981, Figure 108; Hills, Penn and Rickett 1984, Figures 74 and 85; Richards 1992)

vessels, and a social explanation is favoured. The choice of plastic decoration, especially vertical bosses, is more strongly associated with adults than children, men rather than women, and the bones of cows rather than sheep (Figure 7.3). By contrast, incised hanging arches are linked with female children. Richards has also noted a link between the decoration on urns and that on the grave-goods found inside (Figure 7.4), demonstrating how the coded message could be transferred from one medium to another, and from life to death (Richards 1992). The grave-goods and vessels reflect the age, sex or other identity of the deceased, and there was a collective conception of the urn form that was most appropriate for a person from a particular social milieu. Some of the correlations were found at both of the cremation cemeteries studied, others at only one, suggesting that there was an 'Anglian culture' as well as local funerary symbolism.

There were clearly rules governing the age at which individuals might acquire particular objects thereby symbolising their maturity. Late adolescent and adult males were provided with shields and swords (Dickinson and Härke 1992: 68–9) and access to saucer brooches amongst females generally occurred at the same age, 'perhaps at betrothal or marriage' (Dickinson 1993a: 38–9). The analysis of a cemetery at Abingdon (Huggett 1995) also indicated that there were thresholds for acquiring particular objects. Knives and weapons symbolised female and male adulthood respectively. However, the fact that some adults were not buried with appropriate symbols suggests that such distinctions related 'to a state of adulthood that is not achieved by all adults, such as marital status' (ibid.: 189). Those adults without such symbols may have been unmarried and appear in the analysis amongst groups of mixed-sex young individuals, the stage in which they had remained. The important result of the study is that discrimination is based on sex and age. They should be examined together as there were distinctions being made about the identity of individuals within age and sex groups, for instance 'marital status, fertility, parenthood, and warriorhood'. The form of a grave is, as Richards observes (1992), an inscription that we must try to read and it should be read not simply as male and adult but also as incorporating such additional factors, some of which are personal while others are inherited from the individual's family.

DESCENT GROUPS

Affinity with the family in early Anglo-Saxon England was strong and while that strength is apparent in general terms it is very difficult to reconstruct the details of families. The family adds another dimension to the complexity of identity; just how complex has been revealed by the detailed study of weapon burial (Härke 1992b). The incidence of the rite of weapon burial did not coincide with intensive warfare, did not always represent fighting equipment that was practical and was not necessarily chosen for a person's potential or actual combat experience. A person accorded the rite was generally of above average stature, possibly the result of differential access to high-protein food, who was given a funeral involving high investment as a member of a high-status family. This could be demonstrated by the analysis of epigenetic traits in skeletons buried with and without weapons at the cemetery of Berinsfield (Boyle et al. 1996). They clearly fell into two separate groups, each a different descent group (Table 7.4).

Membership of family and tribal groups was also represented in the choice of the form and 'decoration' of artefacts that varies both locally and regionally. Distinctive groups of cremation pottery may also indicate membership of a particular descent group (Figures 5.14, 5.15). The combinations of motifs on brooches, for instance the distinct groups of great square-headed brooches identified by Hines (1984), might point in the same direction (Figures 5.18, 5.19). The manner in which particular motifs are interchanged and new ones occasionally added, on both pottery and metalwork, might, for instance, represent a form of heraldry denoting individual descent groups. It tends to be high-status families that are the most easily observed, for instance a woman

Table 7.4 Epigenetic traits and weapon burials at Berinsfield, Oxfordshire

	Epigenetic traits					
Burials	Metopic suture	Wormian bones	Dental anomaly	Foramen olecranon	Sixth lumbar vertebra	Spina bifida
With weapons						
24					*	
26					*	
28					*	
43/1–2				*		
53				*		
61				*		
69				*		
110						*
Without weapons						
37			*			
67	*	*				
76		*				
101		*				
164		*				

Source: Härke 1990, Table 5

buried at Chessell Down on the Isle of Wight could well have been a member of a family living near, and buried at, the cemetery at Sarre, so strong are the similarities between certain graves. To reconstruct the remainder of the family requires many assumptions.

While the sex and age of individuals are symbolised in the choice of the grave-goods, the nature of the objects themselves appears to indicate a regional or tribal identity. A study of particular brooch types (Welch 1983: 163 ff.) showed how Sussex belonged to a province that included Surrey, west Kent, Essex, the north of the Thames valley, Gloucestershire, Wiltshire and Hampshire. Saucer brooches worn as pairs on the shoulders could be combined in richer burials with square-headed brooches on the chest, with poorer equivalents of these types, the cast disc brooch and the small-long brooch, being more commonly found. The majority of saucer brooches were interred with late adolescents and adults and one of the rare exceptions is the grave of a 6- to 12-year-old girl at Lechlade (Gloucestershire) who was buried with brooches that may have been made in Kent and other objects more typical of a rich female grave in Kent or East Anglia (Dickinson 1993a: 38). There are further examples of disidentification, the transference and/or reinterpretation of the symbols of regional identity.

The identity found in central southern England is in marked contrast to the patterns found to the east in Kent and west in the Isle of Wight. The number of shared traits between these two areas has tempted some to view the link as a result of the Jutish/Kentish settlement of the island documented in the written sources. Analysis of the data suggests that the strength of the connection has been overemphasised. About 13 per cent of the graves at Chessell Down have sixth-century grave-goods that would conventionally be described as 'Kentish'. The significance of that figure can only be appreciated by some consideration of the proportion of female graves with such diag-nostic artefacts in broadly contemporary cemeteries in Kent; the published data from three such cemeteries reveals 5 per cent at Lyminge, 4 per cent at Sarre, and it is only at Bifrons, with 12 per cent, that we come close to the Chessell Down figure. It is possible that such similarities result from the marriage of Kentish people into Isle of Wight families or that the 'Kentish' concept is mistaken. It may be this that lies behind the tradition of 'settle-ment' that is referred to in the later sources (Arnold 1990) and in this way identity could be transplanted and maintained for perhaps a generation or two through kindred alliances (Scull 1993).

Despite the longer-distance movement of some ideas and objects, perhaps through exogamy, most decorative metalwork and dress within a region served to reinforce the tribal identity. Whether living within a region or widely scattered, adherence to a style of dress helped to integrate groups within society by demonstrating their membership of a family and tribe that was 'crucial to the creation and maintenance of social order' (Dickinson 1993a: 39, 1991). The analysis of six cemeteries in the east Midlands and East Anglia has shown how mortuary treatment varied between areas and how some female dress-fasteners, annular and swastika brooches and pins 'emphasised relationships within local communities while simultaneously differentiating community members from those outside the group'. Other dress-fasteners 'may have facilitated interaction between the members of different commu-nities by visually reducing the distance between them' (Fisher 1988: 143–4), or at least symbolised membership of a larger group.

Bede presented a picture of England in which there were particular peoples – the Angles, Saxons and Jutes. What meaning these labels had by the time he was writing or indeed whether they had any meaning earlier is difficult to determine. While the migrants' point of departure and direction of travel will have caused some segregation there must have been some mixing of people. The choice of label in each region may have been determined by the origin of dominant groups later distinguished using geographical labels, such as East Saxon and West Saxon. The distribution of peoples with ethnic labels did not always coincide with political territories and it is unclear whether ethnic labels had a greater or lesser significance than political ones. At some stage they appear to have become blurred. Such ethnicity was given expression in material culture and dress-styles (Owen-Crocker 1986) which have been

Figure 7.5 Reconstruction of sixth-century female Anglian dress and the distribution of sleeve-fasteners (sources: Owen-Crocker 1986, Figure 30 and Parker Pearson, van de Noort and Woolf 1994, Figure 2)

reconstructed from graves. Within each region there were appropriate ways of wearing distinctive objects irrespective of the actual range and number that an individual possessed (Figure 7.5). While they do have geographical currency their boundaries are blurred. There is also clear evidence for the mixing of symbols although this could have been brought about by a variety of means, for instance political motivation (Parker Pearson, van de Noort and Woolf 1994).

Within the complexity of early Anglo-Saxon society there were many possible identities and each individual would have had a particular combination. The relationships between individuals would have articulated a hierarchy of such identities both within and between families. Position within such a hierarchy might be considered as a person's status. There may have been many factors that determined position within such a hierarchy, for instance descent group, control of land and its products, or roles in society. There is considerable evidence for high-status descent groups and individuals whether judged by building size or the nature of funerals. However, while those members of society who wielded considerable power may also have enjoyed above average access to resources reflected in the energy input to the form and content of graves, it does not necessarily follow that all 'rich' graves held members of such an élite, nor that the simplest graves with no grave-goods were all servile. An individual may have had considerable power in society without necessarily being buried with material wealth, for instance the 'cunning woman' identified at Bidford-on-Avon (Dickinson 1993b). Of those graves without grave-goods there is little more that can be said. Although they are often said to be those for slaves they may not represent a single identity group. Of those graves accompanied by many grave-goods there need to be additional reasons for defining them as holding members of a particular identity group, for instance 'high status'. It is those individuals buried with many grave-goods that also have expensive and rare symbolic items who might be considered as members of the more powerful families and as leaders.

There is a variety of ways in which relative status was expressed. Within the repertoire of Style I ornament, ambiguity was a common feature whose use extended beyond mere ornamental function (Leigh 1980; Haseloff 1981); the hidden meaning in such ornament (see Chapter 6) emphasises that it was an instrument of exclusion used by a limited number of people to maintain an élite position. The use of Late Roman motifs in the decoration of early Anglo-Saxon metalwork 'could indicate affiliation to both Roman and Saxon sources of power' (Dickinson 1993a: 29). Female dress appears to have been an important medium for conveying information about status. The sources for some of the designs on saucer brooches are official Late Roman belt sets worn by high-ranking men. The introduction of Style I to saucer brooches in the sixth century appears to have been via Kentish garnet inlaid belt plates. This may suggest that those 'kin-groups were dominated by men, whose status was communicated vicariously through the ornamenting of their womenfolk' (ibid.: 39), and it is often noted how men in cemeteries were buried with fewer objects than their 'equivalent' women (Table 7.6). Thus decorated metalwork integrated and segregated society, 'not just superior from inferior, but also people of equivalent status' (ibid.: 43). The rare runic inscriptions, both magical and secret, may have formed a similar role symbolising preferential access to knowledge and power.

Graves that have an above average number of grave-goods tend also to have elaborate burials. Such elaboration was achieved in a variety of ways, as we have seen, but could be expressed as simply as digging such graves deeper than others (Sherlock and Welch 1992: 91). A high proportion of individuals accorded weapon burial rites were also buried in coffins (Härke 1990). Plank-lined graves have been excavated at Spong Hill (Figure 7.6) (Hills, Penn and Rickett 1984), stone-lined examples at Loveden Hill (Vierck 1972) and there is a wide range of types of barrow burials (Figure 6.6) which

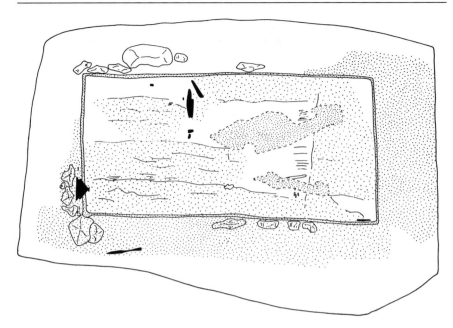

Figure 7.6 Plank-lined grave 31 at Spong Hill, Norfolk (source: Hills, Penn and Rickett 1984, Figure 40)

have been examined as a special form (Shephard 1979). The seventh century saw the use of large barrows over the graves of élite members of society as at Taplow, Asthall and the ship burial of Mound 1 at Sutton Hoo (Figures 4.3 and 7.10). Their use may have been in direct opposition to the growing influence of Christianity (van de Noort 1993), especially amongst élite members of society. Graves that were distinguished from flat graves were more susceptible to robbing as at Finglesham, Kent (Chadwick 1958). While this indicates that the significance of a barrow burial was understood by contemporaries it raises the possibility that an additional statement was being made in robbing a grave over and above personal gain. Some cremation burials were also distinguished by having associated structures.

A number of individual cemeteries have been studied from the perspective of the status of individuals and possible descent groups. A community represented in the 'Anglian' cemetery at Norton appeared to comprise about thirty to forty people spread over three or four generations, indicating a settlement of three or four farms. Six to eight men and women in each generation had distinctive graves representing either one dominant family or the principal adults in each of the families. This was reflected in a variety of factors including the nature and position of grave-goods as well as the position of

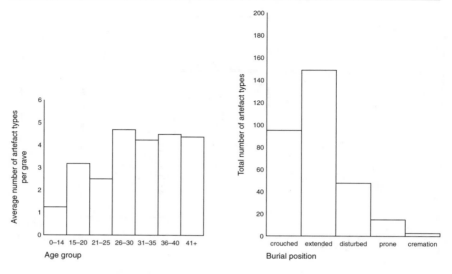

Figure 7.7 The relationship between numbers of artefacts, age and burial position at the cemetery of Norton, Cleveland (source: Sherlock and Welch 1992, Figures 18 and 20)

the body (Figure 7.7) (Sherlock and Welch 1992: 73–102). A similar picture was revealed at Alfriston, Sussex. In the first three-quarters of the sixth century 'the female population was headed by six rich women, representing one, or at the most, two families' (Welch 1983: 199). There were similarities in the type of ornaments worn on the body, suggesting that this symbolised membership of particular families. Their counterparts within the male population are identified with ten men buried with a greater quantity of weaponry. In spatial terms it was noted that the richest females of the sixth century occurred in pairs and there was, in overall terms, a tendency for individuals of the same sex to cluster together.

This demographic pattern is found in many contemporary cemeteries (Table 7.5). Calculations show that most fell within the range of twenty to forty individuals at any one time. The greatest difficulty is estimating the length of time that cemeteries were in use and this may cause much of the variation in the values. Obviously it cannot be assumed that cemeteries served single communities and there are good grounds for believing that in some areas, for instance the east Midlands and East Anglia, the dead were brought from much further afield than, for instance, in southern England (Arnold 1981a: 246–7).

Comparative studies of access to material wealth by examining the average number of types of object in graves within cemeteries emphasise that there is considerable variability (Table 7.6). However, some of that variability may

Table 7.5 Average population figures represented by early Anglo-Saxon cemeteries

Cemetery	No. of graves (p)	Approx. time (t)	$\dfrac{p \times 30}{t}$
Lyminge	44	90	14.6
Bifrons	97	110	26.4
Sarre	192	160	36.0
Gilton	113	100	33.9
Abingdon	122	120	30.5
Berinsfield	95	110	25.9
Long Wittenham I	235	180	39.1
Harnham Hill	76	70	32.5
Petersfinger	63	100	18.9
Ashton Valley	95	80	35.6
Worthy Park	140	160	26.2
Alfriston	129	150	25.8
Chessell Down	110	120	27.5

Table 7.6 The number of types of object in graves in cemeteries in southern and northern England

	No. of graves			No. of types		
	Total	% male	% female	Average, all graves	Average, male	Average, female
Lyminge	44	40.8	40.8	1.7	2.0	1.4
Bifrons	97			2.5		
Sarre	192			1.9		
Gilton	113			2.6		
Kingston	297			1.5		
Polhill	125	33.6	20.0	1.4	1.7	2.0
Abingdon	122	45.8	40.1	1.8	1.2	3.0
Berinsfield	95	28.4	26.3	2.1	2.5	3.0
Long Wittenham I	230	23.8	39.0	1.4	3.1	2.1
Wheatley	47			1.3		
Harnham Hill	76			1.0		
Petersfinger	63	34.7	26.8	3.1	2.5	1.5
Ashton Valley	95	12.6	18.9	2.1	2.7	3.4
Worthy Park	140	14.2	11.3	1.0	2.8	4.0
Winnall II	45	33.3	37.7	2.0	0.5	1.4
Alfriston	129			2.0		
Chessell Down	110			2.0		
Norton	110	15.8	44.1	2.75	4.33	4.37

be the result of the method used to sex the individuals. In some excavation reports a high proportion of the graves are unsexed or there is a possible bias towards a particular sex. The problem arises because the emphasis placed on the various criteria used to determine the sex of individuals and the conclusions that can be drawn have varied. Sometimes assumptions about the sex to which certain grave-goods should belong was taken into consideration whereas in more recent studies it is more likely that the skeletons will be studied independently.

The method indicates the range of items included in graves by mourners and, whatever the significance of individual items, highlights variations in the treatment of the dead on a regional basis. Those graves considered to contain women have on average, with some exceptions, a greater range of types than male graves. Closer scrutiny shows that women tended to be buried with a greater multiplicity of objects rather than variety. For instance a man buried with a sword will tend to have an above average number of types of object, whereas a woman of seemingly equivalent status will be buried with a number of brooches. Clearly the way that status was defined was different for men and women and returns us to the point that a man's status depended on his family which was also communicated through the level of ornamentation on their women. The overall average was 1.8 types and in individual cemeteries varied from 1 to 3.1 types. For Kent, Sussex and the Isle of Wight the average figure was 2, but in the upper Thames valley and central southern counties the value is below average at 1.6 types. In comparison, cemeteries in northern England tend to produce higher averages with less variance between men and women.

The variations between cemeteries and the regional differences that can be discerned in the numbers of types of object deposited in graves may be connected with the development of the social structure, success at wealth generation or access to raw materials. This might be examined using the large number of settlements that have been excavated. However, while patterns are apparent within and between cemeteries there is no good quality data yet available for a comparison of a settlement and its cemetery. Also, many of the functional and even non-functional details of buildings escape recovery, such as the position of windows and, at times, doorways and other elaboration, such as carving, which may have reflected on the status of the occupants. Buildings may be associated with fenced compounds (Figure 3.6) which at Cowdery's Down recurred in each of its three phases. The excavators suggest that this was not simply a reflection of agricultural needs so much as 'a more fundamental division into social units, whether according to kinship, sex or status' (Millett and James 1983: 247) although this raises questions about the use of such building groups, especially at Cowdery's Down which had only one at any particular time. Typically there may be a major building close to, but outside, the enclosure that may represent either a communal house or that of the head of a descent group. We have seen

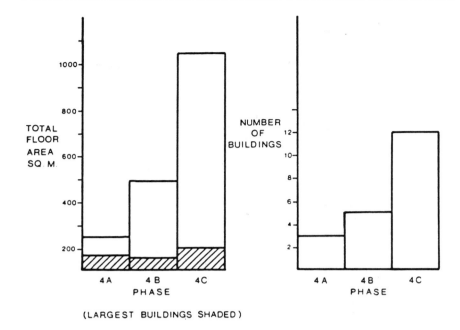

(LARGEST BUILDINGS SHADED)

Figure 7.8 Histograms showing the total available floor area and the number of buildings by phase at the settlement of Cowdery's Down, Hampshire

already that settlements can be divided into two distinct groups (Figure 3.7) on the basis of the size range of the buildings. Some settlements, perhaps the majority, have many small buildings while others have a greater range of sizes. If one examined settlements in more detail it might be possible to discern a development from one form to another. Of those in the former group, West Stow, which was made up of a number of settlement units at any one time, can be placed into phases in which there is no appreciable increase in house size which might be expected if Scull's model (Figure 7.1) was applied literally, although this does not take account of sunken buildings. The latter group (Figure 8.4) includes the documented 'royal' centre at Yeavering and the settlement at Cowdery's Down which comprised only one settlement unit which was rebuilt twice. Each phase sees increasing differentiation in the quality and size of buildings (Figure 7.8) which it is suggested may be linked to increasing social stratification. Hence there are not only two basic types of settlement but they may also have developed in a very different manner.

By whatever means cemetery populations are analysed, one group of graves is always apparent. They are characterised by having elaborate forms of burial structure and many types of, often costly, grave-goods, some of them purely

Table 7.7 The contents of some high-status male graves of the later sixth century

	Weapons						Vessels			Other			
	sword	spear	shield	buckle	axe	arrow	wood	metal	clay	knife	tweezers	shears	toilet imp.
Petersfinger 21	*	*	*	*	*		*			*	*		*
Ashton Valley 47	*	*	*	*	*		*			*	*		
Sarre 39	*	*	*	*	*		*			*			
Alfriston 86	*	*	*	*			*		*	*			
Mucking 600	*	*	*				*			*			
Spong Hill 40	*	*	*	*			*						
Holywell Row 29	*	*	*				*			*			
N. Luffenham	*	*	*				*		*	*	*		
Chessell Down 26	*	*	*			*	*	*		*			
Sarre 54	*	*	*	*						*		*	

symbolic. The energy expended over these persons' graves suggests a complex identity that is normally characterised as 'high status'. Such graves can be placed into three chronological phases, each of about thirty years, during which such burials were given a distinctive form. There are in effect four phases, as the first identified here is preceded by one in which such distinctive graves are not known. There are other examples that might be included but it is difficult at times to distinguish between an incomplete excavation and a different type. The three phases in which such graves are found are:

(a) mid- to late sixth century;
(b) early seventh century;
(c) later seventh century.

The meaning behind such graves is unlikely to have remained constant. There are many such graves belonging to the later sixth century but it is noticeable that the number of such graves diminishes with time. This must in part be the result of the concentration of power in the hands of fewer families with ever increasing territories, as well as the effects of Christianity on burial rites.

The male graves in the sixth century (Table 7.7) are characterised by an extensive array of grave-goods, always including weapons and some form of container (Figure 7.9). There is nothing in these graves that is obviously non-utilitarian, but the frequency of the association distinguishes the graves from the remainder of the population.

The contemporary female graves (Table 7.8) form an equally clear group in most, but not all, regions. They are characterised by richly decorated dress ornaments, as common to this group as weapons are to the men, in most cases by a key or latch-lifter and a coin, and in a few cases by perforated spoons and crystal balls (Figure 7.9). That the same type of grave may be found in areas many kilometres apart has a number of important implications about the mobility of people and ideas, and the spread of fashions and customs through intermarriage between élite families. That the layout of the grave-goods should also be so similar might assure us that it reflects their use in life.

A non-utilitarian aspect may be seen in some of the items. The crystal balls may have had a symbolism similar to that of the orbs surmounted by a cross which were used as royal symbols on the Continent in the sixth century. Minimally a key or latch-lifter, like the males' containers, is a tool, but the frequency of the association may imply much more, for instance, the head of the household, the privilege of privacy and the protection of self and property. Poorer graves that have some of the range of items found in these examples may represent emulation of the élite in richer areas, or different levels of power, but in such a complex society objects may have had different meanings in different contexts. The status of such élite families is most demonstrably being displayed by the women.

Table 7.8 The contents of some high-status female graves of the later sixth century

	brooch	beads	buckle	gold thread	ring	pin	spoon	crystal ball	knife	key	weaving batten	comb	metal/wood vessel	glass vessel	coin
Sarre 4	*	*	*	*	*	*	*	*	*	*	*	*		*	*
Chessell Down 45	*	*	*	*	*		*	*	*	*	*		*		
Bifrons 42	*	*	*		*		*	*	*	*					*
Bifrons 21	*	*		*	*				*	*			*		
Bifrons 29	*	*	*	*	*				*	*					*
Bifrons 41	*	*	*	*	*				*					*	*
Alfriston 62	*	*			*	*	*		*						
Alfriston 43	*	*	*		*									*	*
Lyminge 44	*	*		*			*	*							
Petersfinger 25	*	*	*		*				*	*					*
Abingdon 61	*	*	*		*										
Worthy Park 10	*	*	*		*	*			*	*		*	*		
Long Wittenham I, 71	*	*	*		*				*	*	*				
Holywell Row 11	*	*			*					*	*		*		
Spong Hill 24	*	*	*		?				*	*	*		*		
Empingham II, 73	*	*			*				*	*	*				

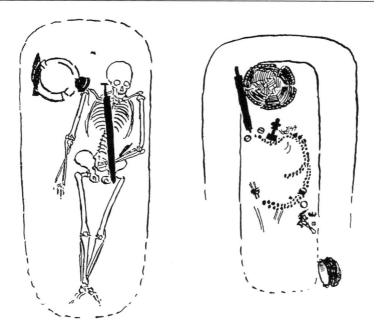

Figure 7.9 Plans of high-status male and female graves of late sixth-century date at Holywell Row, Suffolk (source: Lethbridge 1931, Plan 3)

In the early seventh century the male graves reveal more variety than the earlier examples (Table 7.9) and the group is dominated by three exceptionally rich examples, Taplow, Broomfield and Sutton Hoo mound I (Figures 4.3 and 7.10), which share so many characteristics of context, arrangement and grave-goods (Geake 1992). The major difference between these graves and the earlier examples is that they are under often large mounds. Graves of this general type occur throughout England and their associated grave-goods have been examined in a comparative fashion by Vierck (1972). Excavations at Sutton Hoo suggest that there, at least, such graves represent deposition in a formal burial area reserved for the exclusive use of the élite who were asserting their paganism in the face of Christianity (Carver 1992a: 363–5). Degrees of emulation may be apparent here also as some of the graves contain only what might be taken to be the more available of the items associated with the group, or are much cruder pieces, for instance Lowbury Hill, Berkshire (Atkinson 1916; Fulford and Rippon 1994), and Asthall (Dickinson and Speake 1992). This may, yet again, represent levels of leadership, kings and sub-kings. Other factors may be relevant, such as the circumstances of death and burial or the possibility that objects were deliberately excluded from the burial. There is a consistency in weapons and

Table 7.9 The contents of some high-status male graves of the early seventh century

	Weapons etc.						Vessels					Other			
	sword	spear	shield	buckle	axe	helmet	wood	metal	clay	glass	horn	knife	musical instrum.	game	ring
Cuddesdon	*							*		*					
Coombe Bissett	*	*	*	*				*		*		*			*
Alton 16	*	*	*	*			*					*			
Taplow	*	*	*	*			*	*		*	*	*		*	
Broomfield	*	*	*	*			*	*	*	*		*	*		
Oliver's Battery	*	*						*							
Coombe	*	*						*		*		*			
Sutton Hoo I	*	*	*		*	*	*	*	*		*	*	*		

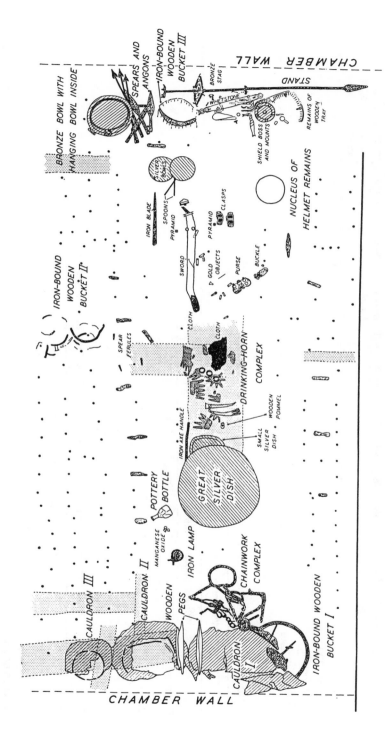

Figure 7.10 Plan of the royal burial chamber in mound I at Sutton Hoo, Suffolk (source: Bruce-Mitford 1966, Plate 24)

Table 7.10 The contents of some high-status female graves of the early seventh century

	brooch	beads	buckle	ring	pin	spoon	knife	key	weaving batten	chatelaine	comb	metal/ wood vessel	glass vessel	coin
Gilton 81	*	*		*			*			*				
Kingston 299	*	*	*	*			*	*		*	*	*		*
Swallowcliffe	*	*	*		*	*					*	*	*	
Sarre	*	*			*		*		*			*		*

Table 7.11 The contents of some high-status male graves of the later seventh century

	Weapon			buckle	pin	Vessel		Other	
	sword	spear	shield			wood	metal	knife	comb
Rodmead	*	*	*	*	*	*	*	*	
Ford	*	*	*	*			*		*
Galley Hills	*	*	*	*			*	*	
Lowbury Hill	*	*	*	*			*	*	

Table 7.12 The contents of some high-status female graves of the later seventh century

	beads	ring	pin	metal/ wood vessel	clay vessel	coin
Winchester 23	*	*				
Roundway Down II	*		*	*	*	*

containers amongst these male graves but rarely is there anything potentially symbolising leadership over and above the combination itself. Sutton Hoo mound I and the female grave (Table 7.10) at Swallowcliffe (Figure 7.11) are the notable exceptions in having a number of non-utilitarian items in addition to their great wealth.

Female graves of this period (Table 7.10) are more rare and are difficult to isolate because of their lack of consistency. The lack of representation of high-status women in burials at this time compared with the previous phase suggests there had been a great change. It is as though women ceased to be vehicles for displaying the status of their husband, who had assumed that role himself.

The rarity of rich graves, both male and female (Tables 7.11 and 7.12), as the seventh century proceeds has been viewed as a reflection of the increasing frequency of Christian burial for the élite, as reported by Bede at Canterbury (Colgrave and Mynors 1969: I 33) and which archaeology is beginning to demonstrate as the pace of church archaeology increases. The known examples are very different from those of the earlier part of the seventh century and may not be truly comparable. They may merely represent relatively high-status, determined pagan families who had been outstripped by their Christian kings.

The rich graves of the period belong, in broad terms, to three chronological phases. These may overlap but there are, nevertheless, clear horizons in the artefacts. This may indicate the level of interaction between nascent kingdoms during the currency of particular fashions and degrees of emulation and competition between individuals. A short time-span is involved in the emergence of kingship, perhaps representing five generations at the most. It is interesting that Dumville has suggested that in the royal genealogies that survive from this period 'only that extent (perhaps four or five generations) which is essential to the smooth running of the social structure will be remembered while more distant ancestors . . . are not recalled in the context of exact genealogical relationships' (1977: 87). If the rich graves isolated above are royal then it could be said that the archaeological evidence would support this and, in addition, would suggest that the genealogies only go back to the time when such leadership existed, prior to which they are a figment, albeit with great propaganda value. Dumville adds that 'there comes a superior limit of immediate credibility and in each case this is somewhere in the second half of the sixth century', and more precisely AD 550–75. Both the genealogies and the archaeological data support the view that this was when some clear form of regional leadership had developed in early Anglo-Saxon England and if any earlier forms of leadership existed they were clearly not memorable and it was not felt desirable to represent their status in a distinctive form at death.

Some of the utilitarian items buried with such rich graves may seem out of place, but they may have had a different significance in this social context.

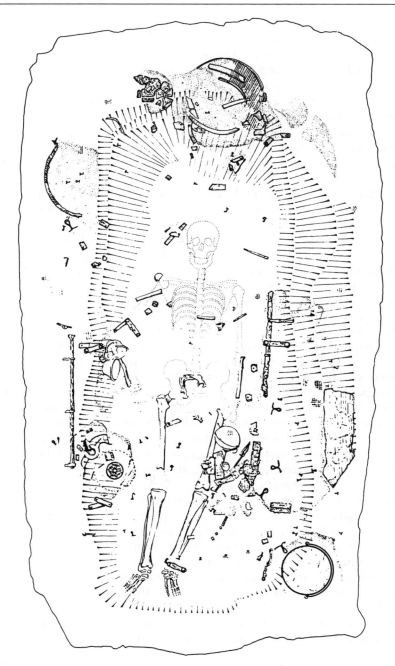

Figure 7.11 Plan of the early seventh-century rich bed burial of a female at Swallowcliffe, Wiltshire (source: Speake 1989, Figure 19)

A piece of weaving equipment that may have symbolised an adult female textile worker in one social context may represent an adult female head of household in another. While certain objects may have had various meanings depending on context, other items buried with these individuals only occur in such graves and do not appear to be utilitarian. These may be viewed as symbols of high status that may have evolved into regalia.

Some of the items buried at Sutton Hoo mound I were labelled regalia very soon after their discovery and presumably the implications of insignia of office and, more precisely, insignia used by royalty at coronations, were fully appreciated. There is no written evidence concerning inauguration rituals for the sixth and seventh centuries and we may have to be content with the probable identification of such symbols. It would be helpful to have an understanding of the meaning behind symbols of office but the sources are principally concerned with rites, especially anointing (Nelson 1977). An even greater problem is that the written sources are concerned with the *installation* of leaders, whereas the archaeological data are concerned with their *funerals*; that such items were being buried only presents a problem if it was assumed that they had to be inherited. Significantly some of the objects at Taplow were old when buried. Heirlooms, relics and regalia are rarely absent from installation ceremonies in anthropological studies that have been made (Fortes 1968). The possession of such objects as a vehicle for the continuity of office is common; after each generation the rites may be redefined, but for periods they may remain fixed. The extent to which such rites may be fixed will also become complicated when centres of power are developing and expanding to incorporate neighbouring territories. Whether the high-status symbols that were buried from the later sixth century onwards are complete sets, parts of sets, or were made especially for the funeral as was the case with cremation urns, will be difficult to determine. An important distinction emerges between earlier and later Anglo-Saxon leadership:

> the significance, political and symbolic, of inauguration rituals arose largely from the fact that no early medieval King succeeded to his kingdom as a matter of course. . . . In no kingdom of the early Medieval west was there quickly established a very restrictive norm of royal succession.
>
> (Nelson 1977: 51)

The date at which a fixed inauguration ritual was introduced is unknown, but a case has been made (Nelson 1977) for elements of West Saxon usage, *ante* AD 856, being preserved in later forms, and 'the relatively early introduction of a fixed rite in England may be explained in terms of the precocious political and ecclesiastical centralisation already achieved by the eighth century' (Nelson 1980: 48). Nelson's research has brought to our attention 'the sceptres of the Saxons, Mercians and Northumbrians' included in a fourteenth-century coronation out of respect for earlier ritual, or, more likely, to give greater legitimacy (1975: 45, 1977: 56). The use of a helmet rather than a crown until *c.* AD 900 (1980: 45) and weapons generally, was common (1975: 59), and Bede describes how Edwin set up bronze drinking cups beside highways for the refreshment of travellers; his majesty was such that banners (*vexilla*) were carried before him in battle, in peacetime his progress was preceded by a standard-bearer, and when walking along roads a standard (*thuf*) was carried before him (Colgrave and Mynors 1969: II 16; Bruce-Mitford 1974: 7–17; Deansley 1943).

The majority of cases where symbols of leadership are present are female graves of the later sixth century and male graves of the early seventh century, the most notable example being Sutton Hoo mound I. Some of the late sixth-century female graves contain perforated spoons and mounted crystal balls but thereafter the burial of symbolic items switches to male graves. Attention has been drawn to Edwin's 'standard' of AD 632 that has been compared with the Sutton Hoo mound I iron 'stand' (Figure 7.12a). The excavator of the mound burial at Benty Grange (Derbyshire) reported a 'six-pronged instrument of iron, in shape much like an ordinary hay-fork' (Bateman 1861: 31). There are pronged, almost rune-like, symbols (Figure 7.12c) beside the diademmed portrait on the obverse of the seventh-century WITMEN gold coinage and its copies (Sutherland 1948: 46–50). An important grave under the threshold of the large hall (A4) at the royal site at Yeavering contained a similar object (Figure 7.12b). A ceremonial significance has also been attached to the whetstone from Sutton Hoo mound I, described as 'an emblem of kingly office' (Bruce-Mitford 1974: 6) and which most commentators refer to as a sceptre, linked with other examples from cemeteries such as Sancton (Figure 6.8) (Bruce-Mitford 1978: 311–93; Evison 1975; Reynolds 1980; Enright 1983). The birds decorating the purse may symbolise the king's sporting privileges (Hicks 1986). The horns may also have carried similar symbolism (Neuman de Vegvar 1992). Helmets are symbols that are especially rare, the only examples belonging to this period being those from Sutton Hoo, Benty Grange with its boar crest (Figure 1.2) and fragments of metal decorated in a similar fashion from Caenby, Lincolnshire (Everson 1993).

Many of these rich funerals were carefully orchestrated to convey complex messages not only to those present but also for the future. The choice of new and old grave-goods and their careful juxtaposition within the grave proclaimed the supreme power of the individual as a leader, as an heir to Roman authority, the defender of his people in war and the provider of food. The contents of Sutton Hoo mound I, with its layered symbolism and ambiguity, have generated the most discussion in this respect (Enright 1983; Mitchell 1985; Nicholson 1986; Neuman de Vegvar 1984; Webster 1992;

Figure 7.12 (right) Possible regalia: (a) the Sutton Hoo mound I iron stand; (b) a grave at Yeavering and (c) obverse of coin with moneyer's name WITMEN (sources: Bruce-Mitford 1966, Figure 3; Hope-Taylor 1977; Sutherland 1973, Plate 2.9)

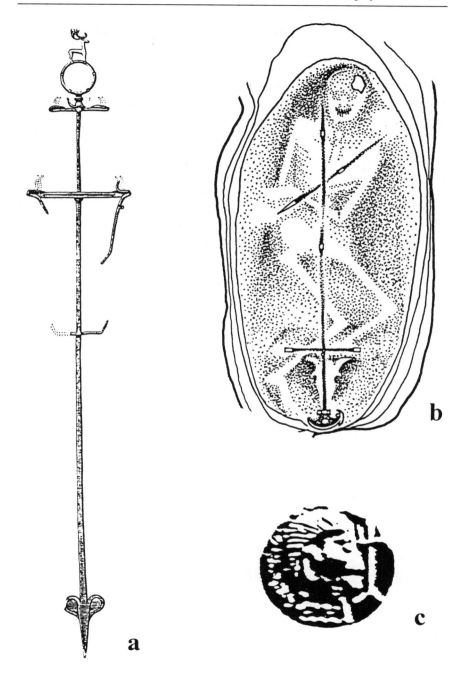

Carver 1992b). Long believed to be the grave of the East Anglian King Rædwald, it has also been argued that it is the grave of the East Saxon King Sæberht (Parker Pearson, van de Noort and Woolf 1994). It is argued that Sæberht is a contender if it is accepted that the funeral was designed to dispose of treasures that symbolised his links with Christianity and the overlordship of Kent. He was succeeded by three sons who may have been responsible for certain of the funerary gifts, three sets of three spears, three cauldrons, three hanging-bowls, three buckets. These were placed outside the area where the body lay as if to distinguish them from his personal possessions. The disposal of the treasures in this manner would have served to 'reduce friction between brothers as to who should inherit the individual items of regalia' (ibid.: 48) and may have been located so as to reassert the boundary between the East Angles and the East Saxons. Whoever was buried in mound I at Sutton Hoo it is one of the most complex funerals of which we have a record, befitting a royal personage in a time of change and uncertainty.

Chapter 8

Kingdoms

The indications of increasing social stratification in early Anglo-Saxon society through the sixth and seventh centuries have to be seen in the context of the development of the documented Anglo-Saxon kingdoms. The development of ranked societies in post-Roman England forms one phase in the formation of the English state. At its roots the process would have been started by successful descent groups who had the ability to attract followers competing with each other. That competition would have been articulated through the acquisition of valuables, conspicuous consumption through both gift-giving and aggression. Theories concerned with the formation of the undeveloped state emphasise the role of conflict between and within societies. There are also integrative processes such as the benefits of public works, redistribution, military organisation that lead to the growth in power of a few members of society (Service 1978; Claessen and Skalnik 1978; Webb 1975). There would be political dominance of the rulers and tributary obligations of the ruled, 'legitimised by a common ideology of which reciprocity is the basic principle' (Claessen 1978: 640). As ruling families achieved control of a region and competed with their neighbours the growth of power could only be achieved by merger that might be brought about by marriage or warfare.

A number of models have been proposed for the development of the early Anglo-Saxon kingdoms at varying levels of generalisation and degrees of emphasis on particular factors (Arnold 1980, 1982b, 1984b, 1987; Dumville 1977; Hodges 1978, 1982a; Sawyer 1978; Scull 1993; Wallace-Hadrill 1971). In an unashamedly processual study Scull has identified four possible stages in the early development of the Anglo-Saxon kingdoms that are principally stages in the political control of increasingly larger areas as a result of competition. The process may have begun (Figure 7.1) with the formation or development of 'ranked lineages'. Competition between them would have resulted in the emergence of 'local hegemonies' with chiefs. Competition between such local chiefs would lead at first to temporary hegemony over regions and then more permanent paramount dynasties with a political hierarchy.

A variety of terms was used by Bede to describe leadership. There appears to have been a distinction between *dux* and *rex* which relates to the cyclical nature of leadership at all levels (Wallace-Hadrill 1971: 15–16; Hodges 1982a: 27; Loyn 1992; Scull 1993). Bede refers to *imperium*, a form of hegemony that passed around the early Anglo-Saxon kings for which a distinct term would be required (Higham 1995). The cycles of leadership and the frequent alliances and annexations creating paramount leaders out of a group of local leaders would have required a complex language to make the necessary distinctions. That need is, of course, also visible in the archaeological record, expressed in the creation of ever more varied burial forms. Sawyer uses such a model in describing the kingdoms of the Heptarchy, albeit in an evolutionary rather than a cyclical form. They were 'created by the fusion of smaller kingdoms which preserved traces of their former independent status in still being described as kingdoms or sub-kingdoms under the rule of *reges*, *reguli* or *subreguli*' (Sawyer 1978: 21). Much of the confusion in the written sources over the earliest leaders (Dumville 1977: 101; Bassett 1989; Yorke 1990) may have arisen, as Sawyer suggested, because a later kingdom originated by the amalgamation of smaller groups each with their own leader.

The seeds of this process were probably brought with the migrants in the form of contacts and relationships. It may have taken some considerable time to reconcile their patterns of allegiance with those of the native population. By the end of the sixth century, as we have seen, 'local chiefdoms and (initially at least) any wider authority are likely to have been hegemonies: a personal or dynastic authority over previously autonomous groups that retained some social and political identity' (Scull 1993: 75). It is not possible to identify such early political structures until there are material correlates in the archaeological record, but regional similarities in material culture need not reflect such structures as they may not have had a 'strong territorial expression' (ibid.). There are, as we have seen, some graves of the later fifth and earlier sixth centuries that are distinct from others and that may represent particular families seeking to reinforce their existing or newly found status. It is only from the late sixth century onwards that élite burials appear with a degree of uniformity, which increases with time. They suggest competition and influence over wide geographical areas, power and status remaining with single descent groups for a number of generations, and strong territorial expression. Scull emphasises the importance of land and its products as a medium for the development of local hegemonies. With a steadily increasing population 'there would be a social imperative towards territorial expansion as individuals in each generation required sufficient land to maintain their status by birth' (ibid.: 77). As more land was required, successive generations would move outwards 'forming the territorial embodiment of a descent group' (ibid.: 78). If power and status within the descent group were maintained and extended the 'folk-land of a descent group might . . . eventually be translated into a territorial unit' (ibid.).

The written sources indicate that seven principal kingdoms were forming during the sixth century. These were Kent, the East, South and West Saxons, the East Angles, Mercia and Northumbria, often referred to as the Heptarchy. A number of factors deemed to be relevant to the control of the emergence of complex ranked societies in early Anglo-Saxon England can be examined using the archaeological data. We have already examined the evidence for increasing specialisation in procurement and production, and increasing access to resources. Settlements and cemeteries point to the emergence of an exploitative, competitive élite. The exchange of goods is clearly in evidence and the negative side of such relations would have been vengeance warfare increasing to warfare for resource acquisition. The development of the type of political hierarchy under examination is a function of the interrelation of the control of population and activity-agglomerates, movement minimisation, and differential accessibility, often emerging in clusters under conditions of mutual competition.

The identification of early Anglo-Saxon population aggregates has been achieved in the past by the combination of a number of forms of evidence – archaeological, documentary and the allied study of place-names (Ekwall 1936; Leeds 1913: 39, map 4; Collingwood and Myres 1936: 353, map VI; Davies and Vierck 1974). The distribution of pagan Anglo-Saxon graves gives an immediate, if potentially misleading, impression of population densities when presented as a trend surface diagram (Figure 8.1). Some of the apparent concentrations result from the existence of large centralised cemeteries, particularly in East Anglia, the east Midlands and Yorkshire. Elsewhere the patterns may be a closer reflection of the distribution of the living population. The fact that the map is one of the dead is, however, inescapable and it is also rather static, being an aggregation of about 300 years of human occupation. To introduce any detail and depth into such a diagram presents difficulties. The total number of graves represented is in the order of 26,000, a figure that stands as a minimum basis for determining the population of early Anglo-Saxon England. Naturally, levels of population must have fluctuated at a national and a local level although most of the models for the development of the kingdoms tend to assume that population was generally on a rising track. This need not be the case as competition alone may have provided the fuel.

Anglo-Saxon politics, with its numerous royal associations, joint kingships and the possible implications for territorial division, are extremely complex. Research on the written records has resulted in an understanding of much of the structure of institutions and the sequence of events but until recently there has been little desire to understand the mechanisms of the development of the kingdoms. This is now changing (Bassett 1989; Yorke 1990). The written sources indicate that before the end of the seventh century there were ten separate royal families ruling simultaneously in England, eight south of the Humber if one includes Sussex and the Isle of Wight. Before the

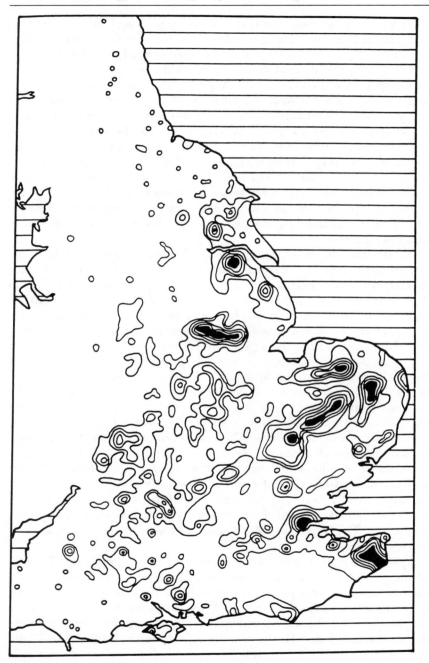

Figure 8.1 Trend surface map of early Anglo-Saxon graves by grid generalisation. Lowest contour 50 graves per 25 sq km, thereafter 100, 200 etc.

end of the seventh century a series of political events had caused the lesser kingdoms to disappear, such as when Caedwalla, King of Wessex, exterminated the dynasty that once ruled the Isle of Wight. Such political activities may have been necessary for the acquisition of resources – especially land and people and what in combination they could produce. Emerging complex societies often developed in close proximity to each other and the competition for land and resources frequently led to aggression and the annexation of smaller groups within the larger. Even making allowance for the fictitious nature of the early entries (Harrison 1976; Yorke 1993) and its southern bias, the *Anglo-Saxon Chronicle* demonstrates the nature of aggression during the period. It provides a sample of confrontations recorded as having taken place between AD 550 and 700 (Figure 8.2). There was a pattern of predominantly 'West Saxon' aggression, not only against the 'Britons' in defence and expansion of their territory, but also against Kent from AD 568 and the South Saxons in AD 607. Problems with their northern frontier with 'Mercia' in the middle years of the seventh century mark the beginning of a decline in the fortunes of the West Saxon kingdom (Yorke 1995). Nevertheless, their aggression continues, being directed towards Kent and the Isle of Wight.

That early Anglo-Saxon society was geared up for warfare is evident from the large quantities of functional weaponry that were manufactured and which were ultimately used in male burials. These include the sword (Davidson 1962), the spear (Swanton 1973, 1974) and the shield (Dickinson and Härke 1992). However, the weapon burials provide a distorted image of the nature of use of such weaponry because of the additional symbolism they bear in that context. Many of the weapon combinations, for instance, are not strictly functional. The nature of weapon burial, and the nature of the persons being accorded such a rite, was changing through the period. Thus Härke has demonstrated that few of those buried with weapons in the first half of the sixth century show signs of involvement in battles and few men were buried with their weapons in the seventh century (1990: 32–3). The greatest incidence of weapon burials occurs in the middle of the sixth century when recorded battles were at their lowest (Figure 8.3). While it might be tempting to see a direct correlation between these two trends it may not simply be a case of the variation in use-value of weapons. There may have been a greater desire to demonstrate the status of leading families through weapon burials during peacetime than when their authority was being exercised in battle. In the seventh century changes occurred in the nature of weapon burials (Härke 1992a) which are of significance to the broader political changes in society. Härke suggests that in the seventh century weapon burials ceased to indicate ethnic affiliation and it was no longer a symbol of family affiliation amongst juveniles. The status of males was no longer indicated by full-size weapons but by substitutes, and weapon burial was, for a time, the preserve of the élite members of society.

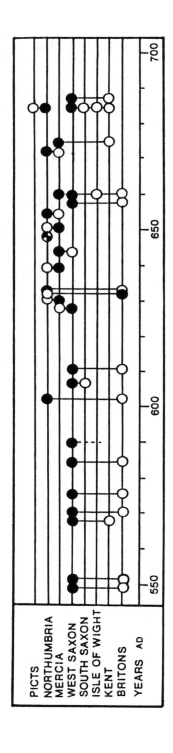

Figure 8.2 Diagram illustrating the incidence of warfare in early Anglo-Saxon England recorded in the *Anglo-Saxon Chronicle*, AD 550–700. The black dots are the recorded aggressors. Imprecise data has been excluded

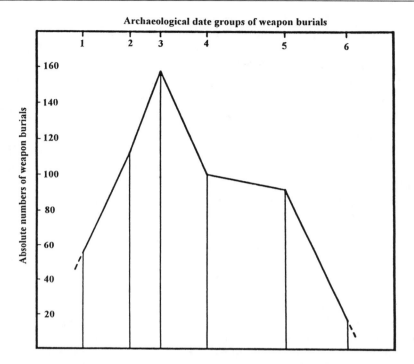

Figure 8.3 The frequency of weapon burials in early Anglo-Saxon England (source: Härke 1990: 30)

There are also regional variations in the nature of weapon burials with a different emphasis on particular weapons in certain areas (Table 8.1). In some areas, for instance the upper Thames valley and north-east England, the sword is poorly represented. In others, for instance counties along the south coast, they are more common.

Table 8.1 Proportions of weapon graves in cemeteries in southern England

%	Graves with weapons (%)	Graves with spear, shield and sword (%)
Berinsfield, Oxon	27	0
Sarre, Kent	24.4	14.8
Alfriston, Sussex	25.5	3.3
Chessell Down, IoW	24.5	18.5

It is difficult to disentangle the meaning behind these differences, for instance whether this represents different ways of symbolising power, the presence or absence of élite families, or other reasons. The relatively high level of weaponry in Kent has been commented on:

Sarre . . . is set apart from the majority by virtue of a high proportion of male burials with weapons, including numerous swords, far in excess of what is normal even in aristocratic cemeteries such as Bifrons. The only truly comparable case in Kent is the cemetery at Buckland, behind Dover. Here then, we have two unusually well-armed communities in strategic positions close to known albeit later ports.

(Hawkes 1969: 191)

It is perhaps not so much that well-armed males are an indication of commerce or incipient ports of trade but that social and political development, and especially the evolution of permanent political hierarchies whose competitiveness was institutionalised in commerce, was more advanced in some areas than others. Such differences may actually have encouraged some emerging kingdoms to be aggressive towards their more 'successful' neighbours in the late sixth and seventh centuries (Figure 8.2).

The existence of a developing form of leadership and kingship at least by the seventh century has led to a search for a settlement type befitting persons of such status. A problem arises in the choice of factors that should be used for the identification of such 'palaces'. Initial, perhaps premature, excitement following the identification of a type of large timber building from aerial photographs (Rahtz 1976: 65–8; Sawyer 1983b) has been tempered by the discovery, from excavation, that the form and size of these buildings are present on many, otherwise ordinary, rural settlements; in one unusual instance excavation showed that the features were medieval rabbit warrens (Clark, Hampton and Hughes 1983). Many writers have taken building size as an indication of high social status. The range of sizes of buildings at some settlements, for instance Cowdery's Down (Figure 3.7), is above the norm, and the largest have been described as 'palaces' (Figure 8.4). Size alone need not make a building the residence of a king and Millett and James suggest that the absence of seed and bone at Cowdery's Down is not so much due to poor preservation but because crop and meat processing may not have taken place there because of the status of its various occupants (1983: 249–50).

The problem is exemplified by two sites, at Northampton and Yeavering. To the east of a series of minster churches in Northampton, dating from the middle-Saxon period onwards, was a rectangular stone hall. It had an internal floor area of 315 m^2 and dates to the eighth century. The building is interpreted as the centre of secular power on the royal estate in the same way that the minster was the seat of ecclesiastical authority (Williams, Shaw and Denham 1985). Below the stone building was a large timber hall of the seventh century with a floor area of 252 m^2, consisting of a rectangular centre with square annexes at either end, which appears to be a highly sophisticated, possibly bayed, structure, which was set with extreme precision. In contexts associated with the eighth-century minster and 'palace' were a bronze shrine

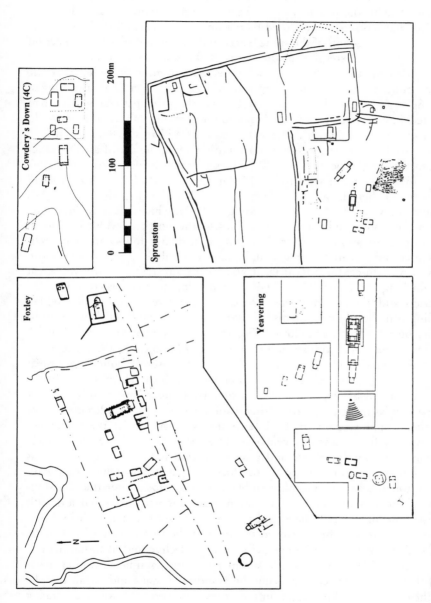

Figure 8.4 Plans of possible royal palaces (sources: Hinchliffe 1986, Figure 1; Millett and James 1983, Figure 27; Hope-Taylor 1977; St Joseph 1982)

fitting, a bronze stylus, glass vessels and a decorated pin; all are relatively unusual items. Yet no such items were associated with the timber predecessor. We are left with the problem of whether the timber structure and the stone building that replaced it were used by persons of a similar status for the same functions. The erection of the stone palace and the church may be a reflection of a change or an extension in the status of the site, from an unexceptional rural settlement to a 'palace'. If size is relevant it must be noted that the timber building was certainly large, being 35 m^2 larger than the biggest building at Cowdery's Down. It may be that the principal change that had occurred was conversion to Christianity following which a secular lord would wish to be associated with ecclesiastical power (Williams 1984a, 1984b).

The problems of interpretation surrounding Yeavering are of an altogether different nature (Hope-Taylor 1977). The settlement is identified with Bede's *Gefrin* that was graced with royal visits and one by Paulinus who preached and baptised there in AD 627. The site was abandoned in the early eighth century in favour of *Maelmin*, according to Bede, which has been identified from aerial photographs a few kilometres to the north at Millfield. Hope-Taylor's interpretation promotes Yeavering as a British folk-centre with religious foci and a 'cattle corral' that became the palace of the Anglo-Saxon kings of seventh-century Bernicia. It was an administrative centre with great halls for king and court. The post-Roman development consisted of wooden buildings and a great enclosure. There was a square enclosure of wooden buildings on the site of a prehistoric stone circle, around which were inhumation burials. This was followed (Figure 8.4) by the construction of major halls, a temple and a timber auditorium or grandstand. At the settlement's height the grandstand was enlarged, the great enclosure rebuilt, and a great hall (A4) was erected. Under its threshold was a grave accompanied by an object identified by the excavator as a surveyor's *groma*, but possibly a ceremonial standard (Figure 7.12b). When Paulinus visited in the 620s the temple was altered and reconsecrated while in the western part of the settlement there was the final phase of a cemetery. The settlement itself was deliberately burnt in the seventh century and a re-occupation followed. This phase was characterised by numerous posts, the foci for graves, and which may have carried 'totemic and zoomorphic emblems of the tribe'. After the abandonment of the western cemetery a church was built with a churchyard with orderly rows of graves. The grandstand was replaced and new halls built. This settlement was also destroyed by fire, but the significance of the site is indicated by four new buildings before a final decline and abandonment.

It is impossible to do justice, in summary, to the magnificent timber structures that were excavated, especially the grandstand, halls and pagan temple, and the details should be sought in the excavator's report. However, a paradox arises again when we contrast the magnificence of contemporary 'royal' burials and the apparent material poverty of Yeavering. Yet this is a characteristic of most settlements of the period. Hope-Taylor emphasises that the *potential* magnificence of the buildings can only be measured by postholes, as the timber and plaster may have been ideal media for decoration by carving and painting. Over and above an acceptance of the identification of Yeavering as Bede's *Gefrin*, the principal factors used to emphasise the settlement's status are the size and nature of the buildings, the great hall having a floor area of 336 m². We must be wary, at present, of being overawed by the range of archaeology at Yeavering when there are so few excavated settlements to compare it with in northern England. Bede also mentions Rendlesham (Suffolk) as a royal palace and its close proximity to Sutton Hoo (6 km) has raised expectations. Similarities in metalwork from the two sites suggest this may be warranted. Recent field walking has demonstrated the existence of a large scatter of Ipswich ware indicating that the settlement was very large and, unlike early Anglo-Saxon rural settlements, demonstrates continuity into the middle-Saxon period as at other royal sites (Newman 1992).

The development of the early Anglo-Saxon kingdoms and leadership might have been symbolised by palatial central places. Contenders for this position have been argued on their individual merits, in the case of Northampton and Rendlesham by site continuity and context, and in the case of Yeavering by historical evidence and the scale and type of the structures. High-status settlements may be expected at major centres, particularly those that achieved ecclesiastical and commercial prominence in the seventh and eighth centuries, such as Winchester, Canterbury and London (above). Both Yeavering and Foxley (Hinchliffe 1986) have buildings that are interpreted as churches. We should, perhaps, be wary of imposing such status on other settlements too readily (Hawkes 1979; Arnold 1982c); to do so makes great assumptions about early Anglo-Saxon society and especially how authority was held, dispensed and symbolised in the material world. Within the pagan world power was demonstrated and symbolised in visible, moveable wealth. This is exemplified by the rich seventh-century burials constructed in direct opposition to Christianity. The construction of magnificent buildings as appropriate housing for such individuals may only have arisen following the establishment of Christianity; the power and authority of the Church were demonstrated in buildings and secular lords may have felt it necessary to match such splendour. Indeed the development of a more institutionalised form of kingship in the later seventh century may owe as much to the influence of the Church as to the evolution of secular institutions.

The chiefdoms and kingdoms of early Anglo-Saxon England, standing side by side in competition with each other, must have had some concept of territory. Naturally, in their volatile condition boundaries may have been disputed and may not have remained fixed for any great length of time. Thus any attempt to reconstruct the boundaries of the developing kingdoms at a particular time is fraught with problems. Even armed with this knowledge a number of writers have not been deterred from producing maps showing the location of tribes and kingdoms (Ordnance Survey 1966). Some writers have chosen to print the relevant names in large font across their maps leaving the boundaries notional. Others have drawn lines separating one kingdom from another. Both practices fossilise 200 or 300 years of political development in a single image even when boundaries were clearly in a constant state of flux.

Nowhere do we have sufficiently complete information to recreate the evolving territories and their infrastructure in a given region. Models for the development of the kingdoms assume the creation of a number of settlements within which certain lineages assumed increasing power over people and land. The centres of secular power may at times have been the rural settlement with its adjacent territory. In the seventh century élite burial and residence, not yet demonstrably adjacent, are at least separated from the remainder of society as power became more institutionalised. Boundaries may have remained fixed for periods but would also have been shifting. Through the process of territorial amalgamation and annexation older centres of power may well have come to lie close to new boundaries and new centres of power near old boundaries. The model assumes, however, that territories expand outwards from their original centres and that centres of power would not lie close to their boundaries.

Archaeologists sometimes view prehistoric burials and their visible covering mounds as territorial markers, reinforcing the real or apparent time-depth of ancestry and ownership. An example of this projected into early Anglo-Saxon England concerns Sutton Hoo. Many of the grave-goods in mound I have strong affiliations with Essex and Kent. The link is so strong that it has been suggested that we should look to the regnal list of the East Saxon royal family for the incumbent of the burial and that the funeral was located as 'a political gesture to restate the nature of the boundary with the East Angles' (Parker Pearson, van de Noort and Woolf 1994: 47). This places a greater emphasis on the distribution of types of decorated metalwork as an indicator of seventh-century royal boundaries than as an indicator of royal alliances.

One method of reconstructing evolving boundaries is by using unweighted Theissen Polygons drawn between rich graves in areas with a seemingly good data-set, for instance southern England, although a number of assumptions have to be made (Arnold 1988c). Naturally the data will not be complete and may not always be strictly contemporary, but the periods over which the locations or graves were venerated may at least have overlapped. The rich graves, being closely dated, also allow territories to be reconstructed in three time-lapse images.

Figure 8.5 (right) Three chronological phases of rich graves in early Anglo-Saxon southern England, acting as centres of territories defined by Theissen Polygons: (a) mid–late sixth century; (b) early seventh century; (c) later seventh century

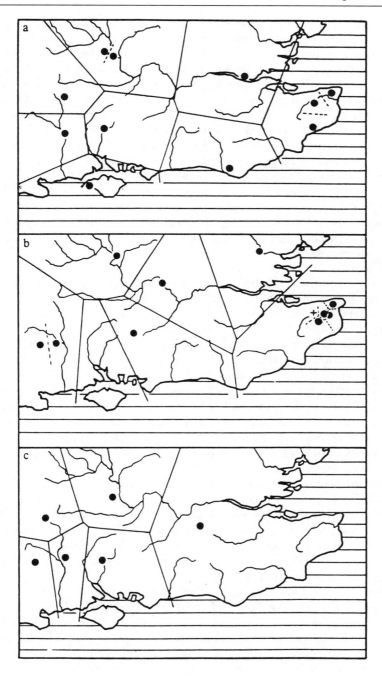

The results of such an approach are stimulating especially when compared with what little is known about competition between the named polities in the written sources (Figure 8.5). During the mid- to later sixth century a number of regions of roughly equal size were created. Many of the hypothetical territory edges corresponded with natural features, particularly rivers. By the late sixth and early seventh century there had been a marked change. The Kent region, for instance, had lost ground on its north-west frontier, but had expanded westwards; Essex appeared as a distinct zone, incorporating part of the area south of the River Thames; Sussex remained as a separate unit extending further westwards, with a new region to the north lying astride the Thames. The Hampshire zone now incorporated the Isle of Wight. Wiltshire and the upper Thames valley remained divided into small units. Finally in the later seventh century Kent, Sussex and Surrey were one with the region to the north; one region remained in the upper Thames valley looking northwards, leaving a large zone comprising Hampshire and the Isle of Wight and, again, the smaller regions in Wiltshire, now extended further westwards.

In the second and third phases the territorial frontiers corresponded less with possible natural examples, and it is more likely that as the political map of southern England became more artificial, there was a greater need to construct artificial boundaries, such as linear earthworks (Figure 8.6). Few such earthworks are closely dated, although some are demonstrably post-Roman. A number of them have been seen as reflecting early Anglo-Saxon period political history; for instance, the eastern section of Wansdyke (Fox and Fox 1958), the east Hampshire complex (Coffin 1975), Bokerly Dyke (Rahtz 1961) and those on the borders of Surrey and Kent near Westerham (Clark 1960) and Crayford (Hogg 1941). There are linear earthworks elsewhere in England, such as those of west Norfolk, which appear to demarcate the boundaries between western East Anglia and eastern Norfolk (Carver 1989; Scull 1992; Yorke 1990: 58–71).

The absence of close dating tends to leave such testimonies of human territoriality floating amongst the details of political history and it is of little value to correlate them speculatively either with historical events or with the hypothetical frontiers generated here, despite there being a number of apparent matches; far worse would be to use such correlations to date the earthworks! (See, for example, Wheeler 1934.) They are, at least, a reflection of the existence of territories.

These maps are not the material for a history of the English kingdoms, just as a correlation with Bede and the *Anglo-Saxon Chronicle* would be very dubious when they rarely mention boundaries. The results do support the model for the growth of a smaller number of larger polities. The alterations to the pattern appear to reflect a demand for control of the coastline that may relate to a desire to control developing ports of trade. It should be noted that it is the more northerly and landlocked kingdoms that are the most

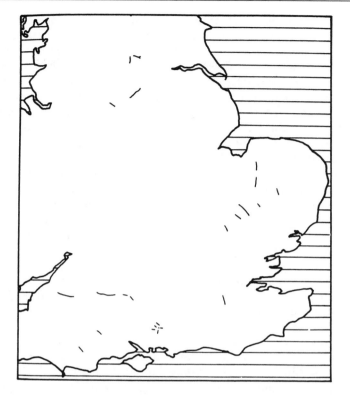

Figure 8.6 The location of possible early Anglo-Saxon linear earthworks in England

belligerent in the later sixth and seventh centuries, attacking the southern groups and annexing them into larger territories.

At the level of more specific historical interpretation we may observe, for instance, that the East Saxons (Yorke 1990: 45–57) are interpreted as having relieved Kent of the London area by the early seventh century (Colgrave and Mynors 1969: II 3), but eventually lost it to Mercian control before AD 700 (ibid.: III 7). The political history of Sussex (Welch 1989) is not at all clear, but it is generally agreed that its independence was under threat by both the Mercians and the West Saxons. For the Isle of Wight and the Meonware to have been given to the south Saxons by Mercia in the seventh century has interesting strategic implications *vis-à-vis* the position of the West Saxons (Yorke 1989, 1990: 128–56, 1995). In the late seventh century Kent (Brooks 1989a; Yorke 1990: 25–44) was apparently very unsettled as it was disputed by the West Saxons and Mercia. By the middle of the seventh century Mercia was the dominant force (Dumville 1989a).

Undoubtedly one of the most important kingdoms in the seventh century was Mercia. We know relatively little about its early development as it lies outside the scope of the written sources until the early seventh century. The kingdom enters the written record when it imposed itself, often violently, on its southern neighbours. Despite this obscurity there are strong similarities with the developments that have been noted elsewhere. By the eighth century this midland kingdom (Dornier 1977; Brooks 1989b; Gelling 1989; Yorke 1990: 100–27) incorporated the river systems of the Warwickshire Avon, Trent and Severn. The southern border lay on the edge of the Chilterns, to the east lay the Fens, beyond which lay other English territories. To the north lay Northumbria (Dumville 1989b; Yorke 1990: 72–99), the frontier possibly protected by a series of linear earthworks near Sheffield (Figure 8.6) (Blair 1948: 120–3). The centre of this territory is normally seen as the upper Trent valley in the eastern part of the Midlands, which is in accordance with the historical tradition of relatively late English settlements in the Midlands from East Anglia in the early sixth century (Davies 1977). The archaeological evidence indicates settlement in the middle Trent and the upper Warwickshire Avon by this time and some types of metalwork, like the pottery, point to a strong connection with East Anglian styles; by the later sixth and seventh century there appears what might be called a Midlands style of metalwork (Leeds and Pocock 1971: 34; Eagles 1979).

Rich graves of the type better known further south are to be found in the east Midlands at Empingham II (Rutland) burial 73 (Table 7.8), dating to the later sixth century (Clough, Dornier and Rutland 1975: 3), and the later barrow burials of Benty Grange and Wigber Low in Derbyshire (Bateman 1861: 28–33; Collis 1983).

The condition of Mercia in the seventh century has been viewed through an obscure text known as the *Tribal Hidage* (Davies and Vierck 1974; Dumville 1989c); its date is difficult to establish, but the contents are consistent with a developed kingdom that had united smaller tribal groupings in its formation and had expanded outwards. It is the very process of uniting smaller groups that creates the obscurity of this kingdom and difficulties arise as there are undoubtedly many focal points within its boundaries. Within Mercia there are sites revealed by aerial photography containing large halls, amongst other buildings, which have been compared in form and function with the examples discussed above (p. 218); Atcham, near Shrewsbury (Shropshire) has not been excavated, but one building at Hatton Rock, near Stratford, indicated a date from the late seventh century onwards. During the seventh and early eighth centuries the secular and ecclesiastical organisation of the heartland of Mercia had been consolidated, providing the base for its outward expansion (Figure 8.7). The contiguance between this map and seventh-century southern England (Figure 8.5) may be no more than coincidence.

The evidence of the seventh century indicates considerable social and economic change. The climax of princely burial and the manifestation of a

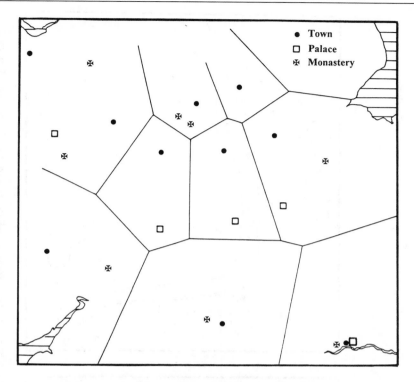

Figure 8.7 The kingdom of Mercia defined by Theissen Polygons, showing the distribution of early towns, monasteries and suggested royal palaces (source: P. Barnwell)

hierarchy in settlements indicate an established authority of large territories. That this creation of an extended settlement hierarchy may have caused considerable dislocation is suggested by the apparent discontinuity between early and middle-Saxon rural settlements. The desire and ability of élites to engage in the circulation of exotic goods amongst their peers within Europe, and to control access to them, would have been a powerful political tool. This sees its ultimate expression in the development of *emporia* or ports-of-trade. The precise mechanism for the initial transportation of foreign imports is not known although as a precursor to the formalised ports Hodges has suggested the existence of incipient trading settlements (1982a, 1989; Hodges and Hobley 1988), which may have been little more than beach markets. The steps towards ports as permanent settlements imply the appearance of new persona in society, those occupying such proto-urban settlements and those moving between them by sea. Amongst the earliest ports-of-trade that have been archaeologically investigated on any scale are Southampton,

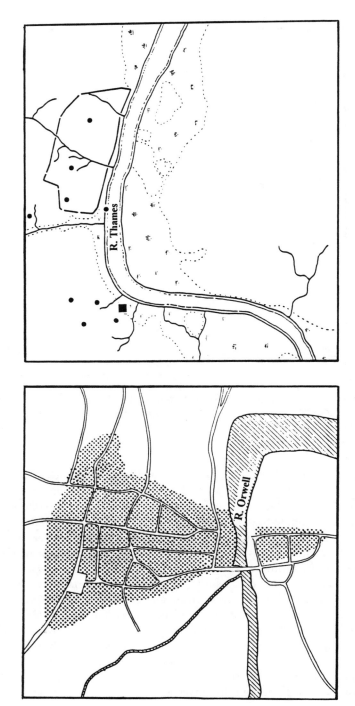

Figure 8.8 Plans of mid-Saxon ports-of-trade, Ipswich and London (sources: Hodges 1982a, Figure 15; Vince 1990, Figure 4)

London, Ipswich and York although others are known or suspected, for instance Fordwich and Sandwich in Kent (Figure 8.8). Such ports were sited to take advantage of natural harbours on navigable rivers, often founded close to, but not inside, the walls of Roman towns and forts. In London a late seventh-century waterfront has been excavated in the Strand area where significant numbers of contemporary artefacts have been found bolstered by the significant name Aldwych, the 'old *wic*' (Vince 1990; Cowie 1992). The trading settlement at York, referred to as *Eoforwic*, is about one kilometre downstream from the Roman town and fort. The extent of the settlement at Ipswich and its pottery industry is gradually coming into focus (Wade 1988).

The most extensive excavations have taken place at *Hamwic*, mid-Saxon Southampton. By the late seventh century *Hamwic* comprised rows of houses built alongside gravel roads along the spine of the Southampton peninsula. On the Continent some such ports developed as dispersed clusters of buildings but the English examples, at present, appear to have been conceived as large units (Vince 1984, 1990; Biddle 1984). Among the many imported goods are glass, quern stones and pottery from a variety of regions in northern France, probably connected with a trade in wine. Many of the more institutionalised activities occurring at such ports can be seen as a continuation of earlier exchange. Likewise the major crafts represented – metalworking, carpentry, weaving and bone working – would earlier have been carried out on rural settlements.

Hodges takes the relationship between the origins of the medieval market and the formation of the state as his central theme (Hodges 1982a, 1982b, 1989; Hodges and Hobley 1988) and while this might overstate its contribution there is little doubt that there was a strong relationship between paramount leaders and such ports. What is unclear is whether such ports developed as a result of the intensification of trade causing a gradual drift from the rural settlements to the new urban environments, or whether the ports were deliberately founded. The geographical association between royal centres and the ports makes their relationship clear (Figure 8.9) and also serves to emphasise how competition between leaders would have made access to such ports a critical factor.

By the end of the seventh century the settlement hierarchy had reached a climax and was a direct reflection of the permanent political hierarchy. Paramount leaders and their administrations were detached from society, albeit in parallel with the growing power and influence of the Church, with international trade and craft production concentrated in new urban foundations, and rural settlements. In the 200 years following the migrations the foundations of medieval society had been laid.

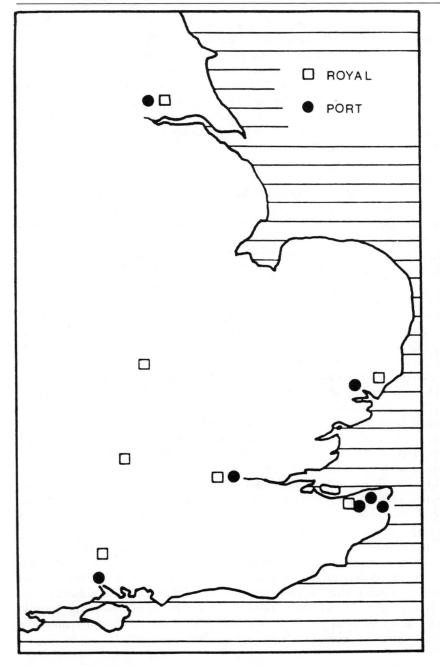

Figure 8.9 The distribution of royal sites and ports-of-trade in early Anglo-Saxon England known from written sources and by excavation

Bibliography

Åberg, N. (1926) *The Anglo-Saxons in England During the Early Centuries after the Invasion*, Uppsala.

Addyman, P.V. (1964) 'A Dark-Age settlement at Maxey, Northants', *Medieval Archaeol* 8: 20–73.

—— (1972) 'The Anglo-Saxon house: a new review', *Anglo-Saxon England* 1: 273–307.

—— (1977) 'York and Canterbury as ecclesiastical centres', in M.W. Barley (ed.), *European Towns: Their Archaeology and Early History*, London: 499–509.

Addyman, P.V. and Hill, D.H. (1968) 'Saxon Southampton: a review of the evidence', Part I, *Proc Hampshire Fld Club Archaeol Soc* 25: 61–93.

—— (1969) 'Saxon Southampton: a review of the evidence', Part II, *Proc Hampshire Fld Club Archaeol Soc* 26: 61–96.

Addyman, P.V., Leigh, D. and Hughes, M.J. (1972) 'Anglo-Saxon houses at Chalton, Hampshire', *Medieval Archaeol* 16: 13–32.

Ager, B. (1990) 'The alternative quoit brooch: an update', in E. Southworth (ed.), *Anglo-Saxon Cemeteries: a Reappraisal*, Liverpool: 153–62.

Akerman, J.Y. (1855) *Remains of Pagan Saxondum*, London.

Alcock, L. (1978) '*Her . . . gefeaht with Walas*: Aspects of the warfare of Saxons and Britons', *Bull Board Celtic Studies* 27: 413–24.

—— (1981) 'Quantity or quality: the Anglian graves of Bernicia', in V.I. Evison (ed.), *Angles, Saxons, and Jutes*, Oxford: 168–86.

—— (1992) 'Messages from the dark side of the moon: western and northern Britain in the age of Sutton Hoo', in M.O.H. Carver (ed.), *The Age of Sutton Hoo*, Woodbridge: 205–15.

Alcock, N.W. and Walsh, D. (1993) 'Architecture at Cowdery's Down: A reconsideration', *Archaeol Journ* 150: 403–19.

Anstee, J.W. and Biek, L. (1961) 'A study in pattern welding', *Medieval Archaeol* 5: 71–93.

Arnold, C.J. (1978) 'George Hillier: an Isle of Wight antiquary', *Proc Hampshire Fld Club Archaeol Soc* 34: 59–64.

—— (1980) 'Wealth and social structure: a matter of life and death', in P. Rahtz, T. Dickinson and L. Watts (eds), *Anglo-Saxon Cemeteries 1979*, Brit Archaeol Rep 82, Oxford: 81–142.

—— (1981a) 'Early Anglo-Saxon pottery: production and distribution', in H. Howard and E.L. Morris (eds), *Production and Distribution: a Ceramic Viewpoint*, Brit Archaeol Rep 120, Oxford: 243–55.

—— (1981b) 'Colonisation and settlement: the early Anglo-Saxon pottery of the Isle of Wight', *Proc Isle of Wight Nat Hist & Arch Soc* 7: 419–35.

—— (1982a) *The Anglo-Saxon Cemeteries of the Isle of Wight*, London.

—— (1982b) 'Stress as a factor in social and economic change', in A.C. Renfrew and S. Shennan (eds), *Ranking, Resource and Exchange*, Cambridge: 124–31.

—— (1982c) 'Excavations at Eastry Court Farm, Eastry, Kent', *Archaeol Cantiana* 98: 121–35.

—— (1983) 'The Sancton-Baston Potter', *Scottish Archaeol Rev* 2: 17–30.

—— (1984a) *Roman Britain to Saxon England*, London.

—— (1984b) 'Social evolution in post-Roman western Europe', in J. Bintliff (ed.), *European Social Evolution*, Bradford: 277–94.

—— (1988a) *An Archaeology of the Anglo-Saxon Kingdoms*, first edition, London.

—— (1988b) 'Early Anglo-Saxon pottery of the "Illington-Lackford" type', *Oxford Journ of Archaeol* 7 (3): 343–59.

—— (1988c) 'Territories and leadership: frameworks for the study of emergent polities in early Anglo-Saxon southern England', in Driscoll and Nieke (eds), Edinburgh: 111–27.

—— (1990) 'The Anglo-Saxon cemeteries of the Isle of Wight: an appraisal of nineteenth-century excavation data', in E. Southworth (ed.), *Anglo-Saxon cemeteries: a reappraisal*, Liverpool:163–76.

—— (1991) 'Metallurgical analysis and the interpretation of modes of production: gold bracteates in Anglo-Saxon Kent', in P. Budd *et al.* (eds), *Archaeological Sciences 1989*, Oxford, 119–24.

—— (forthcoming) 'Early Medieval Wales AD 400–1000', in C.J. Arnold and J.L. Davies (eds), *The Archaeology of Prehistoric and Early Wales*, Edinburgh.

Arnold, C.J. and Wardle, P. (1981) 'Early Anglo-Saxon settlement patterns in southern England', *Medieval Archaeol* 25: 145–9.

Arnold, C.J. and Wilkinson, J.L. (1984) 'Three Anglo-Saxon cremations from Girton', *Proc Cambridge Antiq Soc* 73: 23–7.

Arnold, D.E. (1985) *Ceramic Theory and Cultural Process*, Cambridge.

Arrhenius, B. (1971) *Granatschmuck und Gemmen aus nordischen Funden des Frühen Mittelalters*, Stockholm.

—— (1973) 'East Scandinavian Style I – a review', *Medieval Archaeol* 17: 26–42.

—— (1975) 'Die technischen Voraussetzungen für die Entwicklung der Germanischen Tierornamentik', *Frühmittelalterliche Studien* 9: 93–109.

—— (1978) review of Bruce-Mitford (1975), *Medieval Archaeol* 22: 189–95.

Arthur, B.V. and Jope, E.M. (1963) 'Early Anglo-Saxon pottery kilns at Purwell Farm, Cassington, Oxfordshire', *Medieval Archaeol* 6–7: 1–12.

Astill, G. (1985) 'Archaeology, economics and early medieval Europe', *Oxford Journ of Archaeol* 4 (2): 215–32.

Astill, G. and Lobb, S. (1982) 'Sampling a Saxon settlement site: Wraysbury, Berks', *Medieval Archaeol* 26: 138–42.

Atkinson, D. (1916) *The Romano-British Site on Lowbury Hill in Berkshire*, Reading.

Atkinson, R.J.C. (1953) 'Technical notes on the construction of the swords, scabbards and shields', in Leeds and de S. Shortt (1953): 55–60.

Avent, R. (1975) *Anglo-Saxon Garnet Inlaid Disc and Composite Brooches*, Brit Archaeol Rep 11, Oxford.

Avent, R. and Evison, V.I. (1982) 'Anglo-Saxon button brooches', *Archaeologia* 107: 77–124.

Avent, R. and Leigh, D. (1977) 'A study of cross-hatched gold foils in Anglo-Saxon jewellery', *Medieval Archaeol* 21: 1–46.

Baillie, M. (1994) 'Dendrochronology raises questions about nature of AD 536 dust-veil event', *The Holocene* 4 (2): 212–17.

Bakka, E. (1958) *On the Beginnings of Salin's Style I in England*, Bergen.

Bassett, S. (ed.) (1989) *The Origins of Anglo-Saxon Kingdoms*, Leicester.
Bateman, T. (1861) *Ten Years' Diggings in Celtic and Saxon Grave Hills*, London.
de Baye, J. (1893) *The Industrial Arts of the Anglo-Saxons*, London.
Beck, C.W. (1970) 'Amber in archaeology', *Archaeology* 23: 7–11.
Beckwith, J. (1972) *Ivory Carvings in Early Medieval England*, London.
Beddoe, J. (1885) *The Races of Britain: a Contribution to the Anthropology of Western Europe*, London.
Bell, J.A. (1981) 'A Reconstruction of Anglian Female Dress in Yorkshire and Lincolnshire', unpublished BA dissertation, University of Leeds.
Bell, M.G. (1977) 'Excavations at Bishopstone in Sussex', *Sussex Archaeol Coll* 115.
—— (1978) 'Saxon settlements and buildings in Sussex', in P. Brandon (ed.), *The South Saxons*, Chichester: 36–53.
Biddick, K. (1984) 'Field edge, forest edge: early medieval social change and resource allocation' in K. Biddick (ed.) *Archaeological Approaches to Medieval Europe*, Kalamazoo, Mich.: 105–18.
Biddle, M. (1976) 'Hampshire and the origins of Wessex', in G. de G. Sieveking, I.H. Longworth and K.E. Wilson (eds), *Problems in Economic and Social Archaeology*, London: 323–42.
—— (1984) 'London in the Strand', *Popular Archaeol* 6 (1): 23–7.
Bimson, M. (1985) 'Dark-Age garnet cutting', *Anglo-Saxon Studies in Archaeol and Hist* 4: 125–28.
Bimson, M., La Neice, S. and Leese, M. (1982) 'The characterisation of mounted garnet', *Archaeometry* 24: 51–8.
Black, E.W. (1986) 'Roman-British burial customs and religious beliefs in south-east England', *Archaeol J* 143: 201–39.
Blair, J. (1995) 'Anglo-Saxon pagan shrines and their prototypes', *Anglo-Saxon Studies in Archaeol and Hist* 8: 1–28.
Blair, P.H. (1948) 'The Northumbrians and their southern frontier', *Archaeologia Aeliana* (4th series), 26: 98–126.
Boddington, A. (1990) 'Models of burial, settlement and worship: the final phase reviewed', in E. Southworth (ed.), *Anglo-Saxon Cemeteries: a Reappraisal*, Liverpool: 177–99.
Böhner, K. (1958) *Die fränkischen Altertümer des Trierer Landes*, Berlin.
Bond, J.M. (1993) 'Cremated animal bone', in Timby (1993): 300–9.
—— (1994a) 'The cremated animal bone', in McKinley (1994a): 121–35.
—— (1994b) 'An explanatory note on the identification of the ivory fragments', in C.Hills, K. Penn and R. Rickett, *Spong Hill Part V: Catalogue of Cremations*, Gressenhall: 35–6.
Bonnet, C. and Martin, M. (1982) 'La modèle de plomb d'une fibule anglo-saxonne de Saint-Pierre à Genève', *Archéologie suisse* 5 (4): 210–24.
Bonney, D.J. (1972) 'Early boundaries in Wessex', in P.J. Fowler (ed.), *Archaeology and the Landscape*, London: 168–86.
—— (1976) 'Early boundaries and estates in southern England', in P.H. Sawyer (ed.), *Medieval Settlement*, London: 72–82.
Bourdillon, J. (1979) 'Town life and animal husbandry in the Southampton area, as suggested by the excavated bones', *Proc Hampshire Fld Club Archaeol Soc* 36: 181–92.
Boyle, A., Dodd, A., Miles, D. and Mudd, A. (1996) *Two Oxfordshire Anglo-Saxon Cemeteries: Berinsfield and Didcot*, Oxford.
Bradley, R. and Lewis, E. (1968) 'Excavations at the George Inn, Portsdown', *Proc Hampshire Fld Club Archaeol Soc* 25: 27–50.
Brassil, K.S., Owen, W.G. and Britnell, W.J. (1991) 'Prehistoric and early medieval cemeteries at Tandderwen, near Denbigh, Clwyd', *Archaeol Journ* 148: 46–97.

Brenan, J. (1985) 'Assessing social status in the Anglo-Saxon cemetery at Sleaford', *Bull Institute Archaeol* 21–2 (1984–5): 125–31.
—— (1991) *Hanging Bowls and their Contexts*, Brit Archaeol Rep 220, Oxford.
Brisbane, M.A. (1980) 'Anglo-Saxon burials: pottery, production and social status', in P.A. Rahtz, T.M. Dickinson and L. Watts (eds), *Anglo-Saxon Cemeteries 1979*, Brit Archaeol Rep 82, Oxford: 209–18.
—— (1981) 'Incipient markets for early Anglo-Saxon ceramics' in H. Howard and E.L. Morris (eds), *Production and Distribution: a Ceramic Viewpoint*, Brit Archaeol Rep 120, Oxford: 229–41.
—— (1983) 'The period 4 pottery', *Archaeol Journ* 140: 254–7.
—— (1994) 'The cremation pottery fabrics: a note', in C.Hills, K. Penn and R. Rickett, *Spong Hill Part V: Catalogue of Cremations*, Gressenhall: 36.
Briscoe, T. (1981) 'Anglo-Saxon pot stamps', *Anglo-Saxon Studies in Archaeol and Hist* 2: 1–36.
British Museum (1923) *British Museum Guide to Anglo-Saxon Antiquities*, London.
Brooks, N. (1989a) 'The creation and early structure of the kingdom of Kent', in Bassett (ed.) (1989): 55–74.
—— (1989b) 'The formation of the Mercian kingdom', in Bassett (ed.) (1989): 159–70.
Brown, B.J.W., Knocker, G.M., Smedley, N. and West, S.E. (1957) 'Excavations at Grimstone End, Pakenham', *Proc Suffolk Institute Archaeol* 26: 188–207.
Brown, D. (1974) 'So-called "needle-cases"', *Medieval Archaeol* 18: 151–4.
—— (1977) 'Firesteels and pursemounts again', *Bonner Jahrbücher* 18: 451–80.
—— (1981a) 'Swastika patterns', in V.I. Evison (ed.), *Angles, Saxons and Jutes*, Oxford: 227–40.
—— (1981b) 'The dating of the Sutton Hoo coins', *Anglo-Saxon Studies in Archaeol and Hist* 2: 71–86.
Brown, G.B. (1903–37) *The Arts in Early England I* (1903), *II* (1905), *III–IV* (1915), *V* (1921), *VIi* (1925), *VIii* (1937), London.
Brown, P.D.C. (1976) 'Some notes on grass-tempered pottery', *Records of Buckinghamshire* 20: 191–3.
Browne, T. (1658) *Hydriotaphia, or Urne buriall*, London.
Brownsword, D.R. and Hines, J. (1993) 'The alloys of a sample of Anglo-Saxon square-headed brooches', *Antiq Journ* 73: 1–10.
Bruce-Mitford, R.L.S. (1966) *The Sutton Hoo Ship-Burial*, tenth impression, London.
—— (1970) 'The Sutton Hoo lyre, Beowulf and the origins of the frame harp', *Antiquity* 44: 7–13.
—— (1974) *Aspects of Anglo-Saxon Archaeology*, London.
—— (1975) *The Sutton Hoo Ship Burial I*, London.
—— (1978) *The Sutton Hoo Ship Burial II*, London.
—— (1983) *The Sutton Hoo Ship Burial III*, London.
Brush, K.A. (1988) 'Gender and mortuary analysis in pagan Anglo-Saxon archaeology', *Archaeol Rev from Cambridge* 7 (1): 76–89.
Bullough, R.A. (1965) 'Anglo-Saxon institutions and early English society', *Annali della Fondazione Italiana per la Storia Amministraria* 2: 647–59.
Cameron, E. and Filmer-Sankey, W. (1993) 'A sword hilt of horn from the Snape Anglo-Saxon cemetery', *Anglo-Saxon Studies in Archaeol and Hist* 6: 103–5.
Campbell, E. (1989) 'A blue glass squat jar from Dinas Powys, South Wales', *Bull Board Celtic Studies* 36: 239–45.
Campbell, J.A., Baxter, M.S. and Alcock, L. (1979) 'Radio-carbon dates for the Cadbury massacre', *Antiquity* 53: 31–8.
Capelle, T. (1975) 'Weitere Modeln der Merowinger- und Wikingerzeit', *Frühmittelalterliche Studien* 9: 110–42.

Capelle, T. and Vierck, H. (1971) 'Modeln der Merowinger- und Wikingerzeit', *Frühmittelalterliche Studien* 5: 31–8.

Carnegie, S. and Filmer-Sankey, W. (1993) 'A Saxon "Cremation Pyre" from the Snape Anglo-Saxon cemetery, Suffolk', *Anglo-Saxon Studies in Archaeol and Hist* 6: 107–11.

Carver, M.O.H. (1989) 'Kingship and material culture in early Anglo-Saxon East Anglia', in Bassett (ed.) (1989): 141–58.

—— (1992a) 'The Anglo-Saxon Cemetery at Sutton Hoo: an Interim Report', in M.O.H. Carver (ed.), *The Age of Sutton Hoo*, Woodbridge: 343–71.

—— (1992b) 'The future of Sutton Hoo', in C.B. Kendall and P.S. Wells (eds), *A Voyage to the Other World: the Legacy of Sutton Hoo*, Med. Stud. at Minnesota 5, Minneapolis: 183–200.

Chadwick, H.M. (1905) *Studies in Anglo-Saxon Institutions*, Cambridge.

—— (1907) *Origin of the English Nation*, Cambridge.

Chadwick, S.E. (1958) 'The Anglo-Saxon cemetery at Finglesham, Kent: a reconsideration', *Medieval Archaeol* 2: 1–71.

Childe, V.G. (1933) 'Is prehistory practical?' *Antiquity* 7: 410–18.

Claessen, H.J.M. (1978) 'The early state: a structural approach', in Claessen and Skalnik (eds): 533–96.

Claessen, H.J.M. and Skalnik, P. (eds) (1978) *The Early State*, The Hague.

Clark, A. (1960) 'A cross-valley dyke on the Surrey–kent Border', *Surrey Archaeol Colls* 57: 72–4.

Clark, A.J., Hampton, J.N. and Hughes, M.F. (1983) 'Mount Down, Hampshire: the reappraisal of evidence', *Antiq Journ* 63: 122–4.

Cleere, H. (1972) 'Anglo-Saxon Iron-working debris', in A.C.C. Brodribb, A.R. Hands and D.R. Walker, *Excavations at Shakenoak Farm, near Wilcote, Oxfordshire III*, Oxford: 117–18.

Clough, T. Mc.K., Dornier, A. and Rutland, R.A. (1975) *A Guide to the Anglo-Saxon and Viking Antiquities of Leicestershire and Rutland*, Leicester.

Coffin, S. (1975) 'Linear earthworks in the Froxfield, East Tisted and Hayling Wood district', *Proc Hampshire Fld Club Archaeol Soc* 32: 77–82.

Colgrave, B. and Mynors, R.A.B. (eds) (1969) *Ecclesiastical History of the English People*, Oxford.

Collingwood, R.G. and Myres, J.N.L. (1936) *Roman Britain and the English Settlements*, Oxford.

Collis, J. (1983) *Wigber Low, Derbyshire: a Bronze Age and Anglian Burial Site in the White Peak*, Sheffield.

Cook, A.M. (1974) 'The evidence for the reconstruction of female costume in the early Anglo-Saxon period in the South of England', unpublished MA thesis, University of Birmingham.

Cook, A.M. and Dacre, M.W. (1985) *Excavations at Portway, Andover 1973–1975*, Oxford University Committee for Archaeology Mono 4, Oxford.

Copley, G. (1986) *Archaeology and Place-names in the Fifth and Sixth Centuries*, Brit Archaeol Rep 147, Oxford.

—— (1988) *Early Place-Names of the Anglian Regions of England*, Brit Archaeol Rep 185, Oxford.

Corney, A., Ashbee, B., Evison, V.I. and Brothwell, D. (1967) 'A prehistoric and Anglo-Saxon burial ground, Portsdown, Portsmouth', *Proc Hampshire Fld Club Archaeol Soc* 24: 20–41.

Cowie, R. (1992) 'Archaeological evidence for the waterfront of middle Saxon London', *Medieval Archaeol* 36: 164–8.

Crabtree, P.J. (1985) 'The faunal remains', in West (1985): 85–96.

—— (1989a) 'Sheep, horses, swine, and kine: a zooarchaeological perspective on the Anglo-Saxon settlement of England', *Journ of Field Archaeol* 16: 205–13.

— (1989b) 'Zooarchaeology at early Anglo-Saxon West Stow' in C.L. Redman (ed.), *Medieval Archaeology: Papers of the Seventeenth Annual Conference of the Center for Medieval and Early Renaissance Studies*, New York: 203–15.

Cramp, R.J. (1957) 'Beowulf and archaeology', *Medieval Archaeol* 1: 57–77.

— (1976) 'Monastic sites', in Wilson (ed.) (1976a): 201–52.

Crawford, G. (1983) 'Excavations at Wasperton, third interim report', *West Midlands Archaeology* XXVI: 15–28.

Crawford, S. (1993) 'Children, death and the afterlife in Anglo-Saxon England', *Anglo-Saxon Studies in Archaeol and Hist* 6: 83–91.

Crowfoot, E. and Hawkes, S.C. (1967) 'Early Anglo-Saxon gold braids', *Medieval Archaeol* 11: 42–86.

Crowfoot, G.M. (1952) 'Anglo-Saxon tablet weaving', *Antiq Journ* 32: 189–91.

Cunliffe, B. (1972) 'Saxon and medieval settlement patterns in the region of Chalton, Hampshire', *Medieval Archaeol* 16: 1–12.

Daniel, G.E. (1981) *A Short History of Archaeology*, London.

Daniels, R. (1988) 'The Anglo-Saxon monastery at Church Close, Hartlepool, Cleveland', *Archaeol Journ* 145: 158–210.

Darrah, R. (1982) 'Working unseasoned oak', in S. McGrail (ed.) *Woodworking Techniques before AD 1500*, Brit Archaeol Rep 129, Oxford: 219–30.

Davidson, H.R.E. (1962) *The Sword in Anglo-Saxon England: Its Archaeology and Literature*, Oxford.

— (1992) 'Human sacrifice in the late pagan period in north western Europe', in M.O.H. Carver (ed.), *The Age of Sutton Hoo*, Woodbridge: 332–40.

Davies, S.M. (1980) 'Excavations at Old Down Farm, Andover. Part I: Saxon', *Proc Hampshire Fld Club Archaeol Soc* 36: 161–80.

— (1984) 'The excavation of an Anglo-Saxon cemetery (and some prehistoric pits) at Charlton Plantation, near Downton', *Wiltshire Archaeol Nat Hist Mag* 79: 109–54.

Davies, W. (1977) 'Annals and the origins of Mercia', in A. Dornier (ed.), *Mercian Studies*, Leicester: 17–29.

— (1982) *Wales in the Early Middle Ages*, Leicester.

— and Vierck, H. (1974) 'The contexts of the *Tribal Hidage*: social aggregates and settlement patterns', *Frühmittelalterliche Studien* 8: 223–93.

Day, L.R. and Perkins, D.R.J. (1991) 'Neutron activation analysis of late Roman and Dark Age glass from Kent', in P. Budd *et al.* (eds), *Archaeological Sciences 1989*, Oxford: 16–22.

Deanesley, M. (1943) 'Roman traditionalist influence among the Anglo-Saxons', *English Hist Rev* 58: 129–46.

Denton, G.H. and Karlén, W. (1973) 'Holocene climatic variations: their pattern and possible cause', *Quaternary Research* 3: 155–205.

Dickinson, T.M. (1974) *Cuddesdon and Dorchester-on-Thames*, Brit Archaeol Rep 1, Oxford.

— (1978) 'British antiquity: post-Roman and pagan Anglo-Saxon', *Arch Journ* 135: 332–44.

— (1982) 'Ornament variation in pairs of cast saucer brooches: a case study from the Upper Thames Region', in L. Webster (ed.), *Aspects of Production and Style in Dark Age Metalwork*, London: 21–50.

— (1983) 'Anglo-Saxon archaeology: twenty-five years on', in D.A. Hinton (ed.), *25 Years of Medieval Archaeology*, Sheffield: 38–43.

— (1991) 'Material culture as social expression: the case of saucer brooches with running spiral decoration', *Studien zur Sachsenforschung* 7: 39–70.

— (1992) 'The seventh-century cremation burial in Asthall barrow', in M.O.H. Carver (ed.), *The Age of Sutton Hoo*, Woodbridge: 95–130.

—— (1993a) 'Early Saxon saucer brooches: a preliminary overview', *Anglo-Saxon Stud in Archaeol and Hist* 6: 11–44.

—— (1993b) 'An Anglo-Saxon "cunning woman" from Bidford-on-Avon', in M.O.H. Carver (ed.), *In Search of Cult*, Woodbridge: 45–54.

Dickinson, T.M. and Härke, H. (1992) *Early Anglo-Saxon Shields*, London.

Dickinson, T.M. and Speake, G. (1992) 'The seventh-century cremation burial in Asthall barrow, Oxfordshire: a reassessment', in M.O.H. Carver (ed.), *The Age of Sutton Hoo*, Woodbridge: 95–130.

Dixon, P.H. (1982) 'How Saxon is the Saxon house?' in P.J. Drury (ed.), *Structural Reconstruction*, Brit Archaeol Rep 110, Oxford: 275–87.

—— (1993) 'The Anglo-Saxon settlement at Mucking: an interpretation', *Anglo-Saxon Stud in Archaeol and Hist* 6: 125–47.

—— (1994) *The Reading Lathe*, Newport.

—— (1995) 'Entrances to sunken-floored structures in Anglo-Saxon times', *Anglo-Saxon Stud Archaeol Hist* 8: 99–102.

Done, G. (1993) 'Animal bone from Anglo-Saxon contexts', in Hamerow (1993): 74–9.

Doran, J.E. and Hodson, F.R. (1975) *Mathematics and Computers in Archaeology*, Edinburgh.

Dornier, A. (1977) *Mercian Studies*, Leicester.

Douglas, J. (1793) *Nenia Britannica*, London.

Down, A. and Welch, M. (1990) *Chichester Excavations VII*, Chichester.

Driscoll, S. and Nieke, M. (eds) (1988) *Power and Politics in Early Medieval Britain and Ireland*, Edinburgh.

Dumville, D.N. (1977) 'Kingship, genealogies and regnal lists', in P.H. Sawyer and I.N. Wood (eds), *Early Medieval Kingship*, Leeds: 72–104.

—— (1989a) 'Essex, middle Anglia and the expansion of Mercia in the south-east Midlands', in Bassett (ed.) (1989): 123–40.

—— (1989b) 'The origins of Northumbria: some aspects of the British background', in Bassett (ed.) (1989): 213–24.

—— (1989c) 'The Tribal Hidage: an introduction to its texts and their history', in Bassett (ed.) (1989): 225–30.

Dunning, G.C. (1932) 'Bronze-Age settlements and a Saxon hut near Bourton-on-the-Water, Gloucestershire', *Antiq Journ* 12: 279–93.

—— (1959) 'The Anglo-Saxon plane from Sarre', *Archaeol Cantiana* 73: 196–201.

Eagles, B.N. (1979) *The Anglo-Saxon Settlement of Humberside*, Brit Archaeol Rep 68, Oxford.

Ekwall, E. (1936) 'Some notes on English place-names containing tribal names', *Namn och Bygd* 24: 178–83.

Enright, M.J. (1983) 'The Sutton Hoo whetstone sceptre: a study in iconography and cultural milieu', *Anglo-Saxon England* 11, 119–34.

Esmonde Cleary, A.S. (1989) *The Ending of Roman Britain*, London.

—— (1993) 'Approaches to the difference between late Romano-British and early Anglo-Saxon archaeology', *Anglo-Saxon Stud in Archaeol and Hist* 6, 57–63.

Evans, A.J. (1890) 'On a late-Celtic urn-field at Aylesford, Kent', *Archaeologia* 52: 315–88.

Everson, P. (1993) 'Pre-Viking settlement in Lindsey', in A. Vince (ed.), *Pre-Viking Lindsey*, Lincoln: 91–100.

Evison, V.I. (1955) 'Early Anglo-Saxon inlaid metalwork', *Antiq Journ* 35: 20–45.

—— (1958) 'Further Anglo-Saxon inlay', *Antiq Journ* 38: 240–4.

—— (1963) 'Sugar-loaf shield bosses', *Antiq Journ* 43: 38–96.

—— (1967) 'The Dover ring-sword and other sword rings and beads', *Archaeologia* 101: 63–118.

—— (1968) 'Quoit brooch style buckles', *Antiq Journ* 48: 231–49.
—— (1972) 'Glass cone beakers of the "Kempston" type', *Journ Glass Stud* 14: 48–66.
—— (1975) 'Pagan Saxon whetstones', *Antiq Journ* 55: 70–85.
—— (1979a) 'The body in the ship at Sutton Hoo', *Anglo-Saxon Stud in Archaeol and Hist* 1: 121–38.
—— (1979b) *A Corpus of Wheel-thrown Pottery in Anglo-Saxon Graves*, London.
—— (1987) *Dover: The Buckland Anglo-Saxon Cemetery*, London.
—— (1988) *An Anglo-Saxon Cemetery at Alton, Hampshire*, Hampshire Field Club Monograph 4.
—— (1994) *An Anglo-Saxon Cemetery at Great Chesterford, Essex*, Council Brit Archaeol Res Rep 91, York.
Farley, M. (1976) 'Saxon and medieval Walton, Aylesbury: excavations 1973–4', *Records of Buckinghamshire* 20: 153–290.
Faull, M.L. (1976) 'The location and relationship of the Sancton Anglo-Saxon cemeteries', *Antiq Journ* 56: 227–33.
—— (1977) 'British survival in Anglo-Saxon Northumbria', in L. Laing (ed.), *Studies in Celtic Survival*, Brit Archaeol Rep 37, Oxford.
Fell, C.E. (1975) 'Old English *BEOR*', *Leeds Studies Eng* (new series) 8: 76–95.
Filmer-Sankey, W. (1990) 'A new boat burial from the Snape Anglo-Saxon cemetery, Suffolk', in S. McGrail (ed.), *Maritime Celts, Frisians and Saxons*, London, 126–34.
—— (1992) 'Snape Anglo-Saxon cemetery: the current state of knowledge', in M.O.H. Carver (ed.), *The Age of Sutton Hoo*, Woodbridge: 39–52.
Fisher, G. (1988) 'Style and sociopolitical organisation: a preliminary study from early Anglo-Saxon England', in Driscoll and Nieke (eds) (1988): 128–44.
Foard, G. (1978) 'Systematic fieldwalking and the investigation of Saxon settlement in Northamptonshire', *World Archaeol* 9: 357–74.
Fortes, M. (1968) 'Of installation ceremonies', *Proc Roy Anthrop Inst for 1967*: 5–20.
Fox, A. and Fox, C. (1958) 'Wansdyke reconsidered', *Archaeol Journ* 115: 1–48.
Fox, C. (1923) *The Archaeology of the Cambridge Region*, Cambridge.
Fulford, M.G. and Rippon, S.J. (1994) 'Lowbury Hill, Oxon: a re-assessment of the probable Romano-Celtic temple and Anglo-Saxon barrow', *Archaeol Journ* 151:158–211.
Gaimster, M. (1992) 'Scandinavian gold bracteates in Britain. Money and media in the Dark Ages', *Medieval Archaeol* 36: 1–28.
Geake, H. (1992) 'Burial practice in seventh- and eighth-century England', in M.O.H. Carver (ed.), *The Age of Sutton Hoo*, Woodbridge: 83–94.
Gelling, M. (1978) *Signposts to the Past*, London.
—— (1989) 'The early history of western Mercia', in Bassett (ed.) (1989): 184–201.
Gilchrist, R. and Morris, R. (1993) 'Monasteries as settlements: religion, society, and economy, AD 600–1050', in M.O.H. Carver (ed.), *In Search of Cult*, Woodbridge: 113–18.
Gilmour, B. (1984) 'X-radiographs of two objects: the weaving batten (24/3) and the sword (40/5)', in Hills, Penn and Rickett (1984): 160–3.
Goodier, A. (1984) 'The formation of boundaries in Anglo-Saxon England: a statistical study', *Medieval Archaeol* 28: 1–21.
Green, B. and Rogerson, A. (1978) *The Anglo-Saxon Cemetery at Bergh Apton, Norfolk*, East Anglian Archaeol Rep 7, Gressenhall.
Green, B., Rogerson, A. and White, S.G. (1987) *Morning Thorpe Anglo-Saxon Cemetery, Norfolk*, East Anglian Archaeol Rep 36, Gressenhall.
Green, C. (1963) *Sutton Hoo: the Excavation of a Royal Ship-burial*, London.
Green, C.S. (1987) *Excavations at Poundbury, Volume I: The Settlements*, Dorset Nat Hist Archaeol Soc Mono Ser 7, Dorchester.

Green, F.J. (1983) 'The plant remains', *Archaeol Journ* 140: 259–61.

Grierson, P. (1959) 'Commerce in the dark ages: a critique of the evidence', *Trans Roy Hist Soc* (5th series) 9: 123–40.

—— (1961) 'La fonction sociale de la monnaie en Angleterre au VIIe-VIIIe siècles', *Settimane di studio del Centro italiano di stude sull'alto medioevo* 7: 341–85.

Grierson, P. and Blackburn, M. (1986) *Medieval European Coinage 1, The Early Middle Ages (5th-10th centuries)*, Cambridge.

Griffith, A.F. and Salzmann, L.F. (1914) 'An Anglo-Saxon cemetery at Alfriston, Sussex', *Sussex Archaeol Coll* 56: 16–51.

Hall, D.N. (1979) 'New evidence of modifications in open field systems', *Antiquity* 53: 222–4.

—— (1981) 'The origins of open-field agriculture – the archaeological fieldwork evidence', in T. Rowley (ed.), *The Origins of Open Field Agriculture*, London: 22–38.

Hallam, S. (1961) 'Wash coast-line levels since Roman Times', *Antiquity* 35: 152–5.

Hamerow, H. (1991) 'Settlement mobility and the "Middle Saxon Shuffle": rural settlements and settlement patterns in Anglo-Saxon England', *Anglo-Saxon England* 20: 1–18.

—— (1993) *Excavations at Mucking, Volume 2: the Anglo-Saxon Settlement*, London.

—— (1994) 'Migration theory and the migration period', in B. Vyner (ed.), *Building the Past*, London: 164–77.

Hamerow, H., Hollevoet, Y. and Vince, A. (1994) 'Migration period settlements and "Anglo-Saxon" pottery from Flanders', *Medieval Archaeol* 38: 1–18.

Harden, D.B. (ed.) (1956a) *Dark Age Britain. Studies presented to E.T. Leeds*, London.

—— (1956b) 'Glass vessels in Britain and Ireland, AD 400–1000', in Harden (1956a): 132–70.

—— (1978) 'Anglo-Saxon and later medieval glass in Britain: some recent developments', *Medieval Archaeol* 22: 1–24.

Härke, H. (1981) 'Anglo-Saxon laminated shields at Petersfinger – a myth', *Medieval Archaeol* 25: 141–4.

—— (1989) 'Knives in early Saxon burials: blade length and age at death', *Medieval Archaeol* 33: 144–8.

—— (1990) '"Warrior graves"? The background of the Anglo-Saxon weapon burial rite', *Past and Present* 126: 22–43.

—— (1992a) 'Changing symbols in a changing society: the Anglo-Saxon weapon burial rite in the seventh century', in M.O.H. Carver (ed.), *The Age of Sutton Hoo*, Woodridge: 149–65.

—— (1992b) *Angelsächsische Waffengräber des 5. bis 7. Jahrhunderts*, Cologne.

Härke, H. and Salter, C. (1984) 'A technical and metallurgical study of three Anglo-Saxon shield bosses', *Anglo-Saxon Stud in Archaeol and Hist* 3: 55–66.

Harrison, K. (1976) *The Framework of Anglo-Saxon History to AD 900*, Cambridge.

Haseloff, G. (1981) *Die germanische Tierornamentik der Völkerwanderungszeit. Studien zu Salin's Stil I*, Vorgeschichtliche Forschungen 17, Berlin.

Hatch Wicker, N.L. (1992) 'Swedish–Anglian contacts antedating Sutton Hoo: the testimony of the Scandinavian gold bracteates', in R. Farrell and C. Neuman de Vegvar (eds), *Sutton Hoo: Fifty Years After*, Ohio: 149–71.

Hawkes, C.F.C. (1956) 'The Jutes of Kent', in Harden (1956a): 91–111.

Hawkes, C.F.C. and Smith, M.A. (1957) 'On some bucket mounts and cauldrons of the Bronze and Early Iron Ages', *Antiq Journ* 37: 131–98.

Hawkes, S.C. (1961) 'The Jutish Style A. A study of Germanic animal art in southern England in the fifth century AD', *Archaeologia* 98: 29–74.

—— (1968) 'Richborough – the physical geography', in B. Cunliffe, *Fifth Report on the Excavations of the Roman Fort at Richborough, Kent*, London: 224–30.

—— (1969) 'Early Anglo-Saxon Kent', *Archaeol Journ* 127: 186–92.

—— (1973) 'The dating and social significance of the burials in the Polhill cemetery', in Philp (1973): 186–201.

—— (1977) 'Orientation at Finglesham: sunrise dating of death and burial in an Anglo-Saxon cemetery in East Kent', *Archaeol Cantiana* 92: 33–51.

—— (1979) 'Eastry in Anglo-Saxon Kent: its importance and a newly found grave', *Anglo-Saxon Stud in Archaeol and Hist* 1: 81–114.

—— (1982) 'Anglo-Saxon Kent *c.* 425–725', in P.E. Leach (ed.), *Archaeology in Kent to AD 1500*, Council Brit Archaeol Res Rep 48, London: 64–78.

Hawkes, S.C. and Dunning, G.C. (1961) 'Soldiers and settlers in Britain, fourth to fifth century: with a catalogue of animal ornamented and related belt-fittings', *Medieval Archaeol* 5: 1–70.

Hawkes, S.C. and Page, R.I. (1967) 'Swords and runes in south-east England', *Antiq Journ* 47: 1–26.

Hawkes, S.C. and Wells, C. (1975) 'Crime and punishment in an Anglo-Saxon cemetery?', *Antiquity* 49: 118–22.

Hawkes, S.C. and Pollard, M. (1981) 'The gold bracteates from sixth-century Anglo-Saxon graves in Kent, in the light of a new find from Finglesham', *Frühmittelalterliche Studien* 15: 316–70.

Hawkes, S.C., Merrick, J.M. and Metcalf, D.M. (1966) 'X-ray fluorescent analysis of some Dark Age coins and jewellery', *Archaeometry* 9: 98–138.

Hedeager, L. (1992) 'Kingdoms, ethnicity and material culture: Denmark in a European perspective', in M.O.H. Carver (ed.), *The Age of Sutton Hoo*, Woodridge: 279–300.

Hedges, J.D. and Buckley, D.G. (1985) 'Anglo-Saxon burials and later features excavated at Orsett, Essex, 1975', *Medieval Archaeol* 29: 1–24.

Hedges, M.E. (1977) 'The excavation of the Knowes of Quoyscottie, Orkney', *Proc Soc Antiq Scotland* 108: 130–55.

Hewlett, H.G. (ed.) (1886) *The Flowers of History, by Roger Wendover*, London.

Hicks, C. (1986) 'The birds on the Sutton Hoo purse', *Anglo-Saxon England* 15, 153–66.

—— (1993) *Animals in Early Medieval Art*, Edinburgh.

Higham, N. (1992) *Rome, Britain and the Anglo-Saxons*, London.

—— (1995) *An English Empire: Bede and the early Anglo-Saxon Kings*, Manchester.

Hillier, G. (1856) *The History and Antiquities of the Isle of Wight*, London.

Hills, C. (1977) *The Anglo-Saxon Cemetery at Spong Hill, North Elmham, Part I*, East Anglian Archaeol Rep 6, Gressenhall.

—— (1979) 'The archaeology of Anglo-Saxon England in the pagan period: a review', *Anglo-Saxon England* 8: 297–329.

—— (1980a) 'Anglo-Saxon chairperson', *Antiquity* 54: 52–4.

—— (1980b) 'Anglo-Saxon cremation cemeteries with particular reference to Spong Hill, Norfolk', in P.A. Rahtz, T.M. Dickinson and L. Watts (eds), *Anglo-Saxon Cemeteries 1979*, Brit Archaeol Rep 82, Oxford: 197–208.

—— (1980c) 'The Anglo-Saxon settlement of England', in D.M. Wilson (ed.), *The Northern World*, London: 71–94.

—— (1981) 'Barred zoomorphic combs of the migration period', in V.I. Evison (ed.), *Angles, Saxons and Jutes*, Oxford: 96–125.

—— (1993) 'Where have all the dead Saxons gone?', in M.O.H. Carver (ed.), *In Search of Cult*, Woodbridge: 55–60.

Hills, C. and Rickett, R. (1981) *The Anglo-Saxon Cemetery at Spong Hill, North Elmham, Part II*, East Anglian Archaeol Rep 11, Gressenhall.

Hills, C., Penn, K. and Rickett, R. (1984) *The Anglo-Saxon Cemetery at Spong Hill,*

North Elmham, Part III: Catalogue of Inhumations, East Anglian Archaeol Rep 21, Gressenhall.

—— (1987) *The Anglo-Saxon Cemetery at Spong Hill, North Elmham, Part IV: Catalogue of Cremations*, East Anglian Archaeol Rep 34, Gressenhall.

Hinchliffe, J. (1986) 'An early medieval settlement at Cowage Farm, Foxley, Near Malmesbury', *Archaeol Journ* 143: 240–59.

Hines, J. (1984) *The Scandinavian Character of Anglian England in the Pre-Viking Period*, Brit Archaeol Rep 124, Oxford.

—— (1992a) 'The scandinavian character of Anglian England: an update', in M.O.H. Carver (ed.), *The Age of Sutton Hoo*, Woodridge: 315–29.

—— (1992b) 'The seriation and chronology of Anglian English women's graves: a critical assessment', in L. Jørgensen (ed.), *Chronological Studies of Anglo-Saxon England, Lombard Italy and Vendel-period Sweden*, Copenhagen: 81–93.

—— (1994) 'The becoming of the English: identity, material culture and language in early Anglo-Saxon England', *Anglo-Saxon Stud in Archaeol and Hist* 7, 49–59.

Hinton, D.A. (1990) *Archaeology, Economy and Society: England from the Fifth to the Fifteenth Century*, London.

Hirst, S.M. (1985) *An Anglo-Saxon Cemetery at Sewerby, East Yorkshire*, York.

—— (1993) 'Death and the archaeologist', in M.O.H. Carver (ed.), *In Search of Cult*, Woodbridge: 41–3.

Hockey, S.F. (1977) 'Stolen manuscripts: the case of George Hillier and the British Museum', *Archives* 13: 20–8.

Hodges, H. (1964) *Artifacts. An Introduction to Early Materials and Technology*, London.

Hodges, R. (1977) 'Some early medieval French wares in the British Isles', in D.P.S. Peacock (ed.), *Pottery and Early Commerce*, London: 239–56.

—— (1978) 'State formation and the role of trade in Middle Saxon England', in D. Green, C. Haselgrove and M. Spriggs (eds), *Social Organisation and Settlement*, Brit Archaeol Rep Internat Series 47, Oxford: 439–54.

—— (1982a) *Dark Age Economics. The Origins of Towns and Trade AD 600–1000*, London.

—— (1982b) 'The evolution of gateway communities: their socio-economic implications', in C. Renfrew and S. Shennan (eds), *Ranking, Resource and Exchange*, Cambridge: 117–23.

—— (1989) *The Anglo-Saxon Achievement*, London.

Hodges, R. and Hobley, B. (eds) (1988) *The Rebirth of Towns in the West AD 700–1050*, Council Brit Archaeol Res Rep 68, London.

Hogarth, A.C. (1973) 'Structural features in Anglo-Saxon graves', *Archaeol Journ* 130: 104–19.

Hogg, A.H.A. (1941) 'Earthworks in Joydens Wood, Bexley, Kent', *Archaeol Cantiana* 54: 10–27.

Holdsworth, P. (1976) 'Saxon Southampton: a new review', *Medieval Archaeol* 20: 26–61.

—— (1980) *Excavations at Melbourne Street, Southampton, 1971–76*, Council Brit Archaeol Res Rep 20: 26–61.

Holmqvist, W. (ed.) (1961) *Excavations at Helgö I*, Stockholm.

—— (ed.) (1964) *Excavations at Helgö II*, Stockholm.

—— (ed.) (1970) *Excavations at Helgö III*, Stockholm.

—— (ed.) (1972) *Excavations at Helgö IV, Workshop. Part I*, Stockholm.

—— (1975) 'Helgö, an early trading settlement in central Sweden', in R.L.S. Bruce-Mitford (ed.), *Recent Archaeological Excavations in Europe*, London: 111–32.

Hope-Taylor, B. (1977) *Yeavering: an Anglo-British Centre of Early Northumbria*, London.

Horsfield, T.W. (1835) *History, Antiquities and Topography of Sussex*, Lewes.

Huggett, J.W. (1988) 'Imported grave goods and the early Anglo-Saxon economy', *Medieval Archaeol* 32, 63–96.

—— (1992) 'A computer-based analysis of early Anglo-Saxon inhumation burials', unpublished PhD thesis, Staffordshire Polytechnic.

—— (1995) 'Numerical techniques for burial analysis', in J. Wilcock and K. Lockyear (eds), *Computer Applications and Quantitative Methods in Archaeology 1993*, Brit Archaeol Rep Internat Ser 598, Oxford: 183–90.

Huggins, P.J. (1983) 'Saxon building measurements', in J.G.B. Haigh (ed.) *Computer Applications and Quantitative Methods in Archaeology*, Bradford:103–10.

—— (1991) 'Anglo-Saxon timber building measurements: recent results', *Medieval Archaeol* 35, 6–28.

Huggins, P.J., Rodwell, K. and Rodwell, W.J. (1982) 'Anglo-Saxon and Scandinavian building measurements', in P.J. Drury (ed.), *Structural Reconstruction: Approaches to the Interpretation of the Excavated Remains of Buildings*, Brit Archaeol Rep 110, Oxford, 21–65.

Hughes, M. (1984) 'Rural settlement and landscape in late Saxon England', in M. Faull (ed.), *Studies in Late Anglo-Saxon Settlement*, Oxford: 65–80.

Humphreys, J., Ryland, J., Barnard, E.A.B., Wellstood, F.C. and Barnett, T.G. (1923) 'An Anglo-Saxon cemetery at Bidford-on-Avon, Warwickshire', *Archaeologia* 73: 89–116.

Hunter, J.R. (1985) 'Glass and glass-making', in P. Phillips (ed.), *The Archaeologist and the Laboratory*, Council Brit Archaeol Res Rep 58, London: 63–6.

Hurst, J.G. (1976) 'The pottery', in D.M. Wilson (ed.) (1976a): 283–348.

Hyslop, M. (1963) 'Two Anglo-Saxon cemeteries at Chamberlains Barn, Leighton Buzzard, Bedfordshire', *Archaeol Journ* 120: 161–200.

Jackson, D.A., Harding, D.W. and Myres, J.N.L. (1969) 'The Iron Age and Anglo-Saxon site at Upton, Northants', *Antiq Journ* 49: 202–21.

Jackson, P.M. (1995) 'Footloose in archaeology', *Current Archaeol* 144, 466–70.

James, E. (1977) *The Merovingian Archaeology of South-West Gaul*, Brit Archaeol Rep Supp Series 25, Oxford.

James, S., Marshall, A. and Millett, M. (1984) 'An early medieval building tradition', *Archaeol Journ* 141: 182–215.

Janaway, R.C. (1985) 'Textile fibre characteristics preserved by metal corrosion: the potential of SEM studies', *The Conservator* 7: 48–52.

Jarvis, K., Arnold, C., Janaway, R. and Keepax, C. (1983) 'The Bargates pagan-Saxon cemetery with late Neolithic and bronze age sites', in K. Jarvis (ed.), *Excavations in Christchurch 1969–1980*, Dorset Nat Hist Archaeol Soc Monog 5, Dorchester: 102–44.

Jessup, R.F. (1975) *Man of Many Talents*, London.

Johnson, M. (1993) 'The Saxon monastery at Whitby: past, present, future', in M.O.H. Carver (ed.), *In Search of Cult*, Woodbridge: 85–9.

Johnson, S. (1983) *Burgh Castle: Excavations by Charles Green 1958–61*, East Anglian Arch Rep 20, Gressenhall.

Jolliffe, J.E.A. (1933) *Pre-Feudal England: the Jutes*, Oxford.

Jones, M.U. (1975) 'A clay piece-mould of the Migration Period from Mucking, Essex', *Antiquaries Journ* 55, 407–8.

—— (1979a) 'Saxon Mucking – a post-excavation note', *Anglo-Saxon Stud in Archaeol and Hist* 1: 21–38.

—— (1979b) 'Saxon sunken huts: problems of interpretation', *Archaeol Journ* 136: 53–9.

—— (1980) 'Metallurgical finds from a multi-period settlement at Mucking, Essex', in W.A. Oddy (ed.), *Aspects of Early Metallurgy*, London: 117–20.

Jones, M.U. and Jones, W.T. (1975) 'Crop-mark sites at Mucking, Essex, England', in R.L.S. Bruce-Mitford (ed.), *Recent Archaeological Excavations in Europe*, London: 133–87.

Kemble, J.M. (1863) *Horae Ferales*, London.

—— (1876) *The Saxons in England*, second edition, London.

Kendrick, T.D. (1938) *Anglo-Saxon Art to AD 900*, London.

Kennett, D.H. (1975) 'The Souldern burials', *Oxoniensa* 40: 201–10.

Kidd, D. (1976) review of Myres and Southern (1973), *Medieval Archaeol* 20: 202–4.

Kjølbye-Biddle, B. (1986) 'The 7th century minster at Winchester interpreted', in L.A.S. Butler and R.K. Morris (eds), *The Anglo-Saxon Church*, London: 196–209.

Knocker, G.M. (1957) 'Early burials and an Anglo-Saxon cemetery at Snell's Corner near Horndean, Hampshire', *Papers Proc Hampshire Fld Club Archaeol Soc* 19: 117–70.

Knox, R. (1855) *Descriptions Geographical, Topographical and Antiquarian in Eastern Yorkshire, between the Rivers Humber and Tees*, London.

Kuhn, H. (1940) *Die Germanischen Bügelfibeln der Völkerwanderungszeit in der Rheinprovinz*, Bonn.

Laing, L. (1975) *The Archaeology of Late Celtic Britain and Ireland c. 400–1200 AD*, London.

Lamm, K. (1973) 'The manufacture of jewellery during the Migration Period at Helgö in Sweden', *Bull Hist Metallurgy Group* 7 (2): 1–7.

—— (1980) 'Early medieval metalworking on Helgö in central Sweden', in W.A. Oddy (ed.) *Aspects of Early Metallurgy*, London: 97–116.

Lamm, K. and Lundström, A. (1976) 'East Scandinavian Style I: an answer to Birgit Arrhenius', *Medieval Archaeol* 20: 16–25.

Lancaster, L. (1958) 'Kinship in Anglo-Saxon society', *Brit Journ Sociol* 9: 230–50, 359–77.

Lawson, G. (1978) 'The Lyre from Grave 22', in Green and Rogerson (1978): 87–97.

Leeds, E.T. (1912) 'The distribution of the Anglo-Saxon saucer brooch in relation to the Battle of Bedford AD 571', *Archaeologia* 63: 159–202.

—— (1913) *The Archaeology of the Anglo-Saxon Settlements*, Oxford.

—— (1916) 'An Anglo-Saxon cemetery at Wheatley, Oxfordshire', *Proc Soc Antiq London* 29: 48–64.

—— (1923) 'A Saxon village near Sutton Courtenay, Berkshire', *Archaeologia* 72: 147–92.

—— (1924) 'An Anglo-Saxon cremation-burial of the seventh century in Asthall Barrow, Oxfordshire', *Antiq Journ* 4: 113–26.

—— (1927) 'A Saxon village near Sutton Courtenay, Berkshire (second report)', *Archaeologia* 76: 59–79.

—— (1933) 'The Early Saxon penetration of the Upper Thames area', *Antiq Journ* 13: 229–51.

—— (1936) *Early Anglo-Saxon Art and Archaeology*, Oxford.

—— (1945) 'The distribution of the Angles and Saxons archaeologically considered', *Archaeologia* 91: 229–51.

—— (1947) 'A Saxon village near Sutton Courtenay, Berkshire (third report)', *Archaeologia* 92: 79–93.

—— (1949) *A Corpus of Anglo-Saxon Great Square-Headed Brooches*, Oxford.

—— (1953) 'Anglo-Saxon exports: a criticism', *Antiq Journ* 33: 208–10.

Leeds, E.T. and Harden, D.B. (1936) *The Anglo-Saxon Cemetery at Abingdon, Berkshire*, Oxford.

Leeds, E.T. and Pocock, M. (1971) 'A survey of the Anglo-Saxon cruciform brooches of florid type', *Medieval Archaeol* 15: 13–36.

Leeds, E.T. and Riley, M. (1942) 'Two early Saxon cemeteries at Cassington, Oxon',

Oxoniensa 7: 61–70.

Leeds, E.T.and Shortt, H. de S. (1953) *An Early Anglo-Saxon Cemetery at Petersfinger, near Salisbury, Wilts*, Salisbury.

Leigh, D. (1980) 'The square-headed brooches of sixth-century Kent', unpublished PhD thesis, University College, Cardiff.

—— (1984a) 'Ambiguity in Anglo-Saxon Style I Art' *Antiq Journ* 63: 34–42.

—— (1984b) 'The Kentish keystone-garnet disc brooches: Avent's classes 1–3 reconsidered', *Anglo-Saxon Stud in Archaeol and Hist* 3: 65–74.

—— (1985) 'Differential abrasion and brooch usage', *Science and Archaeol* 27: 8–12.

—— (1990) 'Aspects of early brooch design and production', in E. Southworth (ed.), *Anglo-Saxon Cemeteries: a Reappraisal*, Stroud: 107–24.

Lethbridge, T.C. (1931) *Recent Excavations in Anglo-Saxon Cemeteries in Cambridgeshire and Suffolk*, Cambridge Antiq Soc quarto publications, Cambridge.

Lloyd-Jones, J. (1995) 'Measuring biological affinity among populations: a case study of Romano-British and Anglo-Saxon populations', in J. Huggett and N. Ryan (eds), *Computer Applications and Quantitative Methods in Archaeology 1994*, Brit Archaeol Rep Internat Ser 600, Oxford: 69–73.

Londesborough, the Lord (1852) 'An account of the opening of some tumuli in the East Riding of Yorkshire', *Archaeologia* 34: 251–5.

Losco-Bradley, S. (1977) 'Catholme', *Current Archaeol* 59: 358–64.

Loyn, H.R. (1962) *Anglo-Saxon England and the Norman Conquest*, London.

—— (1974) 'Kinship in Anglo-Saxon England', *Anglo-Saxon England* 3: 197–209.

—— (1992) 'Kings, Gesiths and Thegns', in M.O.H. Carver (ed.), *The Age of Sutton Hoo*, Woodbridge: 75–9.

Macalister, F. (1985) 'The slags', in West (1985): 69.

McDonnell, G. (1989) 'Iron and its alloys in the fifth to eleventh centuries AD in England', *World Archaeol* 20 (3), 373–82.

—— (1993) 'Slags and ironworking residues', in Hamerow (1993): 82–3.

MacGregor, A. (1985) *Bone, Antler, Ivory and Horn: the Technology of Skeletal Materials since the Roman Period*, London.

McKinley, J.I. (1993) 'Cremated bone', in Timby (1993): 287–99.

—— (1994a) *Spong Hill Part VIII: The Cremations*, East Anglian Archaeol Rep 69, Gressenhall.

—— (1994b) 'A pyre and grave-goods in British cremation burials; have we missed something?', *Antiquity* 68, 132–4.

Mackreth, D.F. (1978) 'Orton Hall Farm, Peterborough: a Roman and Saxon settlement', in M. Todd (ed.), *Studies in the Romano-British Villa*, Leicester: 209–38.

Manley, J. (1985) 'The archer and the army in the late Saxon period', *Anglo-Saxon Stud in Archaeol and Hist* 4: 223–35.

Manser, J. (1977) 'A technological study of the "bronze" brooches excavated at Spong Hill, Norfolk, 1972–76', unpublished dissertation, University of London.

Marshall, A. and Marshall, G. (1991) 'A survey and analysis of the buildings of early and middle Saxon England', *Medieval Archaeol* 35: 29–43.

—— (1993) 'Differentiation, change and continuity in Anglo-Saxon buildings', *Archaeol Journ* 150: 366–402.

Meaney, A. (1964) *A Gazetteer of Early Anglo-Saxon Burial Sites*, London.

—— (1981) *Anglo-Saxon Amulets and Curing-Stones*, Brit Archaeol Rep 96, Oxford.

—— (1995) 'Pagan English sanctuaries, place-names and hundred meeting places', *Anglo-Saxon Stud Archaeol Hist* 8: 29–42.

Meaney, A. and Hawkes, S.C. (1970) *Two Anglo-Saxon Cemeteries at Winnall, Winchester, Hampshire*, Soc Medieval Archaeol Mono 4, London.

Meeks, N.D. and Holmes, R. (1985) 'The Sutton Hoo garnet jewellery', *Anglo-*

Saxon Stud in Archaeol and Hist 4: 143–58.

Millett, M. and James, S. (1983) 'Excavations at Cowdery's Down, Basingstoke, Hampshire 1978–81', *Archaeol Journ* 140: 151–279.

Milne, G. and Richards, J. (1992) *Two Anglo-Saxon Buildings and Associated Finds*, Wharram VII: York University Archaeol Publications 9, York.

Mitchell, S.A. (1985) 'The whetstone as symbol of authority in Old English and Old Norse', *Scandinavian Stud* 57, 1–31.

Montelius, O. (1908) 'The chronology of the British Bronze Age', *Archaeologia* 61: 97–162.

Moore, D.T. and Oddy, W.A. (1985) 'Touchstones: some aspects of their nomenclature, petrography and provenance', *Journ Archaeol Sci* 12: 59–80.

Moore, W.J. and Corbett, M.E. (1971) 'The distribution of dental caries in ancient British populations I: Anglo-Saxon period', *Caries Res* 5: 151–68.

Morris, C. (1993) 'Tools', in Hamerow (1993): 69–70.

Morris, C.A. (1982) 'Aspects of Anglo-Saxon and Anglo-Scandinavian lathe turning', in S. McGrail (ed.), *Woodworking Techniques before AD 1500*, Brit Archaeol Rep Int Ser 129, Oxford: 245–61.

Morris, J. (1974) review of Myres and Green (1973), *Medieval Archaeol* 18: 225–32.

Morris, R.K. (1983) *The Church in British Archaeology*, Council for Brit Archaeol Res Rep, London.

Mortimer, C. (1990) 'Some aspects of early medieval copper-alloy technology, as illustrated by a study of the Anglian cruciform brooch', unpublished PhD thesis, University of Oxford.

—— (1991a) 'Northern European metalworking traditions in the fifth and sixth centuries AD', in P. Budd *et al.* (eds), *Archaeological Sciences 1989*, Oxford: 162–8.

—— (1991b) 'A descriptive classification of early Anglo-Saxon copper-alloy compositions: towards a general typology of early medieval copper alloys', *Medieval Archaeol* 35, 104–7.

—— (1994) 'Lead-alloy models for three early Anglo-Saxon brooches', *Anglo-Saxon Stud in Archaeol and Hist* 7, 27–33.

Murphy, P. (1985) 'The cereals and crop weeds', in West (1985): 100–8.

Musty, J. and Stratton, J.E.D. (1964) 'A Saxon cemetery at Winterbourne Gunner, near Salisbury', *Wiltshire Archaeol Mag* 59: 86–109.

Myres, J.N.L. (1969) *Anglo-Saxon Pottery and the Settlement of England*, Oxford.

—— (1970) 'The Angles, the Saxons and the Jutes', *Proc Brit Academy* 56: 145–74.

—— (1977) *A Corpus of Anglo-Saxon Pottery of the Pagan Period*, Oxford.

—— (1978) 'Amulets or small change', *Antiq Journ* 58: 352.

Myres, J.N.L. and Green, B. (1973) *The Anglo-Saxon Cemetery at Caistor-by-Norwich and Markshall, Norfolk*, London.

—— and Southern, W.H. (1973) *The Anglo-Saxon Cemetery at Sancton, East Yorkshire*, Hull.

Namier, L. (1930) *England in the Age of the American Revolution*, London.

Nelson, J.L. (1975) 'Ritual and reality in the early Medieval "ordines"', *Stud Church Hist* 11: 41–51.

—— (1977) 'Inauguration rituals', in P.H. Sawyer and I.N. Wood (eds), *Early Medieval Kingship*, Leeds: 50–71.

—— (1980) 'The earliest royal *Ordo*: some liturgical and historical aspects', in B. Tiernay and P. Linehan (eds), *Authority and Power: Studies on Medieval Law and Government*, Cambridge: 29–48.

Neuman de Vegvar, C. (1984) 'The iconography of kingship in Anglo-Saxon archaeological finds', in J. Rosenthal (ed.), *Kings and Kingship, Acta* 11, Binghampton: 1–15.

—— (1992) 'The Sutton Hoo horns as regalia', in R. Farrell and C. Neuman de Vegvar (ed.), *Sutton Hoo: Fifty Tears After*, Ohio: 63–74.

Newman, J. 1992 'The late Roman and Anglo-Saxon settlement pattern in the Sandlings of Suffolk', in M.O.H. Carver (ed.), *The Age of Sutton Hoo*, Woodbridge: 25–38.

Nicholson, L.E. (1986) '*Beowulf* and the pagan cult of the stag', *Studi Medievali* 27: 637–69.

O'Brien, E. (1993) 'Contacts between Ireland and Anglo-Saxon England in the seventh century', *Anglo-Saxon Stud in Archaeol and Hist* 6: 93–102.

Oddy, W.A. (1980) 'Gilding and tinning in Anglo-Saxon England', in W.A. Oddy (ed.), *Aspects of Early Metallurgy*, London: 129–34.

O'Niell, B.H. St J. (1967) 'Monastic mining and metallurgy in the British Isles', *Metals and Materials* 3: 182–90.

Ordnance Survey (1966) *Britain in the Dark Ages*, Southampton.

Owen, G.R. (1981) *The Rites and the Religions of the Anglo-Saxons*, London.

Owen-Crocker, G.R. (1986) *Dress in Anglo-Saxon England*, Manchester.

Pader, E. (1980) 'Material symbolism and social relations in mortuary studies', in P.A. Rahtz, T.D. Dickinson and L. Watts (eds), *Anglo-Saxon Cemeteries 1979*, Brit Archaeol Rep 82, Oxford: 143–60.

—— (1982) *Symbolism, Social Relations and the Interpretation of Mortuary Remains*, Brit Archaeol Rep Int Ser 130, Oxford.

Page, R.I. (1970) *Life in Anglo-Saxon England*, London.

—— (1973a) *An Introduction to English Runes*, London.

—— (1973b) 'The runic inscription from N 59', in Myres and Green (1973): 114–7.

—— (1995) *Runes and Runic Inscriptions in Anglo-Saxon England*, Oxford.

Parker Pearson, M., van de Noort, R. and Woolf, A. (1994) 'Three men and a boat: Sutton Hoo and the East Anglian kingdom', *Anglo-Saxon England* 22: 27–50.

Peebles, C.S. (1972) 'Monothetic divisive analysis of the Moundville burials: an initial report', *Newsletter of Computers in Archaeol* 8: 1–13.

Pelteret, D. (1981) 'Slave raiding and slave trading in early England', *Anglo-Saxon England* 9: 99–114.

Penny, L.F. (1974) 'Quaternary', in D.H. Rayner and J.E. Hemingway (eds), *The Geology and Mineral Resources of Yorkshire*, Leeds: 145–64.

Philp, B.J. (1973) *Excavations in West Kent 1960–1970*, Dover.

Philpott, R. (1991) *Burial Practices in Roman Britain*, Brit Archaeol Rep British Ser 219, Oxford.

Putnam, G. (1984) 'The human bones', in Hills, Penn and Rickett (1984): 15–17.

Rackham, O. (1986) *The History of the Countryside*, London.

Rahtz, P.A. (1961) 'An excavation on Bokerley Dyke, 1958', *Archaeol Journ* 118: 65–99.

—— (1970) 'A possible Saxon palace near Stratford-on-Avon', *Antiquity* 44: 137–43.

—— (1976) 'Buildings and rural settlement', in D.M. Wilson (ed.) (1976a): 49–98.

—— (1978) 'Grave Orientation', *Archaeol Journ* 135: 1–14.

Reilly, P. (1988) *Computer Analysis of an Archaeological Landscape*, Brit Archaeol Rep 190, Oxford.

Renfrew, C. (1975) 'Trade as action at a distance: questions of integration and communication', in J.A. Sabloff and C.C. Lamberg-Karlovsky (eds), *Ancient Civilisation and Trade*, Albuquerque: 3–60.

Reynolds, N. (1980) 'The king's whetstone: a footnote', *Antiquity* 54: 232–7.

Richards, J.D. (1982) 'Anglo-Saxon pot shapes: cognitive investigations', *Sci and Archaeol* 24: 33–46.

—— (1984) 'Funerary symbolism in Anglo-Saxon England: further social dimensions of mortuary practice', *Scottish Archaeol Rev* 3: 42–55.

—— (1987) *The Significance of Form and Decoration of Anglo-Saxon Cremation Urns*, Brit Archaeol Rep 166, Oxford.

—— (1992) 'Anglo-Saxon Symbolism', in M.O.H. Carver (ed.), *The Age of Sutton Hoo*, Woodbridge: 131–48.

Richards, P. (1986) 'Byzantine vessels in England and Europe: the origins of Anglo-Saxon trade', unpublished PhD thesis, University of Cambridge.

Rigold, S. (1975) 'The Sutton Hoo coins in the light of the contemporary background of coinage in England', in Bruce-Mitford (1975): 653–77.

Rigold, S. and Bayley, J. (1977) 'A group of three sceattas from excavations at Mucking, Essex', *Brit Numism Journ* 47: 127–8.

Robinson, M. (1981) 'The Iron Age to early Anglo-Saxon environment of the upper Thames Terraces', in M. Jones and G. Dimbleby (eds), *The Environment of Man*, Brit Archaeol Rep 87, Oxford: 251–86.

Rodwell, W. (1984) 'Churches in the landscape: aspects of topography and planning', in M.L. Faull (ed.) *Studies in Late Anglo-Saxon Settlement*, Oxford: 1–24.

—— (1993) 'The role of the church in the development of Roman and early Anglo-Saxon London', in M.O.H. Carver (ed.), *In Search of Cult*, Woodbridge: 91–9.

Roosens, H. and Thomas-Goorieckx, D. (1970) 'Die Merowingische Goldscheiben-fibel von Rosmeer', *Archaeol Belgica* 123: 5–18.

Russel, A.D. (1984) 'Early Anglo-Saxon Ceramics from East Anglia: A Microprovenance Study', unpublished PhD Thesis, University of Southampton.

Russell, J.C. (1976) 'The early medieval plague in the British Isles', *Viator* 7: 65–78.

Ryan, M. (1992) 'The Sutton Hoo ship burial and Ireland: some Celtic perspectives', in R. Farrell and C. Neuman de Vegvar (eds), *Sutton Hoo: Fifty Years After*, Ohio: 83–116.

St Joseph, J.K. (1982) 'Sprouston, Roxburghshire; an Anglo-Saxon settlement discovered by air reconnaisance', *Anglo-Saxon England* 10, 191–200.

Salin, B. (1904) *Die altgermanische Thierornamentik*, Stockholm.

Sanderson, D.C.W. and Hunter, J.R. (1980) 'Major element glass type specification for Roman, post-Roman and medieval glasses', *Rev Archéometrie* 3: 255–64.

Sanderson, D.C.W. and Warren, S.E. (1984) 'Energy dispersive X-ray fluorescence analysis of 1st millenium AD glass from Britain', *Journ Archaeol Sci* 11: 53–69.

Sawyer, P.H. (1978) *From Roman Britain to Norman England*, London.

—— (1983a) 'English archaeology before the Conquest: a historian's view', in D.A. Hinton (ed.), *25 Years of Medieval Archaeology*, Sheffield: 44–7.

—— (1983b) 'The royal *tun* in pre-Conquest England', in P. Wormald (ed.), *Ideal and Reality in Frankish and Anglo-Saxon Society*, Oxford: 273–99.

Scull, C. (1985) 'Further evidence from East Anglia for enamelling on early Anglo-Saxon Metalwork', *Anglo-Saxon Stud in Archaeol and Hist* 4: 117–24.

—— (1990) 'Scales and weights in early Anglo-Saxon England', *Archaeol Journ* 147, 183–215.

—— (1991) 'Post-Roman Phase I at Yeavering: a reconsideration', *Medieval Archaeol* 35, 51–63.

—— (1992) 'Before Sutton Hoo: structures of power and society in early East Anglia', in M.O.H. Carver (ed.), *The Age of Sutton Hoo*, Woodbridge: 3–24.

—— (1993) 'Archaeology, early Anglo-Saxon society and the origins of the Anglo-Saxon kingdoms', *Anglo-Saxon Studies in Archaeology and History* 6, 65–82.

Seebohm, F. (1911) *Tribal Customs in Anglo-Saxon Law*, London.

Service, E.R. (1978) 'Classical and modern theories of the origins of government', in R. Cohen and E.R. Service (eds), *Origins of the State*, Philadelphia: 21–34.

Shephard, J.F. (1979) 'The social identity of the individual in isolated barrows and barrow cemeteries in Anglo-Saxon England', in B.C. Burnham and J. Kingsbury (eds), *Space Hierarchy and Society*, Brit Archaeol Rep Int Ser 59, Oxford: 47–80.

Sherlock, S.J. and Welch, M.G. (1992) *An Anglo-Saxon Cemetery at Norton, Cleveland*, Council for British Archaeol Res Rep 82, London.

Sims-Williams, P. (1986) 'The visionary Celt: the construction of an ethnic pre-conception', *Cambridge Medieval Celtic Stud* 11: 71–96.
Smith, C.R. (1848–80) *Collectanea Antiqua* (7 vols), London.
—— (ed.) (1856) *Inventorium Sepulchrale*, London.
Smith, R.A. (1905) 'The evolution of late-Keltic pins of the hand-type', *Proc Soc Antiq London* 20: 344–54.
—— (1923) *A Guide to the Anglo-Saxon and Foreign Teutonic Antiquities*, London.
Speake, G. (1980) *Anglo-Saxon Animal Art*, Oxford.
—— (1989) *A Saxon Bed Burial on Swallowcliffe Down*, London.
Stahl, A.M. and Oddy, W.A. (1992) 'The date of the Sutton Hoo coins', in R. Farrell and C.N. de Vegvar (eds), *Sutton Hoo: Fifty Years After*, Ohio: 129–48.
Stamper, P. (1978) 'Early Anglo-Saxon buckets', unpublished BA dissertation, University of Southampton.
Sutherland, C.H.V. (1948) *Anglo-Saxon Gold Coinage in the Light of the Crondall Hoard*, Oxford.
—— (1973) *English Coinage*, London.
Swanton, M.J. (1973) *The Spearheads of the Anglo-Saxon Settlements*, London.
—— (1974) *A Corpus of Pagan Anglo-Saxon Spear Types*, Brit Archaeol Rep 7, Oxford.
Tainter, J.A. (1975) 'Social inference and mortuary practices: an experiment in numerical classification', *World Archaeol* 7: 1–15.
Taylor, C.C. (1977) 'Polyfocal settlement and the English village', *Medieval Archaeol* 21: 189–93.
—— (1978) 'Aspects of village mobility in medieval and later times', in S. Limbrey and J.G. Evans (eds), *The Effect of Man on the Landscape: the Lowland Zone*, Council Brit Archaeol Res Rep 21, London: 126–34.
—— (1983) *Village and Farmstead*, London.
Taylor, C.C. and Fowler, P.J. (1978) 'Roman fields into medieval furlongs', in H.C. Bowen and P.J. Fowler (eds), *Early Land Allotment in the British Isles: a Survey of Recent Work*, Brit Archaeol Rep 48, Oxford: 159–62.
Tester, P.J. (1968) 'An Anglo-Saxon cemetery at Orpington', *Archaeol Cantiana* 83: 125–50.
Thomas, C. (1986) 'Recognizing Christian origins: an archaeological and historical dilemma', in L.A.S. Butler and R.K. Morris (eds), *The Anglo-Saxon Church*, London: 121–5.
Thompson, F.H. (ed.) (1980) *Archaeology and Coastal Change*, London.
Timby, J. (1993) 'Sancton I Anglo-Saxon cemetery excavations carried out between 1976 and 1980', *Archaeol Journ* 150: 243–365.
Tooley, M.J. (1978) *Sea-level Changes: North-West England during the Flandrian Stage*, Oxford.
Turville Petrie, G. (1964) *Myth and Religion of the North: the Religion of Ancient Scandinavia*, London.
van de Noort, R. (1993) 'The context of early medieval barrows in western Europe', *Antiquity* 67: 66–73.
van der Veen, M. (1993) 'Grain impressions in early Anglo-Saxon pottery from Mucking', in Hamerow (1993): 80–1.
Vierck, H. (1967) 'Ein Relieffibelpaar aus Nordendorf in Bayerisch Schwaben: zur Ikonographie des germanischen Tierstils I', *Bayerisch Vorgeschichts blätter* 32, 104–43.
—— (1972) 'Redwalds Asche', *Offa* 29: 2–49.
—— (1976) 'Ein südskandinavische Relieffibel: zum Felinguss im frühen Mittelalter', in K.J. Narr (ed.), *Aus der Sammlung des Seminars für Ur- und Fruhgeschichte der Universität Munster*, Münstersche Beiträge zur Ur- und Fruhgeschichte 9, Munster: 137–209.

—— (1978a) 'Trachtenkunde und Trachtgeschichte in der Sachsen-Forschung, ihre Quellen, Ziele und Methoden', in C. Ahrens (ed.), *Sachsen und Angelsachsen*, Hamburg: 231–43.

—— (1978b) 'Die anglische Frauentracht', in C. Ahrens (ed.), *Sachsen und Angelsachsen*, Hamburg: 245–53.

—— (1978c) 'Zur seegermanischen Männertracht', in C. Ahrens (ed.), *Sachsen und Angelsachsen*, Hamburg: 263–70.

Vince, A. (1984) 'The Aldwych: mid-Saxon London discovered?', *Curr Archaeol* 93: 310–2.

—— (1990) *Saxon London: An Archaeological Investigation*, London.

Wade, K. (1988) 'Ipswich', in Hodges and Hobley (eds) (1988): 93–100.

Wade-Martins, P. (1980) *Fieldwork and Excavation on Village Sites in Launditch Hundred*, East Anglian Archaeol Rep 100, Gressenhall.

Walker, J. (1978) 'Anglo-Saxon traded pottery', in M. Todd (ed.), *Studies in the Romano-British Villa*, Leicester: 224–8.

Walker, M.J. (1985) 'The Coprolites', in West (1985): 97–100.

Wallace-Hadrill, J.M. (1971) *Early Germanic Kingship in England and on the Continent*, Oxford.

Watson, J. (1994) 'Wood usage in Anglo-Saxon shields', *Anglo-Saxon Studies in Archaeology and History* 7: 35–48.

Watson, J. and Edwards, G. (1990) 'Conservation of metarial from Anglo-Saxon cemeteries', in E. Southworth (ed.), *Anglo-Saxon Cemeteries: a Reappraisal*, Stroud: 97–106.

Webb, M.C. (1975) 'The flag follows trade', in J.A. Sabloff and C.C. Lamberg-Karlovsky (eds), *Ancient Civilisation and Trade*, Albuquerque: 155–210.

Webster, L. (1992) 'Death's diplomacy: Sutton Hoo in the light of other male princely burials', in R. Farrell and C. Neuman de Vegvar (eds), *Sutton Hoo: Fifty Years After*, Ohio: 75–82.

Welch, M.G. (1983) *Early Anglo-Saxon Sussex*, Brit Archaeol Rep 112, Oxford.

—— (1985) 'Rural settlement patterns in the early and middle Anglo-Saxon periods', *Landscape Hist* 7: 13–25.

—— (1989) 'The kingdom of the south Saxons: the origins', in Bassett (ed.) (1989), Leicester: 75–83.

—— (1992) *Anglo-Saxon England*, London.

Wells, C. (1960) 'A study of cremation', *Antiquity* 34: 29–37.

Wells, C. and Green, C. (1973) 'Sunrise dating of death and burial', *Norfolk Archaeol* 35: 435–42.

Werner, J. (1935) *Münzdatierte Austrasische Grabfunde*, Berlin.

—— (1957) 'Zwei gegossene Koptische bronze-flaschen aus Salona', in *Antidoron Michael Abramic' I, Vjesnik ZA archeologija i historiju dalmatinsku* 56–9, 1954–7: 115–28.

—— (1961) 'Fernhandel und Naturalwirtschaft im östlichen Merowingerreich archäologischen und numismatischen Zeugnissen', *Bericht der Römisch-Germanisch Kommission* 42: 307–46.

—— (1970) 'Zur Verbreitung frügeschichtlicher Metallarbeiten', *Early Medieval Stud* 1: 65–81.

—— (1992) 'A review of The Sutton Hoo Ship Burial Volume 3: some remarks thoughts and proposals', *Anglo-Saxon Studies in Archaeol and Hist* 5, 1–24.

West, S.E. (1985) *West Stow: The Anglo-Saxon Village*, East Anglian Archaeol Rep 24, Ipswich.

Wheeler, R.E.M. (1934) 'London and the Grim's Ditches', *Antiq Journ* 14: 254–63.

White, R.H. (1988) *Roman and Celtic Objects from Anglo-Saxon Graves*, Brit Archaeol Rep British Ser 191, Oxford.

Whyman, M. (1993) 'Invisible people? material culture in "Dark Age" Yorkshire', in M.O.H. Carver (ed.), *In Search of Cult*, Woodbridge: 61–8.

Willems, J. (1973) 'Le quartier artisanal gallo-romain et mérovingien de "Batta" à Huy', *Archaeologica Belgica* 148, 57–9.

Williams, D.F. (1994) 'The petrology of the pottery', in Evison (1994): 81–2.

Williams, J.H. (1984a) 'A review of some aspects of late Saxon urban origins and development', in M.L. Faull (ed.), *Studies in Late Anglo-Saxon Settlement*, Oxford: 25–34.

—— (1984b) 'From "palace" to "town": Northampton and urban origins', *Anglo-Saxon England* 13, 113–36.

Williams, J.H., Shaw, M. and Denham, V. (1985) *Middle Saxon Palaces at Northampton*, Northampton.

Wilson, D. (1985) 'A note on OE *hearg* and *weoh* as place-name elements representing different types of pagan Saxon worship sites', *Anglo-Saxon Studies in Archaeol and Hist* 4: 179–84.

—— (1992) *Anglo-Saxon Paganism*, London.

Wilson, D.M. (1957) 'An inlaid iron folding stool in the British Museum', *Medieval Archaeol* 1, 39–56.

—— (1968) 'Anglo-Saxon carpenters' tools', in M. Claus *et al.* (eds), *Studien zur europäischen Vor- und Frühgeschichte*, Neumunster: 143–50.

—— (ed.) (1976a) *The Archaeology of Anglo-Saxon England*, London.

—— (1976b) 'Craft and industry', in D.M. Wilson (1976a): 253–82.

Wood, I.N. (1983) 'The Merovingian North Sea', *Occasional Papers on Medieval Topics* 1: 1–26.

—— (1991) 'The Franks and Sutton Hoo', in I.N. Wood and N. Lund (eds), *People and Places in Northern Europe 500–1600: Essays in Honour of Peter Hayes Sawyer*, Woodbridge: 1–14.

—— (1992) 'Frankish hegemony in England', in M.O.H. Carver (ed.), *The Age of Sutton Hoo*, Woodbridge: 235–41.

—— (1994) *The Merovingian Kingdoms 450–751*, London.

Wylie, W.M. (1852) *Fairford Graves. A Record of Researches in an Anglo-Saxon Burial-place in Gloucestershire*, Oxford.

Yorke, B. (1989) 'The Jutes of Hampshire and Wight and the origins of Wessex', in Bassett (ed.) (1989): 84–96.

—— (1990) *Kings and Kingdoms of Early Anglo-Saxon England*, London.

—— (1993) 'Fact or fiction? The written evidence for the fifth and sixth centuries', *Anglo-Saxon Studies in Archaeology and History* 6, 45–50.

—— (1995) *Wessex in the Early Middle Ages*, Leicester.

Index